Twayne's English Authors Series

Sylvia E. Bowman, *Editor*

INDIANA UNIVERSITY

William Cowper

William Cowper

By WILLIAM N. FREE

University of Toledo

Twayne Publishers, Inc.   ::   New York

FOR ANNE

Preface

Horace Walpole once wrote that the history of England had so often been recounted that "to make it new" a writer had really to "*make* it *new*." Anyone who attempts a book about William Cowper faces the predicament that Walpole described. Almost every area and method of scholarship have been touched by a stream of books which began with Hayley's *Life* and Cowper's own *Memoir*, and extends to the present. Biography has gone from the extreme of Victorian reticence and moralism to that of Freudian speculation and has returned to a healthy interest in the facts of the poet's life and milieu. Criticism has shown the relation between Cowper's biography and poetry, and between the religious context and the experience of the poet. It has also isolated many of the literary influences on Cowper's work. There have been studies of his poetic idiom, and there is even an annotated bibliography to draw together the many currents of Cowper scholarship.

In this book I have attempted not to create a new Cowper but to refocus attention on his literary achievements. Recent scholarship has made clear that such records of personal distress as Cowper's life fascinate the twentieth-century reader. Although I have tried to show why Cowper's biography in itself should interest us, the biographical chapters which follow are intended primarily as a means of explicating *The Task*, Cowper's short poems, and the *Olney Hymns*. Like all lives, Cowper's provides the environment within which his works operate. I have tried to show how the residue of his experience appears in such formal aspects of his poetry as theme, structure, tone, and metaphor. And I have tried to demonstrate that his temperament accounts for much that was new in his use of conventional themes and forms.

Not every aspect of Cowper's literary work could be covered

in a book of this length. I have chosen to omit discussion of his translations, because they are not usually read and were not influential. The same is true of his prose essays. Of necessity I have also limited discussion of his letters, which admittedly deserve fuller notice, to several brief comments in the biographical chapters.

WILLIAM N. FREE

University of Toledo

Contents

Contents

Chronology

1731 William Cowper born on November 15.

1737 Ann Cowper dies, November 12.

1738 At Dr. Pitman's school in Market Street.

1741– At Westminster.
1748

1745 Has smallpox.

1749– Articled to Chapman.
1751

1752 First attack of melancholy.

1754 Called to the bar, January 14.

1755 Moves to Middle Temple.

1756 Contributes five papers to *Connoisseur*. Cannot marry Theodora. Cowper's father dies.

1758 With brother translates Voltaire's *Henriade*.

1759 Commissioner of Bankrupts.

1763 Offered Clerkship of Journals of House of Lords. First mental breakdown.

1765 Leaves St. Albans, June 27.

1766– At Huntingdon with Unwins, September 14. Moves to
1767 Olney.

1770 John Cowper dies, March.

1772– Engaged to marry Mrs. Unwin. Mental breakdown termi-
1773 nates engagement; dreams that he has been damned. Moves to the Vicarage.

1774 Leaves Vicarage, May 23.

1781 Publishes *Anti-Thelyphthora* anonymously.

1782 Publishes first volume of poems, February.

1783 Begins *The Task*, July.

1785 Second volume of poetry published (includes *The Task*), July.

1786 Moves to Weston, November.

1787 Third mental breakdown, January to June.
1791 Publishes translation of Homer, July. Begins edition of Milton, September.
1794 Attack of melancholy.
1795 Leaves Weston, July.
1796 At East Dereham, September. Mrs. Unwin dies, December.
1799 Writes *Montes Glaciales* and *The Castaway*, his last poems.
1800 Cowper dies, April 25.

William Cowper

CHAPTER 1

The Early Years

BIOGRAPHY has always occupied a disproportionately large place in the criticism of the works of William Cowper, not because his life was crowded with momentous events but because his poetry is deeply rooted in the details of his domestic affairs. Therefore, it is suitable for this book to begin with an account of Cowper's life before it turns to criticism of his poems and hymns. In recounting the details of Cowper's life, however, we should remember that in his case, biography serves as more than a footnote to his literary achievements. As well as leading to criticism, it gives form to the religious myth which shaped the mature poet's consciousness and which, because of his typically eighteenth-century notions of propriety, could not find full expression in his literary works. Moreover, in addition to providing insights into an evangelical mind, it also reveals much about the quality of life that an eighteenth-century gentleman knew.

William Cowper was born on November 15, 1731, the son of the Reverend Dr. John Cowper, rector of Great Berkhampstead, who had married Ann Donne in 1728. He was the fourth child, but the first to survive infancy. Two children born after him died young, and the seventh child, John, who was born in 1737, was the only other to live to adulthood. Shortly after the birth of John, his mother died, in the ninth year of her marriage and in the sixth of the poet's life.

Dr. John Cowper came from a family which had distinguished itself for its loyalty to Charles I and for its service to William III, Queen Anne, and George I. His uncle, the third Sir William Cowper—created Baron Cowper of Wingham, Kent, in 1706 and in 1718 Viscount Fordwiche and Earl Cowper—had risen to the offices of Lord Keeper and Commissioner for the Union with Scotland, and then had become the first Lord Chancellor of England in 1702. This office he held until 1710, and again from 1714 to

1718. He had presided at the Sacheverell trial, in 1710, and had been an important adviser to George I, who spoke almost no English and who also knew little about English social and political institutions. Sir William's younger brother, Spencer Cowper, a judge, seems to have distinguished himself chiefly by collaborating with Sir William at the Sacheverell trial.

Ann Donne Cowper, the poet's mother, was descended from a more ancient and noble family which traced its lineage to Henry III and included the seventeenth-century poet John Donne. William Cowper, then, was a gentleman by birth; and it might be suspected that the household in which he began life conducted itself in an atmosphere of breeding and decorum. The prestige of the family, as well as the position held by Dr. John Cowper, undoubtedly made the Cowpers an important family in Great Berkhampstead, then a village of several hundred houses and fifteen hundred inhabitants. Life was not charged with the controversy that surrounded the first Earl Cowper, or, to a lesser extent, Spencer, the poet's grandfather. Around both of these men had developed the lurid legends and political intrigues which go with prominence. John Cowper, although not wealthy, was able to provide for his family a decent but comparatively modest life. He apparently was not an exceptionally pious nor zealous man, but he seemingly followed the pattern of the cultivated, gentlemanly latitudinarian clergyman.

William Cowper seems to have had an especially warm relationship with his mother, whom he describes with great poignance in one of his most famous poems, written in 1790, fifty-three years after her death:

> Those lips are thine—thy own sweet smiles I see,
> The same that oft in childhood solaced me;
> Voice only fails, else, how distinct they say,
> "Grieve not, my child, chase all thy fears away!"
> The meek intelligence of those dear eyes
> . . . .
> Thy nightly visits to my chamber made,
> That thou might'st know me safe and warmly laid;
> Thy morning bounties ere I left my home,
> The biscuit, or confectionary plum;
> The fragrant waters on my cheeks bestow'd
> By thy own hand, till fresh they shone and glow'd

> All this, and more endearing still than all,
> Thy constant, flow of love, that knew no fall,
> Ne'er roughened by those cataracts and brakes
> That humor interpos'd too often makes . . .[1]

In a typical gentle household, such as the poem describes, servants were probably somewhat closer to the children than the parents. But intimacy need not have been necessary, and a certain distance might well have contributed to the idealism of this portrait. That the event could evoke only a sentimental response many years later may well indicate how superficial the relationship between mother and son was. In spite of all his sentiment, she remains a conventional representation of motherhood; Cowper remembers few outstanding qualities of her character and emphasizes his own sense of loss.

Cowper's idealization of his mother probably grew from the feeling that by her death she had abandoned him. His father's decision to send him off to school shortly after her death must have sharpened this feeling of desertion. In *Tirocinium,* a poem attacking public schools, Cowper later dwelt on the cruelty of parents who send their children away to school at a very early age, and lamented the effect of separation upon a child's love for his parents. That he still could not quite comprehend the motives of the father indicates the degree of pain he had felt many years earlier.

For most boys the cruelty of the schools undoubtedly aroused a spirit of adventure and contributed to the pleasure of later recollections; but Cowper, both as a boy and as a man, seems to have felt only that he had been cut off from a quiet world appropriate to his own retiring nature. The school to which his father sent him, Dr. Pitman's in Bedfordshire, provided neither tenderness and security nor a suitable emotional equivalent. One bully in particular seems to have singled Cowper out for harassment:

But my chief affliction consisted in my being singled out from all the other boys, by a lad about fifteen years of age, as a proper object upon which he might let loose the cruelty of his temper. I choose to forbear a particular recital of the many acts of barbarity, with which he made it his business continually to persecute me; it will be sufficient to say, that he had, by his savage treatment of me, impressed such a dread of his figure upon my mind, that I well remember being afraid to lift up my

eyes upon him, higher than his knees; and that I knew him by his shoe-
buckles, better than any other part of his dress. May the Lord pardon
him, and may we meet in glory! [2]

Eventually the bully was expelled, but the rough and tumble existence of the eighteenth-century school proved too much for
Cowper to bear. In 1739, having developed eye trouble, he went
to live with a Mr. Disney, an oculist; but in this home he apparently found little happiness. Neither the people nor the reason for
his being sent favored a congenial atmosphere.

Like the father that Cowper portrays in *Tirocinium,* Dr.
Cowper seems not to have been much worried about his son's
condition. From the relatively few references to him in William's
letters and elsewhere, we have the impression that he certainly
was not a forceful or domineering parent and that he allowed his
children considerable freedom. Social position, the family situation, and the character of the man probably account for this.
Undoubtedly the care of the two children fell to servants, who
were allowed considerable freedom in the control of their
charges, while Dr. Cowper followed his professional interests and
such cultural pursuits as reading and writing poetry. He in no
way compensated for the gentle, understanding nature that Cowper had felt in his mother.

In 1741 Cowper was sent to Westminster. For a child in his
situation, this event would not seem an auspicious one. The conditions under which students lived were not well suited to his physical and emotional weaknesses. In the houses where the boys
boarded, there was little privacy, almost no supervision, and still
less of the security that Cowper's later poem on his mother's picture hints that he craved. And a person with his modest financial
resources would have had even a harder time than others. Furthermore, the education offered by Westminster lacked the order
and content necessary to stimulate and give direction to the students. Nevertheless, these years there were happy ones for him.
Although the poet's reminiscences are clouded by that very tendency to romanticize the past that he deplores in the parent in *Tirocinium,* it seems quite clear that he achieved at least a partial
adjustment to the chaotic world outside of the rectory at Berkhampstead; and he was, perhaps, beginning to experience the
sense of detachment, even coolness, toward family that in *Tiro-*

cinium he considers a most unpleasant result of public school education.

Cowper remembered with greatest affection the usher of the fifth form, an accomplished Latinist named Vincent Bourne. In a letter to William Unwin, Cowper recalled Bourne:

> I love the memory of Vinny Bourne. He was so good natured, and so indolent, that I lost more than I got by him; for he made me as idle as himself. He was such a sloven, as if he had trusted to his genius as a cloak for everything that could disgust you in his person; and indeed in his writings he almost made amends for all. His humor is entirely original; he can speak of a magpie or a cat in terms so exquisitely appropriated to the character he draws, that one would suppose him animated by the spirit of the creature he describes. And with all this drollery there is a mixture of rational, and even religious, reflection at times: and always an air of pleasantry, good nature, and humanity.[3]

Perhaps a clue to Cowper's enjoyment of Westminster lies in his emphasis on Bourne's idle, easygoing nature and his entertaining, harmless wit. Both of these characteristics agreed very well with Cowper's own personality, and they even foreshadow certain humorous passages in *The Task* and other poems.

Cowper had many other friends at Westminster. From their later careers we might guess that they were not of the retiring type expected to be most amenable to his personality. Unlike Horace Walpole, for example, who at Eton belonged to a tight-knit little group, a "quadruple alliance" of boys sharing his interests, Cowper seems not to have been bound by particular friends or personalities, although at least one friendship, that with Sir William Russell, proved later to be deeply founded. Later in Cowper's life, Westminster would evoke memories which gave pleasure, and which reveal to us the energies which are normal in the formative years between the ages of ten and seventeen. In contrast, Cowper's only pleasant memory from the school at Market Street, recorded in his *Memoir,* concerned a moment in which courage suddenly replaced his usual fear and melancholy:

> One day as I was sitting alone on a bench in the school, melancholy, and almost ready to weep at the recollection of what I had already suffered, and expecting at the same time my tormentor every moment, these words of the Psalmist came into my mind, "I will not be afraid

of what man can do unto me." I applied this to my own case, with a degree of trust and confidence in God, that would have been no disgrace to a much more experienced Christian. Instantly, I perceived in myself a briskness of spirits, and a cheerfulness, which I had never before experienced; and took several paces up and down the room with joyful alacrity—*his* gift in whom I trusted. Happy had it been for me, if this early effort towards a dependence on the blessed God had been frequently repeated by me. But alas! it was the first and last instance of the kind, between infancy and manhood.[4]

We must discount as much of this passage as is necessary to illustrate the "pattern" of his life prior to conversion. For our purposes, the description serves only to show that Cowper later remembered those years as having little to redeem them from perpetual gloom. What other feelings he enjoyed came, as it were, from emotional reflex: the inevitable resurgence of good spirits after long periods of depression. But such moments came suddenly and did not last long. If the gloom lightened for a moment, it did not dissipate. Cowper enjoyed no real change in outlook nor any real adjustment, just a spontaneous release of emotion.

Unlike Market Street, Westminster left memories of fairly strenuous activity, of association with others, of a mind not occupied with melancholy subjects:

> The wall on which we tried our graving skill,
> The very name we carv'd, subsisting still;
> The bench on which we sat while deep employ'd,
> Tho' mangled, hack'd, and hew'd, not yet destroy'd:
> Playing our games, and on the very spot;
> As happy as we once, to kneel and draw
> The chalky ring, and knuckle down at taw;
> To pitch the ball into the grounded hat,
> Or drive it devious with a dext'rous pat—
> The pleasing spectacle at once excites
> Such recollection of our own delights,
> That, viewing it, we seem almost t' obtain
> Our innocent sweet simple years again.
> This fond attachment to the well-known place,
> Whence first we started into life's long race,
> Maintains its hold with such unfailing sway,
> We feel it ev'n in age, and at our latest day.[5]

Like any man in his early fifties Cowper could "love" this "play-place" of his early days. In spite of the fact that he identified Westminster with a grotesque situation in which a pet mouse he had been keeping in a drawer littered, and then ate her offspring, he recalled no morbid feeling.

If Cowper's family provided little deep affection during these years, he seems not to have cared much. Probably many of the pleasures he enjoyed at school he found also when he went home. Father and friends alike would have encouraged his activities and his interest in reading and conversing. It might even be in this light that we should see the famous passage from the *Memoir*, the only reference to his father in that document, in which he records how his father and he had once discussed the moral implications of suicide:

> I well recollect too, that when I was about eleven years of age, my father desired me to read a vindication of self-murder, and give him my sentiments upon the question: I did so, and argued against it. My father heard my reasons, and was silent, neither approving nor disapproving; from whence I inferred that he sided with the author against me; though all the time I believe the true motive for his conduct was that he wanted, if he could, to think favourably of the state of a departed friend, who had some years before destroyed himself, and whose death had struck him with the deepest affliction.[6]

Perhaps John Cowper showed too little feeling in introducing a child of eleven to such dark thoughts, but it is entirely possible that he considered the book an interesting topic of speculation for a well-read, bright boy. Certainly, the appearance of the incident in so slanted a work as the *Memoir* is not a fair indication that it had much immediate effect upon the boy's rather tender sensibilities.

The more lurid accusations against himself contained in the *Memoir* portray Cowper as a boy who was immature in religious experience and who at Westminster had fallen into an environment which could only hamper spiritual growth. Perhaps they should be discounted, since writing a *Memoir* was part of the process of conversion, and Cowper had to portray himself as a sinner, as a boy so addicted to lying that he needed several warnings to prevent him from becoming wholly corrupt. One of these "warnings" occurred one evening as he walked through St. Margaret's churchyard. A gravedigger at work threw up a skull which hit Cowper's leg,[7] and shortly thereafter, he suffered an attack of smallpox. If we do not accept the rigid pattern imposed upon these experiences by the enthusiastic convert, we can see in them still more testimony to Cowper's normalcy. Fears, slovenly habits, sentimentality, even morbidity, all typify most boys of this age.

Cowper, like most of his contemporaries at Westminster, enjoyed visits to such places as the Tower of London; and he delighted in the spectacle of Bedlam (Bethlehem Hospital, a lunatic asylum), where, even though he might have sensed the cruelty of the onlookers and the misery of the patients, he thought that "the madness of them had such a humorous air, and displayed itself in so many whimsical freaks, that it was impossible not to be entertained at the same time that I was angry with myself for being so." [8] And, although we have no evidence that he took part in schoolboy pranks of a violent sort—and his memories of his relationship with Vincent Bourne suggest that he didn't—he laughed heartily when the young Duke of Richmond set fire to Bourne's wig and then boxed his ears to put out the flames, and when another boy of gentle family disguised himself as a titled lady and was received with appropriate ceremony by the headmaster. The sense of humor and keen enjoyment of human nature revealed in these reminiscences were accompanied, as in the older Cowper, by a love of nature, which drew him to many a ramble on the banks of the Thames.

In 1750 Cowper began training for the law. His father, probably intent on preserving the family tradition of public service and on having the right acquaintances to guarantee his son at least a successful beginning to his career, articled him to a Mr. Chapman, a solicitor of Ely Place, Holborn, a district of London. The choice of profession was not fortunate; for, aside from the fact that Cowper initially had almost no interest in the law and apparently cared little for whatever prestige the profession of law would have brought him, the system under which one prepared in the eighteenth century to be called to the bar offered little direction, incentive, or discipline. With little direction from outside, the student was thrown almost entirely on his own resources. Of course, success under such conditions could foster the self-direction and control necessary to advancement in the profession and in politics. So it was with Edward Thurlow, articled to Chapman at the same time as Cowper, who had the necessary ambition and love of the law and of work not only to succeed but to become Lord Chancellor. But Cowper had what might be called a gentlemanly disdain for the goals and means by which such ambition expressed itself. Temperament, education, and family background did not prepare him for the inevitable drudgery of study, nor did they offer much encouragement. Without ambition or personal resource, and impelled only by a promise to his father, and perhaps by a vague longing for the security that any objective, no matter how distasteful, would provide, he did only the minimal amount of work necessary and turned his attentions to more interesting pursuits.

While still at Westminster, Cowper had met his uncle Ashley Cowper and his cousins Harriet, Theodora, and Elizabeth. Harriet had immediately impressed him by her wit, vivacity, and charm, as well as by her good sense; but he had fallen in love with Theodora. Cowper's later correspondence with Harriet, even though he destroyed all her letters, and her later handling of his estate and literary remains, reveal much about Harriet's character. But all we know about Theodora is her touching faithfulness to William after the love affair was broken off, and her concern for his welfare throughout his life. The record of the affair contained in Cowper's nineteen Delia poems does not succeed in giving her any identity other than that of the conventional mistress in a long tradition of love poetry which the poet much too closely imitates:

> Delia, th' unkindest girl on earth,
>   When I besought the fair,
> That favour of intrinsic worth,
>   A ringlet of her hair,—
>
> Refus'd that instant to comply
>   With my absurd request,
> For reasons she could specify,
>   Some twenty score at least.
>
> Trust me, my dear, however odd
>   It may appear to say,
> I sought it merely to defraud
>   Thy spoiler of his prey.[9]

Cowper's diction, allusions, and wit are typical of the age and in marked contrast to those of the previous century. Sentiment has replaced ingenuity, and there are no intimate revelations of her (or his) character. Elsewhere, the generalized mistress is worshipped in tropes dictated by the poet's love of truth and nature (in the eighteenth-century sense), not by a love of verbal ingenuity and metaphysical subtlety. A song which begins with typical references to "the sparkling neck" and to "Glossy locks, and brow serene,/Venus' smiles, Diana's mien" takes a political turn with references to beauty, which "maintains/Her empire, and by *union* reigns." [10] But the political theme rests in the context of an allusion to the all-pervading Classical notion that the whole is greater than its parts:

> Each single feature faintly warms,
> But where at once we view display'd
> Unblemish'd grace, the perfect maid
> Our eyes, our ears, our heart alarms.

The last stanza contains the kind of scientific image for which an age brought up on Newton's *Opticks* had an insatiable appetite.

> So when on earth the God of day
> Obliquely sheds his temper'd ray,
>
> Through convex orbs the beams transmit,
> The beams that gently warm'd before,
> Collected, gently warm no more,
> But glow with more prevailing heat.

If a character emerges clearly from the poems, it is that of the lover, not the beloved. He is William, "once a bashful youth," whose quietness caused some to think him too modest; others, to think him lacking in sense, or wanting in spirit; some, to observe, "that though he little said,/He paid it off with thinking." [11] This bashful man with age "grew perter," became more at ease with company, and "dress'd a little smarter." He even attempted wit, "eyed the women," and "made free/To comment on their shapes." This new man was thought to be rough "but now no longer foolish" until miraculously Delia rendered him

> At length, improv'd from head to heel,
> 'Twere scarce too much to say,
> No dancing bear was so genteel,
> Or half so degagé.

Cleverness and "a way with words," which reveal his buoyant spirits in the earlier years of his romantic attachment, give way in 1754, two years after his first severe attack of melancholy, to a more somber tone, matter, and meter. The meter reveals heaviness of spirits, fear of the future, and puzzlement with the self:

> Bid adieu, my sad heart, bid adieu to thy peace,
> Thy pleasure is past, and thy sorrows increase;
> See the shadows of ev'ning how far they extend,
> And a long night is coming, that never may end;
> For the sun is now set that enliven'd the scene,
> And an age must be past ere it rises again.
>
> Already depriv'd of its splendour and heat,
> I feel thee more slowly, more heavily beat;
> Perhaps overstrain'd with the quick pulse of pleasure,
> Thou art glad of this respite to beat at thy leisure;
> But the sigh of distress shall now weary thee more
> Than the flutter and tumult of passion before.
>
> The heart of a lover is never at rest,
> With joy overwhelm'd, or with sorrow oppress'd:
> When Delia is near, all is ecstasy then,
> And I even forget I must lose her again:
> When absent, as wretched as happy before,
> Despairing I cry, I shall see her no more.[12]

A poem written perhaps in 1755 contains vivid memories of the recent period of depression:

> At length if, slumb'ring to a short repose,
> A sweet oblivion frees me from my woes,
> Thy form appears, thy footsteps I pursue,
> Through springy vales, and meadows wash'd in dew;
> Thy arm supports me to the fountain's brink,
> Where, by some secret pow'r forbid to drink,
> Gasping with thirst, I view the tempting flood

> That flies my touch, or thickens into mud,
> Till thine own hand immerg'd the goblet dips,
> And bears it streaming to my burning lips;
> There borne aloft on Fancy's wing we fly,
> Like souls embodied to their native sky;
> Now ev'ry rock, each mountain, disappears,
> And the round earth an even surface wears;
> When lo! the force of some resistless weight
> Bears me straight down from that pernicious height;
> Parting, in vain our struggling arms we close;
> Abhorred forms, dire phantoms interpose;
> With trembling voice on thy lov'd name I call,
> And gulphs yawn ready to receive my fall;
> From these fallacious visions of distress
> I wake; nor are my real sorrows less.[13]

Perhaps there are echoes of some of the real difficulties the romance with Theodora encountered in another poem written in
1755:

> All-worshipp'd Gold! thou mighty mystery!
> Say by what name shall I address thee rather
> Our blessing, or our bane? without thy aid,
> The gen'rous pangs of pity but distress
> The human heart, that fain would feel the bliss
> Of blessing others; and, enslav'd by thee,
> Far from relieving woes which others feel,
> Misers oppress themselves.[14]

But the realities of the poet's precarious financial position are
immediately sublimated in the conventional theme that the only
true wealth is his mistress, and his avarice is directed to the possession of this "worthiest object."

When the affair was terminated in 1756, Cowper's poetic lament foreshadowed the soul-wracking imagery of such future
poems as "The Castaway":

> Oft I have thought the scene of troubles closed,
>   And hop'd once more to gaze upon your charms;
> As oft some dire mischance has interposed,
>   And snatch'd th' expected blessing from my arms.

The seaman thus, his shattered vessel lost,
  Still vainly strives to shun the threatening death;
And while he thinks to gain the friendly coast,
  And drops his feet, and feels the sands beneath:

Borne by the wave, steep-sloping from the shore,
  Back to th' inclement deep again he beats
The surge aside, and seems to tread secure;
  And now the refluent wave his baffled toil defeats.[15]

Although there has been doubt about the depth of Cowper's affection, I don't think that there can be any doubt that he was really in love with Theodora.[16] Much has been said about his failure to correspond with, or even mention, her after 1756; and, of course, there remain surprisingly few references to his love for her. Perhaps a reason for this silence can be seen in a parallel situation, the first rupture in his friendship with Lady Austen. In a letter to William Unwin about thirty years later, Cowper wrote "that when an amicable freedom of intercourse, and that unreserved confidence which belongs only to true friendship, has been once unrooted, plant it again with what care you may, it is very difficult, if not impossible to make it grow. The fear of giving offence to a temper too apt to take it, is unfavourable to that comfort we propose to ourselves even in our ordinary connexions, but absolutely incompatible with the pleasures of real friendship." [17] In this letter, Cowper reflects on a situation not so unlike the earlier one as we might at first think. Significantly, Lady Austen made the overtures which led to reconciliation; and, even though the argument with her was settled, the relationship never returned to its former state. Within two years they had parted, and Cowper rarely mentioned her again.

The actual breaking off of the affair between Theodora and William seems to have been the work of Ashley Cowper. Although his reasons are not known, two seem plausible. In 1752 William had his first severe attack of melancholy, and Theodora is known to have suffered from a similar malady, which, in fact, seems to have afflicted the entire Cowper family. Since Theodora and William were first cousins, there might well have been talk about the dangers not only to the future happiness of the two but to the health of their children. Furthermore, William showed little interest in his profession, and he did not have the independent means to support Theodora properly. Although he had been called to the bar in 1754, and in 1759 became Commissioner of Bankrupts, a job which required responsible action on his part, he by no means offered much promise of success.

When it became clear that he could not marry Theodora, Cowper had to face the very delicate problem of disengaging himself from an intimate relationship in a family with which he wanted to remain on close terms. Good manners and the preservation of harmony within the family demanded that he conduct himself with great restraint. Undoubtedly, once the break had occurred, his personality would not have allowed him to continue the relationship in a way which would have been to him a mockery of past intimacies. The solution, therefore, seems to have been for both lovers to retreat into themselves and to hide their feelings in dignified silence. Years later, when William had moved to Olney, he received many gifts from an anonymous donor, who, he suspected, was Theodora. But again it was characteristic of the sense of decorum which both shared that no direct mention of each other was made. William avoided any statement that might lead to a resumption of a friendship which could turn only into laments about the past. With Harriet, whom Cowper knew in a different way, no such obstruction existed. The intimacies of that friendship were never violated, and could be restored after the first siege of madness in 1763, and then, after a much greater hiatus, in 1785.

The emphasis which the space needed to catalogue Cowper's reversals and misfortunes in the 1750's necessarily gives to the gloomier side of his personality unfortunately distorts his character as we are beginning more and more to know it. The letters and other personal gleanings from these years indicate that he found ample diversion: first, from the tedium of the law, and, later, from his difficulties with Theodora. Activities with Ashley Cowper's family, especially the sisters Harriet, Theodora, and Elizabeth, occupied much of his time during the early years of the decade. We can imagine him with Thurlow, his fellow law student, employed at Ashley Cowper's house in Southampton Row in "giggling and making giggle, instead of studying law." [18]

Later, his merriment took other forms, such as contributing to the *St. James Chronicle* and *The Connoisseur,* and associating in the Nonsense Club with Bonnell Thornton, George Colman, and Robert Lloyd.[19] Another companion and classmate at Westminster, Charles Churchill, would achieve fame as a rake and satirist in the next decade. The letters of this period show the effect of this company on Cowper's mental habits and style. However, they do not reflect the dissolute behavior in which some members of the club indulged in later years, especially when Wilkes began to associate with them. The gay life in Southampton Row and with the Nonsense Club should serve as a dominant theme in the description of Cowper during the 1750's, even though the fit of depression in 1752, his unhappiness with the law, the end of his romance with Theodora in 1756, and the death of his father in the same year, seem more important when viewed from the perspective of his illness in 1763.

In 1752 Cowper moved from Ely Place to the Middle Temple. Soon after he had settled there, he experienced "such a dejection of spirits, as none but they who have felt the same, can have the least conception of. Day and night I was upon the rack, lying down in horror, and rising up in despair. I presently lost all relish for those studies, to which before I had been closely attached; the classics had no longer any charms for me; I had need of something more salutary than amusement, but I had no one to direct me where to find it." [20] A vacation at Southampton with his cousin Harriet and her fiancé Sir Thomas Hesketh helped remove some of the gloom.

In a letter Cowper later recalled many details of this holiday which help us see what kind of person he was during these years.[21] In all the times he went to Southampton, he wrote, he never was in the assembly room. Although he had no moral objections to dancing and card playing, he had too little fondness for company to indulge in such activities. If he shunned society, however, he was no recluse. He took part in the recreations of Thomas Hesketh's party, especially sailing; but he enjoyed much more greatly a walk through the countryside (probably with a few intimate friends). We immediately think of the later Cowper, the poet, and his deep love of nature. More important, however, from the standpoint of this letter, is the fact that the vacation is recalled in a link between a brief comment on the medicinal value of sea bathing and a longer discussion of his claustrophobic tendencies. Countryside becomes a means of liberating the spirit, whether from the assembly, the confines of a boat, or the city and the law. Cowper's recollections of his less than enthusiastic participation in Hesketh's boating parties leads naturally to a few observations on the "wearisomeness that attends a sea life":

I never was fond of company, and especially disliked it in the country. A walk to Netley Abbey, or to Freemantle, or to Redbridge, or a book by the fire-side, had always more charms for me than any other amusement that the place afforded. I was also a sailor, and being of Sir Thomas Hesketh's party, who was himself born one, was often pressed into service. But though I gave myself an air, and wore trousers, I had no genuine right to that honour, disliking much to be occupied in great waters, unless in the finest weather. How they contrive to elude the wearisomeness that attends a sea life, who take long voyages, you know better than I; but for my own part, I seldom have sailed so far as from Hampton river to Portsmouth, without feeling the confinement irksome, and sometimes to a degree that was almost insupportable. There is a certain perverseness, of which I believe all men have a share, but of which no man has a larger share than I;—I mean that temper, or humour, or whatever it is to be called, that indisposes us to a situation, though not unpleasant in itself, merely because we cannot get out of it. I could not endure the room in which I now write, were I conscious that the door were locked. In less than five minutes I should feel myself a prisoner, though I can spend hours in it, under an assurance that I may leave it when I please, without experiencing any tedium at all. It was for this reason, I suppose, that the yacht was always disagreeable to me. Could I have liked it well enough; but being surrounded with water, I was as much confined in it as if I had been surrounded by fire, and did not find that it made me any adequate compensation for such an abridgment of my liberty. I make little doubt but Noah was glad when he was enlarged from the ark; and we are sure that Jonah was, when he came out of the fish; and so was I to escape from the good sloop the *Harriet*.[22]

If there was a link between the Cowper of the town and the enjoyer of the country, it lay in the facts that both moved in a rather small circle of friends of long standing and both found great pleasure in "a book by the fire-side."

From the distorted perspective of the *Memoir*, begun in 1765, the Nonsense Club and the law represented a hardening of the sinful character formed in the earlier years and at Westminster. The only saving lights were Ashley Cowper's family, who were hardly made in the best evangelical image, and an emotional experience at Southampton. In Mr. Chapman's office he

. . . might have lived and died, without hearing or seeing anything that might remind me of a single Christian duty, had it not been that I was at liberty to spend my leisure time (which was well nigh all my time) at my uncle's in Southampton Row. By this means I had the opportunity of seeing the inside of a church, whither I went with the family on Sundays, which probably I should otherwise never have seen.[23]

But during his several months at Southampton he felt other movings deep within his spirit:

Soon after our arrival we walked to a place called Freemantle, about a mile from the town; the morning was clear and calm; the sun shone bright upon the sea; and the country on the borders of it was the most beautiful I had ever seen. We sat down upon an eminence, at the end of that arm of the sea, which runs between Southampton and the New Forest. Here it was, that on a sudden, as if another sun had been kindled that instant in the heavens, on purpose to dispel sorrow and vexation of spirit, I felt the weight of all my weariness taken off; my heart became light and joyful in a moment; I could have wept with transport had I been alone. I must needs believe that nothing less than the Almighty fiat could have filled me with such inexpressible delight; nor by a gradual dawning of peace, but, as it were, with a flash of his life-giving countenance. I think I remember something like a glow of gratitude to the Father of mercies, for this unexpected blessing, and that I ascribed it to his gracious acceptance of my prayers. But Satan, and my own wicked heart, quickly persuaded me that I was indebted for my deliverance, to nothing but a change of scene. By this means he turned the blessing into a poison; teaching me to conclude, that nothing but a continued circle of diversion, and indulgence of appetite, could secure me from a relapse.[24]

Clearly Cowper in his twenties knew both a lighter and darker side of life, but I do not think that this metaphor should be applied in the conventional, evangelical sense. The struggle existed not between salvation and damnation, between the Heavenly and Hellish forces, as he called them in the *Memoir*, but between happiness and depression. Any sensitive person would have found enough in eighteenth-century life to upset him, and Cowper had

himself experienced many harsh and cruel circumstances. He had
also discovered the misery of being forced into a way of life not at
all congenial to him. There had been no escape from Dr. Pitman's
school—only a few moments, when, as if by emotional reflex,
gloom had temporarily been lifted. At Mr. Disney's there had
been little affection or few attempts to make the environment attractive. Westminster had provided little besides a smattering of
learning and some friendships. Berkhampstead had offered no retreat, not only because Cowper's relations with his father were not
particularly warm, but because a stepmother for whom he had
little feeling had replaced the mother he had idolized. Now, with
nowhere but Ashley Cowper's house in Southampton Row to go,
he had to face a career which he found unrewarding, and which
had settled upon him obligations that he could not fulfill, not the
least of them the desire to please his father.

Nevertheless, Cowper managed to learn some law; and, by
paying the fines assessed against him for habitually absenting
himself from what few activities were required of students, he
made himself ready to be called to the bar in 1754. We may pre-
sume that following this event he continued much as before.
Whatever tensions were caused by the breaking off of his love
affair and by the death of his father in 1756 and that of his closest
friend Sir William Russell in 1757 were undoubtedly dissipated by
his friendships with such people as Joseph Hill and Clotworthy
Rowley and the wits: Thornton, Lloyd, and Colman. However,
the very real problem of how he was going to support himself
remained. It served as the subject of at least one witty letter of
this period.

This world is a shabby fellow, and uses us ill; but a few years hence
there will be no difference between us and our fathers of the tenth
generation upwards. I could be as splenetic as you, and with more
reason, if I thought proper to indulge that humour; but my resolution
is (and I would advise you to adopt it), never to be melancholy while
I have a hundred pounds in the world to keep up my spirits. God
knows how long that will be; but in the meantime *Io Triumphe!* If a
great man struggling with misfortunes is a noble object, a little man
that despises them is no contemptible one; and this is all the philosophy
I have in the world at present. It savours pretty much of the ancient
Stoic, but till the Stoics became coxcombs, they were, in my opinion,
a very sensible sect.

If my resolution to be a great man was half so strong as it is to despise the shame of being a little one, I should not despair of a house in Lincoln's Inn Fields, with all its appurtenances; for there is nothing more certain, and I could prove it by a thousand instances, than that every man may be rich if he will . . .

. . . Upon the whole, my dear Rowley, there is a degree of poverty that has no disgrace belonging to it; that degree of it, I mean in which a man enjoys clean linen and good company; and if I never sink below this degree of it, I care not if I never rise above it. This is a strange epistle, nor can I imagine how the devil I came to write it: but here it is, such as it is, and much good may you do with it. I have no estate as it happens so if it should fall into bad hands, I shall be in no danger of a commission of lunacy.[25]

As in his later correspondence, Cowper here writes with spontaneity, putting ideas down as they come to his mind. If the letter differs in tone from those of later years, it is testimony to the influence of his witty acquaintances. It is ironic that the insanity he jokes about should within a year have turned into somber reality.

Attempts to give Cowper a more solid financial status resulted in his appointment as Commissioner of Bankrupts in 1759 at a salary of sixty pounds per annum. This income could not even begin to cover his expenses, and by the time he moved to the Inner Temple, also in 1759, he had spent most of the money inherited from his father's estate. Repeated jests about these matters, and such details as the sale of a house he and his brother had inherited, show that, to his closest friends, Cowper maintained an air of confidence which seems surprising to many who look at these years from the perspective of the mental breakdown in 1763.

In order to make himself more secure financially, Cowper asked his cousin Major Cowper (a son and successor to William Cowper, and Clerk of the Parliaments) for the appointment, if it should become vacant, as Clerk of the Journals of the House of Lords, a position to which Major Cowper held the patent. Shortly thereafter, the post became vacant through the death of the clerk. At the same time, the office of Reading Clerk and Clerk of Committees, which the Major also controlled, became vacant; and Major Cowper offered these two clerkships to William, who accepted. Then, having second thoughts, he withdrew his acceptance and repeated his request for the other office. Both the Reading Clerk and Clerk of Committees participated directly in the function of the House of Lords, and apparently Cowper did not care for the nature of the activities, the prominence and the kind of personal relationships involved. The Clerk of the Journals could discharge his duties in comparative privacy.

Cowper's right to the clerkship was not to go unchallenged, however. The eighteenth-century system of patronage and sine-cures encouraged abuses of privilege and laxness in the carrying out of duties, and Major Cowper proved to be no exception in the exercise of his patents. Once before the Cowper interests had been challenged, and a committee of the House had even passed a motion of censure. Now a party opposed to the Cowpers decided to support a candidate for the clerkship who had greater experience but no legal claim to the office. The only way to resolve this conflict was for both men to be examined at the bar of the House. In his *Memoir* William tells of his reaction to this development.

All the horror of my fears and perplexities now returned: a thunderbolt would have been as welcome to me as this intelligence. I knew, to demonstration, that upon these terms the clerkship of the journals was no place for me. To require my attendance at the bar of the House, that I might there publicly entitle myself to this office, was, in effect, to exclude me from it. In the meantime, the interest of my friend, the honour of his choice, my own reputation and circumstances, all urged me forward: all pressed me to undertake that which I saw to be impracticable. They whose spirits are formed like mine, to whom a public exhibition of themselves, on any occasion, is mortal poison, may have some idea of the horror of my situation; others can have none. My continual misery at length brought on a nervous fever: quiet forsook me by day, and peace by night; a finger raised against me, was more than I could stand against.[26]

There can be no doubt that Cowper was highly agitated, but his anxieties need not have risen from some of the more exotic causes suggested by the more romantic biographers of the nineteenth century.[27] Instead, they should be attributed to a combination of extremely unpleasant circumstances and to an unsettled state of mind.

In a sense, the impending examination threw upon him the task of defending the family honor, which abuse of the rights of patronage had called into question. As Cowper himself wrote, "it appeared plain, that if we succeeded at last, it could only be by fighting our ground by inches. Every advantage, I was told, would be sought for, and eagerly seized, to disconcert us." [28] Not only did he have to justify the Major's choice (and thus both their characters), but he had to cover up a not completely reputable record of which all would be aware. Personal relationships were also at stake. He could not betray the confidence of his cousin, nor could he refuse the offer of a job that he had sought. Moral scruples complicated the issue. Not only was the appointment tainted, but it placed him in the embarrassing position of accepting the benefits of the kind of prerogative which, at least in later years, he would attack on moral grounds:

> Lucrative offices are seldom lost
> For want of pow'rs proportion'd to the post;
> Give e'en a dunce th' employment he desires,
> And he soon finds the talents it requires;
> A business with an income at its heels
> Furnishes always oil for its own wheels.[29]

If he felt that he had no right to the job merely on the grounds of his privileged status and that the other candidate was better qualified than he, he also felt the burden of his own lack of experience. Moreover, constitutional reserve caused him to abhor the idea of making a spectacle of himself.

From the summer of 1763, when he learned that he would have to face the examination, to November, when he suffered his first attack of insanity, Cowper lived in an agitated state. He tried to prepare himself for the inquiry by going to the office and examining the journals, but in his condition he could not absorb what he felt to be an adequate amount of information. On August 9 he wrote to Harriet of his profound distrust of himself.

I have a pleasure in writing to you at any time, but especially at the present, when my days are spent in reading the Journals, and my nights in dreaming of them—an employment not very agreeable to a head that has long been habituated to the luxury of choosing its subject, and has been as little employed upon business, as if it had grown upon the shoulders of a much wealthier gentleman. But the numscull pays for it now, and will not presently forget the discipline it has undergone lately. . . . Certainly I am not an absolute fool; but I have more weaknesses than the greatest of all the fools I can recollect at present.

In short, if I was as fit for the next world as I am unfit for this, and
God forbid I should speak it in vanity, I would not change conditions
with any saint in Christendom.

The second paragraph of the letter mentions a trip to Margate, a
seaside resort, which he hoped would restore his spirits. But no
vacation could remove the source of distress or alter a character
"fixed" and "riveted fast." [30] Nor could it stem a growing conviction that he would not prove competent in the examination. As
November approached, his anxieties increased, and his mind
turned more than once to possible means of escape. He thought
again of asking Major Cowper to withdraw the appointment, but
the arguments against this course of action remained. He even
thought of suicide, but at first moral scruples prevented serious
consideration of it. As he came closer to the moment of crisis,
however, death, of which he had the usual fears, began to seem
more attractive. Then, curiously enough, conversations with
strangers in chophouses and coffeehouses began to turn toward
the subject of suicide; and Cowper at least twice found such casual acquaintances defending it. He even recalled the conversation
many years earlier in which his father had defended a treatise on
the subject.

Seemingly there was no one to bring him out of himself. His
acquaintances of earlier years were forming new friendships, and
he was forced more and more to fall back upon his own resources.
On his own, Cowper began to fancy that the world had turned
against him. In the last month before the examination he began to
detect in perfect strangers signs that they were aware of his guilty
and hopeless condition. Perhaps a wayward glance, a fleeting expression to which he attached personal significance, a few words
heard out of context, added to the notion that his most private
concerns were the subject of almost universal mirth. One morning, two days before his ordeal, he found in the newspaper a letter
advocating suicide which he took to be an affront by a person who
wished him dead. Tormented by a sense of his own inadequacy
and by his fears that he would be exposed—reactions now transformed to the belief that the world already knew his weaknesses
—he attempted suicide.

Five days earlier he had purchased a bottle of laudanum from a
druggist, who, he fancied, had looked suspicious and had hesi-

tated for a moment. Perhaps unnerved by his own boldness, Cowper had waited day after day for some lucky event to provide an escape for him. When he read the letter in the newspaper, he rushed from the coffeehouse saying within himself, "Your cruelty shall be gratified, you shall have your revenge." Drowning suddenly appearing to be a more expedient method than laudanum, he started out for one of the fields at the edge of London to throw himself into a ditch. But, before he had proceeded far, he decided that he could gain peace and security without violence and dishonor by going to France and entering a Roman Catholic monastery. He went home, began to pack, then again decided to drown himself; but, when he arrived at Tower Wharf, he found a porter sitting on a pile of goods, as if to prevent him.

While returning to the Temple in a coach, he tried to take the laudanum. Suddenly a "convulsive agitation" deprived him of the use of his hands. He was torn between longing for death and fear, between moral convictions and desire for escape, between cowardice and the will to order his destiny. Again and again he raised the bottle to his lips but could not drink. Now desperate, he flung himself into a corner of the coach, and there the fumes from the laudanum, especially from a few drops which had been dashed from the bottle, began to have a "stupefying effect." Still he could not summon up the will to destroy himself, and still he regretted his lack of courage.

When he arrived at his room in the Temple, he poured the laudanum into a small basin; put it beside the bed; partially undressed; and lay down between the blankets. Reproaching himself for his fear of death, he tried to subdue the voice within which continued to tell him to "consider and live." At length he reached for the basin, but again his hands became useless. Although his arms were not paralyzed, he was puzzled at his loss of control of his hands, and lay back to contemplate it. But, when his laundress's husband entered the outer room of the apartment, his arrival shattered Cowper's hysteric fit. He started up from bed, dressed, hid the basin, and tried to restore his composure. When the man left, Cowper's state of mind had completely altered. His hysteria having given way to horror and anger, he emptied the basin into a container of dirty water and threw it out the window.

He still could not face the examination nor himself, and new waves of panic followed the old ones. The horror with which he viewed his actions seems to have come not from any deep moral awakening but from the fact that he had almost been discovered. During the rest of that day and the following one, he was too exhausted by his nervous agitation to do more than mechanically follow his normal daily routine. When "a most intimate friend" called upon him in the evening to wish him well on his decision to keep the office, the friend's cheerfulness could not dispel the gloom, although Cowper feigned a lighter manner.

Early the next morning he again attempted suicide by leaning all of his weight upon the extended blade of a penknife that he had taken into bed with him. Again he could not gather up enough will to make the dulled point of the knife penetrate. When the clock struck seven, he realized that he had to subdue his fear of pain and death and summon the will to settle his affairs once and for all. He twice tried to hang himself, but failed. A third attempt, the first which allowed him to hang at full length, instead of with his legs pulled up, would probably have succeeded had the halter not broken. When he regained consciousness in a few minutes, he stumbled into bed. The laundress, hearing him fall, ran into the room. Cowper, now beyond the ability to worry about detection, sent her for a friend to whom he related the whole affair and who was sent to inform Major Cowper.

The Major's reaction was one to be expected of a man with both the family reputation and his own prerogatives in peril. "My dear Mr. Cowper, you terrify me," he said, "to be sure, you cannot hold the office at this rate—where is the deputation?" Having procured the needed document, the Major hurried away to sever as neatly as possible William's connection with Parliament. When the Major had left, the sudden removal of the cause of anxiety and the sense of total failure must have been as overwhelming as the feeling of moral degradation into which, apparently, all other concerns were channeled. His claustrophobia, linked with the sense of being rejected, latent since his mother's death, led him to fancy that God had closed him in as a foretaste of the eternal imprisonment that awaited him. In the days that followed his attempts at suicide, whenever he opened a book, he found it filled with allusions to his condition and with details and rhetorical figures that seemed addressed to him. In the streets people seemed to avoid him or laugh at him. When he met friends, they seemed to treat him with reserve, to hint at his sin in conversation, and to mock him as soon as they had turned their backs to him.

What had previously seemed to him to be a respectably idle life, the main defect of which was its lack of financial security, now became a history of sin and of divine vengeance. His sense of failure and personal degradation were transmuted to the wrath of God punishing the worst of sinners, as he tried to cope with the feeling of being closed in by himself, his fears and personal limitations, and therefore closed out of a world indifferent to his needs. In the only poem of this period, his anguish poured out:

> Hatred and vengeance, my eternal portion,
> Scarce can endure delay of execution,
> Wait, with impatient readiness, to seize my
> > Soul in a moment.
>
> Damn'd below Judas: more abhorr'd than he was,
> Who for a few pence sold his holy Master
> Twice betrayed Jesus me, the last delinquent,
> > Deems the profanest.
>
> Man disavows, and Deity disowns me:
> Hell might afford my miseries a shelter;
> Therefore hell keeps her ever hungry mouths all
> > Bolted against me.
>
> Hard lot! encompass'd with a thousand dangers;
> Weary, faint, trembling with a thousand terrors;
> I'm called, if vanquish'd, to receive a sentence
> > Worse than Abiram's
>
> *Him* the vindictive rod of angry justice
> Sent quick and howling to the centre headlong;
> *I*, fed with judgment, in a fleshly tomb, am
> > Buried above ground.[31]

The death of the former Clerk of the Journals he took to be God's way of compounding Cowper's original sin of avarice. Having "murdered" the clerk by coveting his job, he must now face punishment for a double crime.

Shortly after he had given up the idea of suicide, William wrote a letter to his brother John to inform him of his condition. Three years before, John had been elected a fellow of what is now Corpus Christi College, Cambridge. He had gained considerable prestige for his academic attainments and, though apparently hypersensitive, could provide calm and rational advice and the balm of a gentle personality. None of these would avail, however; for intellectually and emotionally William could not accept any persuasion to hope. He called in his cousin Martin Madan, a prominent evangelical and Calvinist. But, if Madan, robust in body and spirit, could arouse emotion by his eloquence and zeal and could calm William's fears by discoursing sonorously on the universal depravity of man, he could only agitate him by continual references to a need for a lively, even joyful, commitment to Jesus Christ. In the darkness of his depression Cowper could not entertain even the possibility of divine light penetrating his condition. His reason could not respond to the idea of divine compassion, nor deep within him were there any stirrings beneath the heavy weight of despair. When Madan told him that he must have faith, and that Madan thought that God would vouchsafe it to Cowper, he could only answer, "I wish he would."

The zeal of Madan had temporarily lightened Cowper's depression, however; and John asked him to return. This restorative could at best be temporary, and after the second visit Cowper experienced both a mental and physical relapse.

Satan plied me closely with horrible visions, and more horrible voices. My ears rang with the sound of torments, that seemed to await me. Then did the pains of hell get hold on me, and, before daybreak, the very sorrows of death encompassed me. A numbness seized the extremities of my body, and life seemed to retreat before it. My hands and feet became cold and stiff; a cold sweat stood upon my forehead; my heart seemed at every pulse to beat its last, and my soul to cling to my lips, as if on the very brink of departure. No convicted criminal ever feared death more, or was more assured of dying.

A few hours later John called upon him, and about an hour after his arrival the "distemper of mind" for which Cowper had so ardently prayed as an escape actually seized him.

While I traversed the apartment, in the most horrible dismay of soul, expecting every moment, that the earth would open and swallow me

up; my conscience scaring and the avenger of blood pursuing me, and
the city of refuge out of reach and out of sight; a strange and horrible
darkness fell upon me. If it were possible, that a heavy blow could
light on the brain, without touching the skull, such was the sensation
I felt. I clapped my hand to my forehead, and cried aloud through
the pain it gave me. At every stroke, my thoughts and expressions became more wild and incoherent; all that remained was the sense of
sin, and the expectation of punishment.

When John Cowper decided that William would have to be
placed in an asylum, the one decided upon was Dr. Nathaniel
Cotton's "Collegium Insanorum" at St. Albans. Dr. Cotton was a
gentle, kind, cheerful man who had studied under Boerhaave in
Leyden, written a treatise on scarlet fever, and dabbled in poetry
and sermon writing. His character and training probably made his
home, in which he treated his patients, one of the more humane
hospitals in an age when treatment usually was barbaric. In this
environment Cowper gradually began to recover. To what extent
Cotton and his religious enthusiasm were responsible we cannot
say, but it is entirely possible that in the serene atmosphere of St.
Albans he merely grew out of his depression. For the first five and
one-half months he remained in a state of extreme withdrawal,
persuaded that at any moment God would plunge him into Hell.
But the certainty of damnation eventually made its prospect,
though not less terrible, somewhat less able to excite hysteria. Day
after day Cowper awoke to find himself not in Hell but in the
cheerful atmosphere of Dr. Cotton's *Collegium,* and at length his
depression began to lift.

In July, 1764, when John Cowper arrived to see the patient, his
first impression could not have been favorable. On his asking how
William found himself, he replied, "As much better as despair can
make me." During a walk in the garden, John tried to persuade
him that his fear of impending judgment was unfounded. Apparently he expressed himself with enough of the right kind of feeling
to penetrate for a moment the shell of despair into which William
had retired, for in response he burst into tears and cried out, "If it
be a delusion, then I am the happiest of beings."

The stirrings of hope needed to be confirmed by reason before
Cowper could entirely recover, and this occurred in two characteristic ways. One morning he dreamed that a beautiful child "just
out of leading strings" but able to walk steadily came to his bed-

side and that, upon seeing this apparition, his heart was filled with
peace. Although the vision appeared to be a sign of divine favor,
Cowper still needed to know where to turn for a more abiding
comfort. In a few days two other signs brought with them this
knowledge. As he walked in the garden one morning, he happened upon a Bible. He opened it to the account of the raising of
Lazarus in Chapter 11 of the Gospel of St. John, and almost shed
tears at the revelation of "so much benevolence, mercy, goodness,
and sympathy with miserable men, in our Saviour's conduct."

After lamenting that he had forfeited God's mercy, he returned
to his room with "heart softened, though not yet enlightened." In
a few hours he again turned to the Bible, opening it this time to
III Romans 25: "Whom God hath set forth to be a propitiation
through faith in His blood, to declare His Righteousness for the
remission of sins that are past, through the forebearance of God."
Suddenly his mind was convinced, and the last obstruction was
removed from the joy that had been welling up within him. He
felt that he would die with gratitude and happiness. His "eyes
filled with tears," and his "voice choked with transport." He
"could only look up to heaven in silent fear, overwhelmed with
love and wonder." In this state of exaltation all worldly concerns
dropped away; he knew only an insatiable desire for communion
with God, and praise of the Lord poured forth from him:

> But at length a word of Healing
>   Sweeter than an angel's note,
> From the Saviour's lips distilling
>   Chas'd despair and chang'd my lot.
>   Sweet the sound of Grace Divine,
>   Sweet the grace which makes me thine.
>
> 'Twas a word well tim'd and suited
>   To the need of such an hour,
> Sweet to one like me polluted,
>   Spoke in love and seal'd with pow'r.
>   Grace Divine, how sweet the sound,
>   Sweet the grace that I have found.
>
>   .   .   .   .
>
> All at once my chains were broken,
>   From my feet my fetters fell,

> And that word in pity spoken,
> Snatch'd me from the gates of Hell.
> Grace Divine, how sweet the sound,
> Sweet the grace that I have found.[32]

It is interesting that this poem, celebrating his liberation, should have been the first one to follow the "Lines Written During A Period Of Insanity," the product of his claustrophobia. Imagery, diction, tone, and the use of the ecstatic refrain reveal the completeness of the change.

For many weeks tears were ready to flow whenever Cowper mentioned the Gospel or the name of Jesus. "Joy unspeakable" and "glory" made him want to spend every moment in prayer and thanksgiving. In the "ardour" of his "first love" he burned with such desire to run "in the way of [the] commandments" that he could hardly spare time to sleep. How Dr. Cotton responded to this hysterical joy, we do not know; but for about a year after his recovery, Cowper remained in the asylum spending much of the time in "sweet communion" with Cotton "concerning the things of our salvation." Undoubtedly Cowper had little desire to leave the company of the man who had broken his "chains" and provided him warmth and security. Moreover, he had no place to go. Never again did he want to set foot in the Temple or even go to London.[33]

Not only did the Temple raise horrible memories of the past, but it represented a way of life which Cowper now found morally reprehensible. "God made the country, and man made the town" had deep personal meaning for him, for with conversion came rejection of the worldly pursuits and pleasures of the previous decade and a cleaving to a quieter, more serene way of life conducive to religious contemplation and devotion.[34] The old life was a

> . . . constant revolution, stale
> And tasteless, of the same repeated joys,
> That palls and satiates, and makes languid life
> A pedlar's pack, that bows the bearer down.[35]

This life caused health to suffer and spirits to ebb. A new environment which would freshen his thoughts and constantly raise his mind to God was needed.

The major obstacle separating Cowper from the idyllic existence which he sought was the same problem that had dogged
him for years and had contributed to his mental breakdown. As
yet he had found no way to give order and stability to his financial
condition. Now he was also faced with the expenses incurred during his illness, with a patrimony almost entirely depleted, and
still with no prospects of a steady income. In spite of this condition he decided, probably on moral grounds, to resign his post as
Commissioner of Bankrupts. And, when it came time to leave Dr.
Cotton's, he not only took as a valet one of the servants in the
asylum, but also adopted the six-year-old son of a brutal, drunken
cobbler. The means of supporting this establishment he left to the
devices of his relatives, to his friend Joseph Hill, and to Providence.

His reliance on Providence, of course, resulted from his conversion. By resigning his appointment as Commissioner, he had reduced himself to an income which he realized was barely sufficient to sustain life, but he preferred starvation to the prospect of
offending his Saviour. In return he felt assured that "while I live,
'bread shall be given me, and water shall be sure' according to His
gracious promise." All would come from "the great mercy of God,
who has since raised me up such friends as have enabled me to
enjoy all the comforts and conveniences of life." [36] Cowper's family, of course, would not allow one of its members to fall beneath
that "degree of poverty that has no disgrace belonging to it"; but,
when William himself turned benefactor and at first proved incapable of living within the annual income raised for him by sub-
scription, his relatives expressed displeasure.

It had been decided that Cowper should live near Cambridge,
where his brother could look after him. After a visit of a few days,
in which we can be sure that William's religious enthusiasm annoyed a brother who not only was gaining more prominence in
the academic world, but also shared his brother's rather irritable
temperament, William moved on to Huntingdon, a town fifteen
miles away, where the brothers could exchange visits once a week.
Huntingdon proved to be a fortunate choice. A trim and attractive
town of two thousand people with substantial buildings and good
roads, it had the bustle of thriving commercial enterprises without
great masses of people, and it provided easy access to the countryside.

Although Cowper found the landscape uninteresting, he immediately developed a fondness for the River Ouse, "the most agreeable circumstance in this part of the world." As if to demonstrate his triumph over the past and the environment he had rejected, he insisted that the Thames was in no way superior.

. . . at this town it is I believe as wide as the Thames at Windsor; nor does the silver Thames better deserve that epithet, nor has it more flowers upon its banks, these being attributes which in strict truth belong to neither. Fluellen would say, they are as like as my fingers to my fingers, and there is salmon in both. It is a noble stream to bathe in and I shall make that use of it three times a week, having introduced myself to it for the first time this morning.[37]

The reference to Fluellen shows the high spirits that Cowper enjoyed. But, if the letters to Hill sparkle with a wit which revealed that internal order had been regained, others show a more evangelical kind of joy. His letters to Harriet flow one into another, as his pen, impelled by his rapture, pours out testimony of his conversion and races to glean his emotions. He could not say enough to assure her of his happiness, of his restoration to mental stability, and of his continued affection for her. So well provided was his new world that, if he were to starve, "it must be through forgetfulness, rather than scarcity." [38] The day after he arrived in Huntingdon, he attended church and found it difficult to contain his rapture. His heart, filled with love for the congregation, discovered an intensity of bliss that prevented him from singing the Psalm. When the Gospel was read, "the sound of it was more than I could well support." [39] He felt a direct communion with God which did not permit coherent prayer and meditation, but found expression in heightened feeling and fragmentary outbursts.

These rapturous feelings; Cowper's new preoccupation with churches and churchyards; his ecstatic discourse; his new habit of praying spontaneously, of falling on his knees in the fields around Huntingdon; and his new acquaintances—all of them devout and some to the point of eccentricity—seem to have made such intimate friends as Lady Hesketh fear that perhaps he had not thoroughly recovered, that one form of hysteria had merely replaced another. She apparently tried to persuade Cowper to control his emotions and modify his most extravagant outbursts of enthusiasm. Cowper's letter to her, dated September 14, 1765, clearly was intended to answer her doubts about his protestations of guilt:

You say, you hope it is not necessary for salvation, to undergo the same afflictions that I have undergone. No! my dear cousin. God deals with His children as a merciful Father; He does not, as He Himself tells us, afflict willingly the sons of men. Doubtless there are many, who, having been placed by His good providence out of the reach of any great evil and the influence of bad example, have from their very infancy been partakers of the grace of His Holy Spirit, in such a manner as never to have allowed themselves in any grievous offence against Him. May you love Him more and more day by day; as every day, while you think upon Him, you will find Him more worthy of your love: and may you be finally accepted with Him for His sake, whose intercession for all His faithful servants cannot but prevail!

The letter of July 4, 1765 seems to reply to a rather tactful hint:

It gives me some concern, though at the same time it increases my gratitude, to reflect that a convert made in Bedlam is more likely to be a stumbling-block to others, than to advance their faith. But if it had that effect upon any, it is owing to their reasoning amiss, and drawing their conclusions from false premises. He who can ascribe an amendment of life and manners, and a reformation of the heart itself, to madness, is guilty of an absurdity that in any other case would fasten the imputation of madness upon himself; for by so doing he ascribes a reasonable effect to a unreasonable cause, and a positive effect to a negative. But when Christianity only is to be sacrificed, he that stabs deepest is always the wisest man. You, my dear cousin, yourself will be apt to think I carry the matter too far, and that in the present warmth of my heart I make too ample a concession in saying, that I am *only now* a convert. You think I always believed, and I thought so too; but you were deceived, and so was I. I called myself indeed a Christian; but He who knows my heart knows that I never did a right thing, nor abstained from a wrong one, because I was so; but if I did either, it was under the influence of some other motive. And it is such seeming Christians, such pretending believers, that do most mischief to the cause, and furnish the strongest arguments to support the infidelity of its enemies: unless profession and conduct go together, the man's life is a lie, and the validity of what he professes itself is called in question.

The complete lack of humor in Cowper's replies shows the intensity with which he clung to his former belief in his damnation. Far from giving up the ideas which occurred to him in the earliest stages of madness, he merely assimilated them into the new myth of his narrow escape.

Cowper had no difficulty forming acquaintances in Huntingdon. Most of the people he met seem to have noticed him in church or on his walks in the country. Since he was a stranger, etiquette demanded that those attracted by his gentlemanly appearance and his reserved manner should make an effort to welcome him; but he seems to have made no attempt on his own to widen his circle. Among those who introduced themselves to him was a young man, twenty-one years of age, named William Cawthorne Unwin, who stopped Cowper one morning as he was leaving church. Cowper was charmed by the friendliness and sincerity of Unwin, who in turn found that Cowper's habitual aloofness immediately disappeared. They agreed to have tea together that afternoon. During this interview they discovered in each other the same "spiritual and lively" notions of religion.

As Cowper later wrote to Lady Hesketh, Unwin was

one of the most unreserved and amiable young men I ever conversed with. He is not yet arrived at that time of life when suspicion recommends itself to us in the form of wisdom, and sets everything but our own dear selves at an immeasurable distance from our esteem and confidence. Consequently he is known almost as soon as seen, and having nothing in his heart that makes it necessary for him to keep it barred and bolted, opens it to the perusal even of a stranger.[40]

Through William, Cowper gained access to the rest of the "race of Unwins," consisting of father, mother, and sister. He discovered a family in which there was a "most remarkable cordiality between the members, a habitual cheerfulness, and a lively sense of religion. There were no stiffness and formality in their manners"; and, though he first felt somewhat awkward in their company, he soon became accustomed to being treated "more like a near relation than a stranger." More and more he became a regular inhabitant of a household that was always open to him. The Reverend Morley Unwin, who often carried him to Cambridge in his chaise, was "a man of learning and good sense, and as simple as

Parson Adams." His wife Mary had "a very uncommon understanding, has read much to excellent purpose, and is more polite
than a duchess." In addition, Cowper thought that "the son who
belongs to Cambridge, is a most amiable young man, and the
daughter quite of a piece with the rest of the family." Cowper
was pleased that the Unwins "see but little company," so that "go
when I will, I find a house full of peace and cordiality in all its
parts, and I am sure to hear no scandal, but such discourse instead
of it as we all are better for." He was reminded of "Rousseau's
description of an English morning," for "such are the mornings I
spend with these good people; and the evenings differ from them
in nothing, except that they are still more snug, and quieter." So
enthralled was he that he was "apt to think I should find every
place disagreeable that had not an Unwin belonging to it." [41]

However warm the relationship was with the rest of the family,
it was with Mary Unwin, William's mother, that he formed the
strongest attachment. Within a few days after his introduction to
the family, he had met Mrs. Unwin in the street and had gone
home with her to walk nearly two hours in the garden and have a
conversation which did him more good than he "should have received from an audience of the first prince in Europe." She
seemed "a blessing to me, and I never see her without being the
better for her company." [42]

Within a month Cowper had entered into an agreement to
lodge and board in the Unwin household. The reasons for the
move that he gave in a letter to Joseph Hill were that he could no
longer proceed in his present course "without danger of bank-
ruptcy," that "the family are the most agreeable in the world," and
that "they live in a special good house, and in a very genteel
way." [43] An agreeable family, living in a genteel way, in a "special
good house": how reminiscent of the past.

Indeed many of the considerations which caused him to assert
himself in this way had been permanent fixtures of his life. He
had not been able to bring order and stability to his personal
finances. One of his most amusing letters concerns his inability
during the first days after his arrival in Huntingdon to keep
house.

My butcher's bill for last week amounted to four shillings and ten-
pence. I set off with a leg of lamb, and was forced to give part of it

away to my washerwoman. Then I made an experiment upon a sheep's heart, and that was too little. Next I put three pounds of beef into a pie, and this had like to have been too much, for it lasted three days, though my landlord was admitted to a share of it. Then as to small beer, I am puzzeled to pieces about it. I have bought as much for a shilling as will serve us at least a month, and it is grown sour already.[44]

Although he probably learned after a while how to purchase food in the proper quantities for his small household, he did not learn to live within his rather meagre allowance. Living with the Unwins seemed a more economical method of solving his domestic problems. But the severe emotional and spiritual stress which the *Memoir* tells us he experienced while deliberating the move indicates that much deeper concerns were involved.[45] It was natural that after four months in Huntingdon he should begin to long for something more satisfying than his solitary lodgings and for the steady and intimate relationships of a family. For him this requirement involved communion with intimates who shared his deepest religious convictions. Just as growing discomfort with living conditions inevitably led to a deadening of religious impulse so restoration of domestic order would furnish the environment for a continuation of the "lively and spiritual" religion he desired. Undoubtedly, Cowper hoped that the piety of the Unwin home would restore some of the joy that had been dissipated by the tedium of his life.

Cowper's breeding, innate shyness, and warmth of response to the good nature of the Unwins must have made negotiations an embarrassment for all involved; for, when the idea first occurred to him that he might take the place of one of Morley Unwin's pupils who had just left for Cambridge, he regarded his temerity as a "want of submission to the Lord's Will." The lack of assertiveness which had been his from his youth had now received a religious sanction, but in a strangely inverted way. If he regarded his former inability to create an orderly life as a rejection of God, an act of will instead of an absence of it, he now regarded any initiative as rebellion. Apparently he was to wish for nothing, to have no will but God's, and to have no certain way of discovering that will. Fortunately, at this rather perilous juncture, a phrase, "The Lord God of truth will do this," impressed itself so firmly on his mind that he regarded it as assurance of divine favor. He began negotiations, and in a few days concluded the arrangements.

His new lodgings proved to be entirely satisfactory. In a letter to Major Cowper's wife he describes the fairly rigorous evangelical regimen of life in the Unwin home with an air of contentment which shows that at last he had found the peace and security for which he had longed:

As to amusements, I mean what the world calls such, we have none; the place indeed swarms with them, and cards and dancing are the professed business of almost all the *gentle* inhabitants of Huntingdon. We refuse to take part in them, or to be accessories to this way of murdering our time, and by so doing have acquired the name of Methodists. Having told you how we *do not* spend our time, I will next say how we do. We breakfast commonly between eight and nine; till eleven, we read either the Scripture, or the sermons of some faithful preacher of those holy mysteries; at eleven we attend divine service, which is performed here twice every day; and from twelve to three we separate and amuse ourselves as we please. During that interval I either read in my own apartment, or walk, or ride, or work in the garden. We seldom sit an hour after dinner, but if the weather permits adjourn to the garden, where with Mrs. Unwin and her son I have generally the pleasure of religious conversation till tea-time. If it rains, or is too windy for walking, we either converse within doors, or sing some hymns of Martin's collection, and by the help of Mrs. Unwin's harpsichord make up a tolerable concert, in which our hearts, I hope, are the best and most musical performers. After tea we sally forth to walk in good earnest. Mrs. Unwin is a good walker, and we have generally travelled about four miles before we see home again. When the days are short, we make this excursion in the former part of the day, between church-time and dinner. At night we read and converse, as before, till supper, and commonly finish the evening either with hymns or a sermon; and last of all the family are called to prayers. I need not tell *you*, that such a life as this is consistent with the utmost cheerfulness; accordingly we are all happy, and dwell together in unity as brethren. Mrs. Unwin has almost a maternal affection for me, and I have something very like a filial one for her, and her son and I are brothers. Blessed be the God of our salvation for such companions, and for such a life; above all, for a heart so like it.[46]

Mrs. Unwin's "maternal affection" must have been an important contributing factor. In her, Cowper found many of the things that had been missing from his life since the death twenty-nine years before of his mother. As important as she proved to be, however, Mary Unwin never becomes more than a shadowy figure, even in Cowper's voluminous correspondence. We know only that her religious spirit, intelligence, and competence impressed him as well as her calm and "cordial" nature. For her he must have provided qualities she found lacking in her marriage and family. About seven years older than Cowper, who at their first meeting was just about to turn thirty-five, she was married to a clergyman much older than herself who, far from the evangelical ideal, followed the not unusual practice of delegating his duties to others and pursuing his own interests, among them preparing students for the universities. Undoubtedly Cowper filled a need for companionship. In addition, he would fill the void left when her son William left to go to Cambridge.

The pattern of Cowper's daily life apparently did not change much as he became more and more a part of the Unwin family. Before, his days had consisted mostly of walking and bathing in the River Ouse; of religious devotions, both public and private; and of domestic tasks. The description of life at the Unwin's in the letter to Mrs. Cowper shows that this pattern remained. But the companionship of Mary, and often William, revivified his daily routine; and, although it could not bring back the ecstasy of the initial stages of his conversion or the first days in Huntingdon, it did create a more abiding serenity. The *Memoir* ends with an affecting tribute to the Unwin home as "a place of rest prepared for me by God's own hand, where He had blessed me with a thousand mercies—and communion with his dear disciples." [47]

Whatever liberties the *Memoir* takes with the facts of Cowper's life, and no matter how it distorts their meaning, it is in itself a symbol of the writer's state of mind at this point. The work itself followed a conventional form in which the evangelical for his own sake, and sometimes for the edification of others, traced his conversion from iniquity. To suit this purpose, Cowper's life had to be interpreted as a struggle between his corrupt will and a merciful God, ending with his perfect submission. Out of the internal chaos, brought about by his pride and a corrupting environment, came spiritual order; and that order was confirmed by "God's own hand," which had prepared for him a "place of rest." But what the *Memoir* treats as a primarily religious solution to his problem was much more than that. At last his domestic affairs had been put in order, and his future held out the hope of a modest but stable existence. Furthermore, the rather narrow basis of his religious conversion had been broadened and made more capable of sustaining him over a long period of time. He had fallen into a way of life which promised few irritations, and his naturally shy personality apparently was going to be allowed to retreat to a world wholly in proportion with it. Not only did he have the retired existence which meant security, but that very retirement promised to enrich the intimate kind of friendship which his personality craved.

The only threat to Cowper's equilibrium in the early years with the Unwins was his religious enthusiasm, which could not easily be confined to the narrow limits of his orderly world. In 1766, when he thought of taking Holy Orders, his shyness prevailed; and he returned to "his place of rest." In the letter to Mrs. Cowper already mentioned, he wrote:

I have had many anxious thoughts about taking orders, and I believe every new convert is apt to think himself called upon for that purpose; but it has pleased God, by means which there is no need to particularize, to give me full satisfaction as to the propriety of declining it; indeed, they who have the least idea of what I have suffered from the dread of public exhibitions, will readily excuse my never attempting them hereafter. In the meantime, if it please the Almighty, I may be an instrument of turning many endeavors to the truth in a private way, and I hope that my endeavors in this way have not been entirely unsuccessful. Had I the zeal of Moses, I should want an Aaron to be my spokesman.[48]

The first real trial of the new arrangements that Cowper had made occurred in the summer of 1767. On July 2, 1767, as Morley Unwin was going to his cure, he was flung from his horse and suffered a fractured skull. He died five days later. Although Cowper felt deeply the pathos of this event, it did not upset the order into which his life had so recently settled. Groping for a way to explain his grief to so good a friend as Joseph Hill, he described movingly the spectacle of a man, "perfect in health, and as likely to live twenty years as either of us," suddenly "stretched speechless and senseless upon a flock bed, in a poor cottage."[49] Cowper had "heard his dying groans, the effect of great agony, for he was a strong man, and much convulsed in his last moments."

But Cowper's composure was not disturbed: he described to Hill the effect upon his circumstances as "only . . . a change of a place of abode." He intended, "by God's leave," to stay with Mrs. Unwin, "whose behaviour to me has always been that of a mother to a son." A letter to Mrs. Cowper ends on a note of optimism which might seem incongruous to some.

By this afflictive Providence it has pleased God, who always drops comfort into the bitterest cup, to open a door for us out of an un-evangelical pasture, such as this is, into some better ministry where we may hear the glad tidings of salvation, and be nourished by the sincere milk of the Word. We know not yet where we shall settle, but we trust that the Lord, whom we seek, will go before us, and prepare a rest for us.[50]

Providence again intervened in the form of a visit from John Newton, the evangelical curate of Olney. Newton, who had been told by a mutual friend of Mrs. Unwin's bereavement, made the journey to Huntingdon to offer his condolences. Immediately there rose a warm friendship with both Mary and William, and Newton returned home intent on persuading them to move to Olney. After prayerful consideration, Mrs. Unwin decided that Olney was the best of the evangelical ministries in which to settle; and on September 14 she, her daughter, and Cowper moved to Newton's rectory where they lived until the house on the market place which Newton had found for them was ready.[51]

Because of Newton, Olney was in many ways an ideal choice for Cowper. As a town it had neither the tidiness nor bustle of Huntingdon; it was quiet, dusty, and impoverished. But Newton could offer both the religious comforts and intimate friendship that he needed. Newton shared the evangelical belief that true religion is founded not on intellectual conviction—on the rationality that had in the past led to violent disputes over doctrinal differences—but on a profound sense of conversion, a persuasion too deep for words or tears. He could share with Cowper an experience and a manner of discourse for which a person like John Cowper would have no sympathy. Newton himself had experienced conversion only after a life far more profligate than Cowper's, and only after a struggle to subdue his unruly nature. He, according to his memoir, had ignored the initial, faint awakenings of his soul and had persisted in a sinful life as a sailor. He had educated himself, both in the secular and religious sense, and had followed his final calling with a zeal born of a far more vital and hearty nature than Cowper's. His piety—supported by an intelligent, vigorous, and energetic nature—revived Cowper's own spirit and provided assurance and direction.

The effect of Newton was seen in Cowper's renewed devotion to religion and in a new interest in good works. Cowper became involved in charitable activities, especially among the poor lacemakers of Olney, and helped in the religious activities which Newton had brought into being. He wrote sixty-four hymns during the years 1771 and 1772. Typically, Newton wrote far more (281), but they were of less literary value. In 1779 the work of both men appeared in a collection known as *Olney Hymns.*

To Cowper, then, Olney must have appeared to be a refuge from the distresses of the past and an opportunity to cultivate his newly discovered, but already flagging, religious feelings. Although he did not talk a great deal about his move in the letters written during the last days in Huntingdon, the mood of his correspondence for the next several years suggests that a more tranquil outlook had replaced the fervor of the period following his departure from St. Albans. Olney and the friendship with Newton could promise order and stability, not to speak of the obscurity which Cowper now felt essential to internal peace.

CHAPTER 2

Olney and After

THE move to Olney began a period in which Cowper wrote
what are now considered his best and most characteristic
letters. To discuss Olney and Cowper in these years is to talk
about these letters, for in them he not only achieved mastery of a
literary form but also learned to express himself with a naturalness
revealing perfectly both the man and his world. As I pointed out
in Chapter 1, the letters show us much about Cowper's frame of
mind in the crucial years after he left St. Albans. They constitute
what might be called a "romantic" period in his letter writing, for
they come as close as anything in English literature to being a
"spontaneous overflow of powerful feelings." Sentences pour out
in a rush of joy:

How happy it is to believe, with a steadfast assurance, that our peti-
tions are heard even while we are making them; and how delightful to
meet with a proof of it in the effectual and actual grant of them!
Surely it is a gracious finishing given to those means, which the Almighty has been pleased to make use of for my conversion. After having been deservedly rendered unfit for any society, to be again qualified for it, and admitted at once into the fellowship of those whom God
regards as the excellent of the earth, and whom, in the emphatical language of Scripture, he preserves as the apple of his eye, is a blessing
which carries with it the stamp and visible superscription of divine
bounty—a grace unlimited as undeserved; and, like its glorious Author,
free in its course, and blessed in its operation! [1]

The life he was leading at the time shows how close to the surface
his feelings were. Only a person in a heightened state of religious
fervor could have endured the daily routine of Scriptural readings, private devotions, religious conversations, hymns, sermons,
and prayers to which he subjected himself. Clearly, as he mentions in the last lines of Book V of *The Task*, the inner light of
the spirit was gilding the external world. Extravagant joy might

55

find expression in happy acceptance of domestic arrangements, in
rapturous statements about his spiritual state, or in violent condemnation of his former self. The clichés and homilies which clog
the Huntingdon letters demonstrate how greatly taste and judgment had been overcome by feeling.

The evangelical idiom ceased to seem natural once Cowper's
religious enthusiasm had passed. He no longer felt a need to write
in this way, although on occasions, such as the death of Morley
Unwin, religious formulations could still provide security and
comfort. As a result, the letters of the Olney period become more
"classical" in tenor. As Cowper's attention turns outward to the
world around him, his feelings, as well as changing in nature, become more subdued. A revival of humor and detachment is captured in many brilliant anecdotes, pointing up the absurdities of
his placid, retired life and of the small world around him. Darker
feelings appear often but in a manner more reminiscent of Gray's
Elegy or Thomson's *Seasons* than of Cowper's *Memoir*. Torment
and anguish give way to melancholy reflection on more general
subjects. Much later, in the 1790's, a new phase would open. Again
personal feeling sweeps away reason and detachment, and the letters again reflect not the world outside but the tormented mind of
the writer. However, in 1767 such a future was only a distant
shadow, apprehended in moments of depression but incapable of
dimming the pleasant prospect of life in Olney.

The jaunty tone of a brief letter to Joseph Hill written on July
31, 1769, shows Cowper's optimism. It also suggests that Cowper,
by virtue of his family name, gentlemanly bearing, and perhaps
philanthropic position in the community, had made a name for
himself.

Sir Thomas crosses the Alps, and Sir Cowper, for that is his title
at Olney, prefers his home to any other spot of earth in the world.
Horace, observing this difference of temper in different persons, cried
out a good many years ago, in the true spirit of poetry, "How much
one man differs from another!" This does not seem a very sublime
exclamation in English, but I remember we were taught to admire it
in the original.

A little more than thirteen years later "Sir Cowper" had
enough prestige to warrant an unexpected visit from a candidate
for Parliament, looking not for his vote, for Cowper had none,

but wishing only that he would use his influence with those who
did have:

As when the sea is uncommonly agitated, the water finds its way
into creeks and holes of rocks, which in its calmer state it never reaches,
in like manner the effect of these turbulent times is felt even at Orchard Side, where in general we live as undisturbed by the political
element, as shrimps or cockles that have been accidentally deposited
in some hollow beyond the water mark, by the usual dashing of the
waves. We were sitting yesterday after dinner, the two ladies and
myself, very composedly, and without the least apprehension of any
such intrusion in our snug parlour, one lady knitting, the other netting,
and the gentleman winding worsted, when to our unspeakable surprise
a mob appeared before the window; a smart rap was heard at the
door, the boys haloo'd, and the maid announced Mr. Grenville. Puss
was unfortunately let out of her box, so that the candidate, with all
his good friends at his heels, was refused admittance at the grand
entry, and referred to the back door, as the only possible way of
approach.
Candidates are creatures not very susceptible of affronts, and would
rather, I suppose, climb in at a window than be absolutely excluded.
In a minute the yard, the kitchen, and the parlour were filled. Mr.
Grenville advancing toward me shook me by the hand with a degree
of cordiality that was extremely seducing. As soon as he and as many
more as could find chairs were seated, he began to open the intent
of his visit. I told him I had no vote, for which he readily gave me
credit. I assured him I had no influence, which he was not equally
inclined to believe, and the less, no doubt, because Mr. Ashburner,
the draper, addressing himself to me at this moment, informed me
that I had a great deal. Supposing that I could not be possessed of
such a treasure without knowing it, I ventured to confirm my first assertion by saying, that if I had any I was utterly at a loss to imagine
where it could be, or wherein it consisted. Thus ended the conference.
Mr. Grenville squeezed me by the hand again, kissed the ladies, and
withdrew. He kissed likewise the maid in the kitchen, and seemed
upon the whole a most loving, kissing, kind-hearted gentleman. He is
very young, genteel, and handsome. He has a pair of very good eyes
in his head, which not being sufficient as it should seem for the many
nice and difficult purposes of a senator, he has a third also, which he
wore suspended by a ribband from his buttonhole. The boys haloo'd,
the dogs barked, Puss scampered, the hero, with his long train of
obsequious followers, withdrew. We made ourselves very merry with
the adventure, and in a short time settled into our former tranquility,
never probably to be thus interrupted more.[2]

Well-turned anecdotes like this one testify to the writer's frame
of mind and outlook, as well as to his mastery of the art of letter
writing. An amused acceptance of himself and Olney can be seen
in his juxtaposition of his own retiring nature with that of the
energetic, extroverted Grenville, who bursts in upon the overly
snug and placid household at Orchard Side. Satire is nicely balanced with personal revelation.

The gentleness of the humor with which Cowper records the
event suggests that he accepted his role as Sir Cowper with good
grace and generosity—if with some degree of shyness and embarrassment. Undoubtedly there were many ways in which he could
have been of service to the community. His knowledge of the
law, however sparse and however much he might depreciate it,
put him in a good position to be an adviser. Through his connections he eventually was able to aid charitable enterprises by raising money and by pleading the cause, as we have already noted,
of the impoverished lacemakers of Olney in some eloquent letters.
He aided in religious activities and helped to distribute the items
donated by local benefactors. To him sometimes fell the task of
determining who was worthy of charity. "Olney," he wrote in
1782, was "a populous place inhabited chiefly by the half-starved
and the ragged of the earth." [3] The relief of their misery was so
large an operation that the small party of which Cowper was a
member could not hope to make its efforts and limited resources
"felt among such numbers."

These years were not free of tension, however. There were
difficulties in the household. As Cowper continued to live with
the Unwins, the problem of regularizing his relationship with the
family arose. As the children grew older and left—William (having gone up to Cambridge before Morley's death) to become rector of Stock, in Essex, in 1769; Susanna eventually to marry Mat-
thew Powley in May, 1773—it became necessary for Cowper at
least to propose marriage to Mary. Although William Unwin
might well have approved, his sister did not. She had grown to
think of Cowper as an interloper, and his attempts to laugh away
her attitude as a deficiency in her sense of humor could well have
covered a more serious concern about the tensions that his presence created.

This family crisis was complicated by other concerns. The moments of darkness and doubt which interrupted the happiness of

the convert even before he wrote his *Memoir* continued to burden his nerves. Although the move to Olney, which brought the relief of Newton's friendship, at first strengthened him, its effect could not be permanent. Indeed, his inability to sustain in himself the zeal with which Newton abounded might have done more harm to him than the example of Newton did good. Aside from these problems stands the fact that again, in 1770, he had to face the death of a member of his family, his brother John. Although there seems to be no doubt that the brothers did not grow more intimate as one continued in his new evangelical way of life, and the other, increasingly more ill, pursued his academic career, the death of John moved William deeply. His sorrow might have been lessened, however, by his strenuous attempts to assure himself that his brother died in a proper spiritual state, attempts which seemed rewarded by John's behavior in his last hours of life. Although John had previously given no one cause to believe that he had undergone conversion after the evangelical pattern, he had smiled to his brother a few hours before he died; and, though in great pain, he had uttered the words, "Brother, I am as happy as a king." Newton was able to rejoice in a sermon at Olney at this proof of the younger Cowper's salvation.[4]

The chief anxiety, though, concerned Cowper's betrothal and approaching marriage to Mrs. Unwin. Of course there was no reason that this change had to alter the nature of the relationship between the two. Apparently, however, Cowper's nerves could not bear even the prospect of undergoing a formality which probably was intended more to quiet gossip than to alter the bond between the two. The marriage was supposed to take place in February or March, 1773. But on January 24 Cowper again lost his sanity.

What form his illness took is not very clear. We know from Newton's journal that the curate was called to Orchard Side at four in the morning and that Mrs. Newton remained there all day. Cowper himself described his condition only as "a melancholy that made [him] almost an infant." [5] This depression of spirits did not respond to Newton's warm-hearted, genial ministrations. Then, about a month after the onset of the illness, William had a dream in which a word which he took to be a divine utterance so impressed itself on his mind that he never again could hope for salvation. He never told anyone the word, but its meaning he once gave in a letter to Newton: *actum de te, periisti* ("it is over with thee; thou hast perished").[6] In his misery he turned against both Newton and Mrs. Unwin, refusing to visit one and accusing the other of trying to poison his food.

Then, on April 12, Cowper appeared at the vicarage to seek refuge from the noise of Olney. He stayed for thirteen months. Mrs. Unwin also moved in to minister to him. Throughout the spring and summer Cowper demanded strict attention. The prayers and reasoning of Newton and Mrs. Unwin could not remove the deep-seated causes of his distress; and, despite the pleas of Mrs. Unwin, he refused to return to Orchard Side. Slowly, however, he returned to a calmer state. His improvement came about not through a return of hope but through adjustment to despair. Eventually his melancholy thoughts lost their ability to inspire hysteria. It proved as difficult for his melancholy to sustain itself as it had been for the ecstasy which had followed his conversion.

By October the improvement in Cowper's condition seemed great enough to Newton to allow him to leave Olney for a short time. During his absence William suddenly became possessed with the idea that he should "after the example of Abraham, perform an expensive act of obedience, and offer not a son, but himself." [7] What form the act took or how it was prevented we do not know, but the failure succeeded only in filling him with new ideas of his guilt. Convinced that his condition was hopeless, he, as in 1763, began to think that God had singled him out from the rest of humanity for punishment. He was certain of the ultimate justice of God and was so overwhelmed by his own misery, however, that his reason could envision no escape from his predicament. Although his Calvinistic heritage taught him that man cannot know with absolute certainty the will of God, his inability to experience even the vaguest awakening of hope forced upon him the notion that there could be no mercy in his case. He had failed to carry out God's will by not destroying himself, and God would punish him by not giving him another chance.

How hope could yield so completely to despair we cannot know without possessing more of the materials necessary for a complete psychological study. There are some valuable indications, however, in the always close relationship between Cowper's various emotional states and the forms of his religious experience. His conversion came at the time of a powerful emotional reflex to the extended depression of 1763 and 1764. To use his own prevailing metaphor, in a psychological instead of religious context, the sun had obliterated darkness. Now darkness had again prevailed. If his conversion, founded at least in part on other than spiritual grounds, had allowed him to see the world in a light entirely different from before, so his new darkness concealed all the signs that had formerly pointed to salvation and had kept him from seeing a way out of his misery. It is possible that evangelicalism won him so completely because it could make sense of the victory that his nervous state had gained over the forces of darkness. If this is so, the new, bizarre religion succeeded his evangelical phase for the same reason: that new psychological realities excluded all but it.

Why didn't Cowper try to reconcile his former convictions with his present despairing thoughts? And why didn't his next resurgence of good spirits bring with it a renewed faith? Again we can only speculate. In 1765 reason had finally confirmed what his emotions had seemed to be urging. Both the almost hysterical stage of conversion and the more durable one which followed had needed the assurance of the religious doctrine that evangelicalism taught. It was possible to rationalize his conversion by forcing it into a pattern, by seeing it as a growth from sin to the state of grace. His new loss of hope, both in its religious and psychological implications, could not fit into this pattern. Once his good spirits returned, he still could not revert to his former beliefs because reason could no longer accept them. Since his religious heritage told him that God does not turn his back on those whom he has elected, his lack of spiritual vitality could only mean that his former state of blessedness had been a sham. If Cowper first placed a fairly demented construction upon his misery—seeing it as the result of his failure to commit suicide, to perform the act which in a dream God had required—he could pattern it, when a saner frame of mind returned, in a more orthodox manner as a confirmation of his lack of grace. We do not know what guilty memories the new suicide attempt had aroused, but it seems likely that the knowledge of what he had done prevented his reason from ever again accepting the idea that God intended to be merciful to him. It would have been hard enough for him to rationalize thoughts of suicide as being merely a temptation. How much harder would it be to reconcile himself to the perverse manner in

which the idea had proposed itself to him? It could not be interpreted as the backsliding into which any normal Christian might
fall.

The durable form into which reason poured the new complexity of tensions was, therefore, one which foreboded only the most
miserable destiny. Perhaps this condition also gained durability
(for it never entirely left him) from his age (he was forty-one at
the onset of his second major illness), which deprived him of the
emotional resilience that had before been his salvation. It is ironic
to think that he had now made his God over in his own image.
His inability to control himself became the work of a vengeful
God. Henceforth, he could not conceive of God or of himself in
a different way. He could only get used to the idea of his eventual
destruction and, when day after day it did not arrive, take heart
from its remoteness.

Happiness did return. Although it never reached the ecstatic
heights that marked his recuperation in 1764, it did create the
conditions under which he could write most of the poems which
we now consider his most characteristic—and best. Until then he
had limited himself chiefly to occasional verse, most of it fairly
lifeless imitations of various traditions, and the *Olney Hymns,*
written with Newton. The hymns especially show that Cowper
never grew beyond regret of those "peaceful hours I once
enjoy'd." [8] They had "left an aching void,/The world can never
fill." But pain and emptiness seem to have intensified the calmness
and serenity of the era in which Cowper's poetic genius reached
maturity.

Cowper's recovery from the mental collapse of 1773 was
marked by an urge to create. Although he constantly depreciated
his muse, we must accept his word that the desire to create was at
first hardly more than a compulsion to fill the void left by his loss
of faith. He could maintain stability as long as he remained busy.
There was no sense of dedication to art, no overwhelming desire
to express himself, no vision to communicate. As soon as he was
capable, he "commenced carpenter, made cupboards, boxes,
stools." When these activities no longer interested him, he began
to make birdcages. Wearying of this occupation, he next turned
to gardening, which he later "intermingled with . . . drawing."
But, finding that the latter occupation injured his eyes, he decided
to become a poet. Writing letters and poetry not only occupied

his mind but also allowed his better nature to come forth.[9] He once wrote that, had he understood music, he might never have written verse, but "lived on fiddle-strings." That he didn't pleased him because a poet could "be of a little use in the world, while a musician, the most skillful, can only divert himself and a few others." [10]

Cowper's lack of high seriousness about what we would now consider a vocation undoubtedly sprang in part from his gentlemanly disdain for what a greater commitment would entail. But his psychological state also accounted for it. As he once wrote to Newton,

Such nights as I frequently spend are but a miserable prelude to the succeeding day, and indispose me, above all things to the business of writing. Yet with a pen in my hand, if I am able to write at all, I find myself gradually relieved; and as I am glad of any employment that may serve to engage my attention, so especially I am pleased with an opportunity of conversing with you, though it be but upon paper. This occupation above all others assists me in that self-deception to which I am indebted for all the little comfort I enjoy; things seem to be as they were; and I almost forget that they never can be so again.[11]

Letter-writing, birdcage construction, composing poetry: all sprang from the same motives.

In a letter to William Unwin, he lightheartedly referred to his "scribbling humour," which at that time had been "entirely absorbed in the passion for landscape drawing." But, although he found it "a most amusing art," he thought it required too much practice and attention. "Excellence," he wrote,

is providentially placed beyond the reach of indolence, that success may be the reward of industry, and that idleness may be punished with obscurity and disgrace. So long as I am pleased with an employment, I am capable of unwearied application, because my feelings are all of the intense kind. I never received a *little* pleasure from any thing in my life; if I am delighted, it is in the extreme. The unhappy consequence of this temperature is, that my attachment to any occupation seldom outlives the novelty of it. That nerve of my imagination that feels the touch of any particular amusement, twangs under the energy of the pressure with so much vehemence, that it soon becomes sensible of weariness and fatigue. Hence I draw an unfavourable prognostic, and expect that I shall shortly be constrained to look out for something else. Then perhaps I may string the lyre again, and be able to comply with your demand.[12]

This passage must be taken in its context as good-humored apology for a temporary failure of his muse. Unwin apparently had asked for more of the verse which obviously had a therapeutic value for Cowper as well as entertainment value for his intimates. Cowper then treats his poetry as a "task," an exercise of the mind, which differs from others only in that it more fully engages the intellect and has more satisfying results. Hence, in a letter to John Newton, he could attribute his ability to compose poetry on subjects that his mind could not otherwise entertain to the fact that "the search after poetical expression, the rhyme, and the numbers, are all affairs of some difficulty; they amuse, indeed but are not to be attained without study, and engross perhaps a larger share of the attention than the subject itself." [13]

Writing belonged in the regimen of his daily life for these reasons and undoubtedly contributed to the serenity which pervades his best poetry. As *The Task* indicates, the years after 1774 were also filled with good-humored observation of life at Olney and of nature; and both provided subjects for the scores of letters which served as another means of filling the "aching void." No detail escaped his notice, from the controversy over whether the new town pump should have a lamp on top of it "in order that people may not run their heads against it in the night" to an informal meeting of "the *quidnuncs* of Olney" to discuss English foreign policy.[14] The view of the market place and the activities in Olney often opened out to the larger world, and the onlooker assumed graver tones as he commented on the impending collapse of the Empire. Patriotism mixed with indignation as he deplored the weakness of a corrupt society in England and with compassion as he regarded the plight of the newly independent colonies.[15] Severe as his moral commentary might become, it was usually touched with humor:

What a medley are our public prints, half the page filled with the ruin of the country, and the other half filled with the vices and pleasures of it;—here an island taken, and there an empire lost, and there an Italian opera, or the Duke of Gloucester's rout on a Sunday! [16]

. . . .

But you think Margate more lively. So is a Cheshire cheese full of mites more lively than a sound one: but that very liveliness only proves its rottenness. I remember, too, that Margate, though full of company, was generally filled with such company, as people who were nice in the choice of their company, were rather fearful of keeping company with. The boy went to London every week, loaded with mackerel and herrings, and returned loaded with company. The cheapness of the conveyance made it equally commodious for Dead fish and Lively company.[17]

His delight in small things might be attributed to his lack of stamina and his delicate nervous condition:

Swift's darling motto was, *Vive la bagatelle*—a good wish for a philosopher of his complexion, the greater part of whose wisdom, whencesoever it came, most certainly came not from above. *La bagatelle* has no enemy in me, though it has neither so warm a friend, nor so able a one, as it had in him. If I trifle, and merely trifle, it is because I am reduced to it by necessity—a melancholy, that nothing else so effectually disperses, engages me sometimes in the arduous task of being merry by force. And, strange as it may seem, the most ludicrous lines I ever wrote have been written in the saddest mood, and, but for that saddest mood, perhaps had never been written at all. To say truth, it would be but a shocking vagary, should the mariners on board a ship buffeted by a terrible storm, employ themselves in fiddling and dancing; yet sometimes much such a part act I.[18]

Cowper did not always speak, or write, as a detached moralist. During his first days in Olney he took upon himself many tasks of an unpoetic nature. His charitable endeavors continued, for he distributed clothing and blankets and wrote appeals for financial aid. And, of course, the daily needs of the household had to be satisfied. Because Mary Unwin's income had dwindled until it barely exceeded Cowper's, the value of the garden became more than aesthetic; and animals other than the many pets were kept at Orchard Side.

The impression that most of the letters and poems of this period create differs from that made by continual assertions, especially in the letters to Newton, of Cowper's despair. It is true that at times the poet lacked such "strength of body" that he could not "bear much thinking." When "a long thought" would find its way into "the meshes of that fine network, the brain," which in him were "composed of such spinner's threads," it would "twang" and "bustle" about "at such a rate as seems to threaten the whole contexture." [19] He could not content himself with physiological explanations of these periods of inactivity; they had to have spiritual causes which would fit in the pattern first established by the dream that had foretold his damnation. For this reason he continually described his state as that of one who must continually struggle not against despair itself but against the effects of a condition he could not avoid. But, even in talking about his gloom, he often adopted a tone which revealed the presence of a happier state of mind.

The serenity which prevailed for the most part had both a negative and positive side. In the letters which refer to his melancholy, Cowper usually wrote as one for whom the threat of damnation had lost its former vitality. Although his "nightly instructors"—the dreams, the words, and ideas which periodically impressed themselves upon his mind as if sent by some external power—continued to remind him that "I am a foreigner to the system I inhabit," daylight brought new interests, if not hope.[20] When he felt most depressed, usually during the dreary months of December, January, and February, he experienced not a lively fear of what the future held but a weariness from which there could be no relief.

He constantly sought out means of alleviating the dullness of his condition: "Dissipation itself would be welcome to me, so it were not a vicious one: but however earnestly invited, is coy, and keeps at a distance." [21] Sometimes he withdrew entirely into himself:

But the effect of such continual listening to the language of a heart hopeless and deserted, is, that I can never give much more than half of my attention to what is started by others, and very rarely start anything myself. My silence, however, and my absence of mind, make me sometimes as entertaining as if I had wit. They furnish an occasion for friendly and good-natured raillery; they raise a laugh, and I partake of it.[22]

This growing insensitivity and the refusal of the world outside to allow Cowper to indulge his misery constitute the negative side of the order which rose from the ruins of 1773–1774. But, although he often had to be drawn out of himself, he did find a new kind of joy in the life of Olney, of the household, and especially of the garden, and in the landscape which extended beyond. Significantly, his gloomiest letters were written during the winter months, when weather forced him to be less active. When weather permitted him to walk and encouraged work, he naturally felt better. Even when he was writing his most melancholy letters, the very act of composition seems at times to have lightened his misery and stirred his numbness. In the darkest moments humor peeks through:

It is well for those about me that I am neither very subject to fevers, nor apt to lose my senses when I have one. My ravings would be those of a man more conversant with things beneath than with things above, and if they bore any resemblance to my habitual musings, would serve only to shock bystanders. I heard lately of a clerk in a public office, whose chief employment it was for many years to administer oaths, who being lightheaded in a fever, of which he died, spent the last week of his life in crying day and night—"So help you God—kiss the book—give me a shilling." What a wretch in comparison with you, and how happy in comparison with me! [23]

The long poems entitled "Table Talk," "The Progress of Error," "Truth," "Expostulation," "Hope," "Charity," "Conversation," and "Retirement," written in 1780 and 1781, were motivated by the poet's desire to keep busy. They followed one another at two or three month intervals, as if they were exercises; and, indeed, some of them, written at the urging of Mrs. Unwin, were exactly that. Having completed them, he turned in the summer of 1783 to a much longer effort, *The Task*, with the same motivation. He completed this poem in September, 1784.

This emphasis on keeping busy gives a strongly personal meaning to the praise of work in the first book of *The Task*. When we think of the many letters in which the poet bewailed his lack of accomplishments and when we contemplate his leisurely pace and his deliberate withdrawal from life to the seclusion of Orchard Side, the celebration of labor in "The Sofa" might seem hypocritical:

> Thump after thump responds the constant flail,
> That seems to swing uncertain, and yet falls
> Full on the destin'd ear. Wide flies the chaff.
> The rustling straw sends up a frequent mist
> Of atoms, sparkling in the noon-day beam.

Come hither, ye that press your beds of down
And sleep not: see him sweating o'er his bread
Before he eats it.—'Tis the primal curse,
But soften'd into mercy; made the pledge
Of cheerful days, and nights without a groan.[24]

Obviously, we here see labor not from the viewpoint of the
worker but from that of an observer who, because of his detachment, can appreciate each detail of sound and sight and can contemplate the relationship of what he sees to the moral law and the
cosmos:

By ceaseless action all that is subsists.
Constant rotation of th' unwearied wheel
That nature rides upon maintains her health,
Her beauty, her fertility. She dreads
An instant's pause, and lives but while she moves.
. . . .
The law, by which all creatures else are bound,
Binds man the lord of all. Himself derives
No mean advantage from a kindred cause,
From strenuous toil his hours of sweetest ease.
The sedentary stretch their lazy length
When custom bids, but no refreshment find,
For none they need: the languid eye, the cheek
Deserted of its bloom, the flaccid, shrunk,
And wither'd muscle, and the vapid soul,
Reproach their owner with that love of rest
To which he forfeits ev'n the rest he loves.
Not such th' alert and active. Measure life
By its true worth, the comforts it affords,
And their's alone seems worthy of the name.[25]

The idea that the laws by which the universe operates have a
moral value bespeaks both the eighteenth-century emphasis on
order and the Christian heritage, both Calvinist and otherwise, as
well as the insularity of the gentle class; but it also testifies to the
importance placed by Cowper on activity. Universal order and
social stability might be founded upon "ceaseless action," but so
was the personal stability that the poet had achieved. The title of
The Task is an important personal revelation, and it is significant
that, in the first book of the poem, sofas, leisure, and London are
contrasted with nature, action, and retirement.

Contemplation, writing, gardening, and the many other tasks which engaged Cowper at Olney were supplemented by long walks with Mary out into the countryside. *The Task* also celebrates this kind of activity and gives us some idea of the means by which the poet kept his mind occupied. Close observation of detail, both in limited areas (a flower bed, a pool, a mill-race) and in panoramic views of landscape; constant searching for things as yet unnoticed or newly changed; religious and moral speculation; contemplation of man and his relationship to nature: all of these filled the poet's time. Then, of course, came the pleasurable task of committing all of his impressions to language, of making words not only convey ideas but give some sense of the "feeling," the "texture" of ideas. In a century noted for the emphasis it placed on making sound conform to sense, certainly Cowper must stand near the top in his choice of diction, his arrangement of words, and his modulation of sentences to dramatize meaning. Few sentences, no matter how unassuming, escaped his attention:

> Here Ouse, slow winding through a level plain
> Of spacious meads with cattle sprinkled o'er,
> Conducts the eye along its sinuous course
> Delighted.[26]

> Nor rural sights alone, but rural sounds,
> Exhilarate the spirit, and restore
> The tone of languid Nature. Mighty winds,
> That sweep the skirt of some far-spreading wood
> Of ancient growth, make music not unlike
> The dash of ocean on his winding shore,
> And lull the spirit while they fill the mind;
> Unnumber'd branches waving in the blast,
> And all their leaves fast flutt'ring, all at once.[27]

In *The Task* the serenity born of productive action is not directly contrasted to the poet's melancholy and despair but, in keeping with contemporary poetic theory, to subjects of more general, or more public, interest. Opposed to the "speculative height" from which he exults, both actually in his improved view of landscape and metaphorically in his broader understanding of nature, are the ugliness of "the great ones of mankind" and the tedium of London. The former, like the mole, "disfigures earth;

and plotting in the dark,/Toils much to earn a monumental pile,/ That may record the mischiefs he has done." [28] As in the letters, poetry does not take the form of lyric so much as satiric commentary. Instead of a "spontaneous overflow," the poet presents a much more conventional comparison between the world of the great and retirement, between London and the country.

But, although like many predecessors Cowper might offer his personal experience as an alternative to a way of life that he was forced to reject and to a corruption that for almost a century it had been the role of poetry to deplore, his enthusiasms obviously differed from those of the traditional satirist. Almost everyone could agree with his analysis of the problems facing contemporary society, but only a few could accept the new life that he synthesized, although many would feel a sentimental interest in it. To anticipate criticism, he cheerfully acknowledges the limitations of his world. He will only assert that he has found an existence suitable to him and, what is more, that he knows that the work born of his retirement has a permanent and general value. The extent of his enthusiasm is seen in the way he turns the tables upon his opponents. For years it had been the practice to celebrate the joys of urban life and to characterize the rural retreat as a place where quiet could renew one's spirits but, if prolonged, would deaden them. Cowper makes the country not only a haven but a place of "ceaseless action" and infinite variety. The city, where dullness and the spleen prevail, offers no variety but mere repetition of the same amusements. [29]

The long poems written in 1780 and 1781, and a few others, including the well-known "Boadicea" and "Verses Supposed To Be Written By Alexander Selkirk," were published in February, 1782. Although these poems were not the first he had written for publication, they were the first upon which his reputation as a poet could be founded. During the 1750's he had published several witty essays; in 1779 the *Olney Hymns* had first appeared; and in 1781 he had anonymously published *Anti-Thelyphthora*, a humorous poem of 206 lines, which answered a tract defending polygamy by his cousin Martin Madan. Cowper thus was known only as a writer of hymns, and to a small circle of friends as a wit. The poems of 1782 revealed both the older Cowper and the writer of the *Olney Hymns*. His muse, although imbued with religious fervor, had turned to secular and moral subjects, and often expressed itself with the ease and urbanity prized by wits. The most obvious trait of the volume, however, and the one that bound it most clearly to the years that immediately preceded its publication, was its high seriousness of purpose. One of the epigraphs on the title page did refer to the "sportive" nature of the contents:

> Sicut aquae tremulum labris ubi lamen ahenis
> Sole reperdussum, aut radiantis imagine lunae,
> Omnia pervolitat late loca, jamque sub auras
> Erigitur, summique ferit laquearia tecti.

> So water trembling in a polish'd vase,
> Reflects the beam that plays upon its face,
> The sportive light, uncertain where it falls
> Now strikes the roof, now flashes on the walls.[30]

The image refers not to a dancing wit or pervading gaiety but to the varied contents and the loose conversational structure of the long poems. Like Aeneas, the poet, tossed about by his anxieties, seeks ways of solving the problems of himself and his age. Taken in conjunction with the other motto, from the Marquis Caraccioli, the light imagery also signifies that truth, like sunlight, can best be born when it is reflected from an earthly medium such as a poet's imagination or poetry. The passage by Caraccioli, roughly translated, indicates that, although man is born for truth, he is not able to tolerate its approach. It can speak only through figures, parables, and emblems, since the reader fears that it will reveal his faults too frankly. Truth is not so dazzling as it is embarrassing. Because it informs with too little discretion, one wants, in receiving it, to have it disguised. Poetry, then, becomes a way of persuading a cowardly humanity to contemplate serious ideas.[31]

John Newton contributed a preface to *The Task* which, because of its religious cast, was omitted at the request of Joseph Johnson, the publisher, until the fifth edition in 1793.[32] This preface is of interest, however, because it elaborates on some of the implications of the epigraphs to which I have referred. While affirming his friendship for the poet, in whose company for almost seven years, "though we were seldom seven successive waking hours separated, I always found new pleasure," Newton treats the poems as a part of the poet's religious experience. Having rejected the world, the poet, according to Newton, passed through affliction; and now the dawn (both mental and spiritual, one suspects he means) has arrived. Newton points out that "in his principal subjects, the same acumen which distinguished him in the early period of life, is happily employed in illustrating and enforcing the truths of which he received such deep and unalterable impressions in his mature years." [33] He also notes the mildness and benevolence of his satire, which is (like the operations of the skillful and humane surgeon, who wounds only to heal) "dictated by a just regard for the honor of God, an indignant grief excited by the profligacy of the age, and a tender compassion for the souls of men." [34]

Newton continues with a sermon exhorting all to turn, like Cowper, to the Bible as a refuge from "painful and unavoidable anxieties" and as a foundation for "stable peace" and "solid hope." He also defends Enthusiasm, or "experimental" religion, against the ridicule of those who believe that little deserves to be considered knowledge that will not stand the test of a different kind of experiment, that of the scientists or philosophers. It is perhaps ironic that a defense of religion based upon "inward feelings" should precede poems many of which were written in an attempt to alleviate the misery brought about by excessive dependence on experimental religion.

The reception of the 1782 volume was on the whole favorable. *The London Magazine* for May contained a brief item characterizing it as "an entertaining collection upon a variety of subjects, temporary, moral, and satirical; composed with sound judgment, good taste, and no small share of wit and humour." [35] It found the shorter poems, or "lively sallies, called by the French *jeux d'esprit*," more entertaining than the "laboured pieces of considerable length." "The Report Of An Adjudged Case Not To Be Found In Any Of The Books" and "The Cricket" were printed in the poetical department "for the entertainment of our readers." The reviewer of *The Gentleman's Magazine* reported that he had "perused, with great pleasure, both the serious and humorous pieces, the Latin and English, of which this collection consists." [36] But his opinion might well have been prejudiced by the fact that he knew "the author . . . to have been a keen sportsman in the classic fields of Westminster, and was a coadjutor of the celebrated Mr. Town in *The Connoisseur*. The short article contained the "Adjudged Report" and the poem on the burning of Lord Mansfield's library.[37]

Edmund Cartwright's criticism in *The Monthly Review* began on a formidable tone: "What Pope has remarked of women, may, by a very applicable parody, be said of the general run of modern poets, *Most poets have no character at all;* being, for the chief part, only echoes of those who have sung before them." [38] But, in a sudden reversal of tone, it found Cowper "a poet *sui generis,*" not like others who confine "themselves, like pack horses to the same beaten track and uniformity of pace" with bells "jingling along in uninterrupted unison . . ." Cartwright appreciated Cowper's spontaneity and his humor: "Hence his very religion has a smile that is arch, and his sallies of humour an air that is religious, and yet motley as is the mixture, it is so contrived as to be neither ridiculous nor disgusting."

The *Critical Review* was less favorable.[39] An article in its April issue began by acknowledging that Cowper "seems to be a man of sober and religious turn of mind, with a benevolent heart, and a serious wish to inculcate the precepts of morality," but went on to say that "he is not . . . possessed of any superior abilities or powers of genius, requisite to so arduous an undertaking, his verses are, in general, weak and languid, and have neither novelty, spirit, nor animation, to recommend them; that mediocrity so severely condemned by Horace . . . pervades the whole; and, whilst the author avoids every thing that is ridiculous or contemptible, he, at the same time, never rises to any thing that we can commend or admire." The reviewer censured Cowper's many "coarse, vulgar, and unpoetical" expressions, such as *parrying, pushing by, spitting abhorrence;* and he found his attempts at humor "faint," "awkward," and "prosaic." The short poems at the end seemed a welcome relief, and he felt that it was "a pity that our author had not confined himself altogether to this species of poetry, without entering into a system of ethics, for which his genius seems but ill adapted."

Cowper was depressed by the censure of the *Critical,* but he soon began to regard it as the result of prejudice against his "opinions and doctrines." Whatever was the effect of the review, however, it was quickly dispelled by a letter to a friend from Benjamin Franklin in which Franklin praised the poems highly: "The relish for reading of poetry had long since left me, but there is something so new in the manner, so easy, and yet so correct in the language, so clear in the expression, yet concise, and so just in the sentiments, that I have read the whole with great pleasure, and some of the pieces more than once." [40]

Aside from Cowper's various labors and the pleasing variety which he found in life at Olney, he owed the continued happiness and stability of the years 1781 to 1784 to his acquaintance with Lady Austen. She had first gone to Olney to visit her sister, a Mrs. Jones, who lived about a mile from Olney; but, as Cowper wrote to Newton, desiring retirement, and admiring the Reverend Thomas Scott, Newton's successor, she had decided to stay for a longer time. Upon meeting Cowper and Mrs. Unwin, she decided that when the lease on her town house should expire in about two years, she would move to Orchard Side. Her vivacity and wit, combined with piety, generosity, and a deep sense of gratitude that brought tears to her eyes whenever a kindness was done to her, endeared her to the residents of Orchard Side. [41]

Quite clearly she was most drawn to Cowper. Although she treated both Mary and him "with as much unreservedness of communication, as if we had been born in the same house, and educated together," it became clear by letters she wrote after her departure from Olney that she possessed "a sort of romantic idea of our [i.e. his] merits, and built such expectations of felicity upon our friendship, as we were sure that nothing human could possibly answer." As a result, Cowper "wrote to remind her that we were mortal, to recommend it to her not to think more highly of us than the subject would warrant, and intimating that when we embellish a creature with colours taken from our own fancy, and so adorned, admire and praise it beyond its real merits, we make it an idol, and have nothing to expect in the end, but that it will deceive our hopes, and that we shall derive nothing from it but a painful conviction of our error." [42]

Needless to say, Lady Austen took offense at Cowper's letter. She wrote an answer, "but such an one as [he] could by no means reply to." There ended for the time being "a friendship that bid fair to be lasting; being formed with a woman whose seeming stability of temper, whose knowledge of the world, and great experience of its folly, but above all, whose sense of religion and seriousness of mind (for with all that gaiety, she is a great thinker), induced us both, in spite of that cautious reserve that marks our characters, to trust her, to love and value her, and to open our hearts for her reception." [43] In two weeks Lady Austen, as a conciliatory gesture, sent Cowper three pairs of worked ruffles and advised him that he would soon receive a fourth. He responded by "laying . . . at her feet" his newly published volume of poems.[44]

Not long after she had first arrived at Olney, Lady Austen had taken up residence at the vicarage. In the spring of 1782 she returned there. Between the vicarage and the back of Cowper's house lay his garden, an orchard and the garden belonging to the vicarage. To facilitate communication, Cowper and Lady Austen had doors made in the garden walls. This made the trip shorter and also saved Lady Austen the trouble of going through Olney, a muddy journey during the winter. Eventually Lady Austen, Mary, and Cowper began to dine with each other alternately every day but Sunday.

Lady Austen encouraged Cowper's poetic endeavors. She suggested that he write a poem on the theme and story which became "John Gilpin," gave him the idea of translating Homer, and persuaded him to try his hand at blank verse. She even, in an offhanded way, suggested a topic for a blank verse poem, a sofa. From this playful suggestion grew his most famous work, *The Task*, a poem in six books, which he began in July, 1783.

Aside from inspiring the poet to write, Lady Austen's wit undoubtedly helped to dispel his chronic melancholy. But it had less healthy effects too. It drew Cowper away from Mrs. Unwin, against whose lack of vivacity much of Lady Austen's raillery was apparently directed. Eventually a domestic crisis occurred, the outcome of which was Lady Austen's departure from Olney. Although Cowper never again saw or corresponded with his "Sister Anna," as he had affectionately named her, the parting seems to have been amicable. The poet returned to the less stimulating company of Mrs. Unwin without apparent regret.[45]

The Task was published in July of 1785 in a volume which bore the name of this poem. Also included were "Tirocinium; Or A Review Of The Schools" and "John Gilpin" which had appeared anonymously in *The Public Advertiser* of November 14, 1782. "John Gilpin" was already a great success, and *The Task* received a somewhat warmer reception than the long poems of the 1782 edition. Like Cartwright's review of the 1782 poems, that of Sam-

uel Badcock in *The Monthly Review* for June, 1786, began omi-
nously with an analogy with Pope's second *Moral Essay* and a
comment on the "vacant insipidity" of modern poetry.[46] Badcock
then characterized *The Task* as "an entertainment that mingles
delight and improvement." Cowper is "always moral, yet never
dull: and though he often expands an image, yet he never weakens its force. If the same thought occurs, he gives it a new form;
and is copious, without being tiresome. He frequently entertains
by his comic humour; and still oftener awakens more serious and
more tender sentiments, by useful and pathetic representations;—
by descriptions that sooth and melt the heart, and rouse and
terrify guilt in its closest retreats."

Badcock pointed to the suddenness with which Cowper often
turned from earnestness to humor, from sober moralism to ridicule. But he felt that ridicule was well balanced by compassion,
and although he could perceive no unity of tone, he felt that religion had thrown "a shade of melancholy" over the whole. None-
theless, he detected "an amiable and generous principle shining
through the cloud, and struggling to overcome the evils which it
deplores."

Badcock's review is typical of its age in its praise of "natural
and unforced" language, censure of "careless and prosaic" passages, and approval of a style "seldom rich or ornamented, yet
. . . vigorous and animated" and able to carry "the thought
home to the heart with irresistible energy." Other familiar aspects
are the reviewer's enjoyment of the sublime, the terrible, of noble
and pathetic ideas, and his defense of science against Cowper's
strictures. That Badcock quoted amply from the "Crazy Kate"
and "stricken deer" passages testifies to the influence of sentimental literature.

A more interesting side of Badcock's review is that his appreciation of the benevolent but melancholy personality of the poet
makes him willing to overlook "occasional inelegance, repetition,
and incongruity." So "sound, beautiful, and striking an imagination ought not," he held, "be controlled and confined within the
bounds that criticism prescribes." The most important quality of
The Task, according to the review, becomes the "noble and generous mind"; the "tender, virtuous, and good" character; and
the "enraptured imagination which inform it and give to it sublimity and pathos." It is fitting that a work so rich in feeling

should cause the critic to respond with fervor instead of cool analysis. More than four pages of quotation end with an apology for Badcock's failure to pay proper attention to the shorter pieces; he had no room for a particular account of them, because he had "got on fairy ground, and *had eaten Lotus.*"

Other critics were less enthusiastic. One letter, signed *Phila-retes,* to *The Gentleman's Magazine,* appearing in April, protested that Cowper's rhapsodic religiosity had suppressed the Christian virtues of charity and humility.[47] Apparently the writer wished for a return from the sentimentalist's emphasis on the heart to the Neo-Classical championing of reason. These two strains run through the rest of the criticism, one attacking and the other praising, but neither answering the other. Neo-Classical strictures on looseness of structure, weakness of argument, and lack of conciseness dominated some reviews; but others praised the "glowing imagery," the poet's humanity, and the warm sensibility of his good heart.[48]

Occasional poetry; translation of the poetry of the French Quietist, Madame Guion (1782); and the beginning of the translation of Homer (1784) took much of Cowper's time—but he still could pursue his avocations of gardening and walking, which seem to have increased in importance after Lady Austen left. One of the places in which Cowper and Mrs. Unwin walked was the pleasure grounds owned by the Throckmortons at Weston, about a mile from Olney. Cowper had had the "range" of these grounds for several years but had never "had any intercourse with the family." In the spring of 1784 he received an invitation from John Throckmorton, who had recently succeeded his elder brother to the estate, in which Throckmorton announced that he would attempt to fill a balloon and would be happy to have Cowper attend the event. The endeavor, "very philosophically made," failed, but Mrs. Unwin and Cowper were received in a most flattering manner.[49] Indeed, more notice was taken of them than of any of the other guests. The Throckmortons, as William later wrote to Unwin, "even seemed anxious to recommend themselves to our regards."

Later, other cordialities were extended by the Throckmortons, who obviously considered the poet to be a person of distinction, and who enjoyed his company. But, although Cowper was obviously pleased, he had some reservations:

I should like exceedingly to be on an easy footing there, to give a morning call, and now and then to receive one, but nothing more. For though he is one of the most agreeable men I ever saw, I could not wish to visit him in any other way, neither our house, furniture, servants, or income, being such as qualify us to make entertainments; neither would I on any account be introduced to the neighboring gentry, which must be the consequence of our dining there, there not being a man in the country, except himself, with whom I could endure to associate. They are squires, merely such, purse-proud and sportsmen. But Mr. T. is altogether a man of fashion, and respectable on every account.[50]

The Throckmortons' Catholicism seems not to have bothered Cowper, especially since the two men appeared to be well adjusted to the militant Protestantism, which was the temper of the times. As aggressively Protestant as any Englishman, Cowper could not find a trace of bigotry in his new friends. The company of the Throckmortons helped fill the gap created by the departure of Lady Austen, and it inspired one of Cowper's best poems, the mock elegy on the death of Mrs. Throckmorton's bullfinch.

In the autumn of 1785 Cowper received a letter from his cousin Harriet, now Lady Hesketh and a widow, one of his closest friends and confidants in the days before his first illness.[51] Her husband, Thomas Hesketh, had died in 1778, leaving the poet a small bequest; but Harriet, who had been offended by Cowper's evangelical fervor, had not at that time desired to revive their friendship. Now, seven years later, she apparently was overcome by curiosity about the poet's condition, especially now that he had become famous. Cowper's affecting response ran from one letter into another, as he tried to assure her that, despite occasional dejection of spirits, he was happy in the quiet, unchanging world of Olney. Apparently Lady Hesketh's letter had been filled with pointed, practical inquiries; for, in addition to a description of his mental state, it elicited accounts of his activities, acquaintances, personal finances, physical appearance, and later his religious sentiments. Subsequently, he wrote of the progress of his translation of Homer in a letter which closes with the proud comment that "Dr. Johnson read, and recommended my first volume." [52]

The correspondence which followed these initial letters contains a wide variety of subject matter: illnesses, household remedies, reminiscences, politics—indeed, all of the topics on which the two had to make up for the years of silence. A number of gifts were sent by Harriet, the most important of which was a desk to replace the shaky card table upon which the poet had formerly written.

But the most interesting themes running through the correspondence with Lady Hesketh concern the translation of Homer and the visit to Olney which in January, 1786, she decided to make. Cowper's reaction to the proposed visit was ecstatic:

And now, my dear, let me tell you once more, that your kindness in promising us a visit has charmed us both. I shall see you again. I shall hear your voice. We shall take walks together. I will show you my prospects, the hovel, the alcove, the Ouse, and its banks, everything that I have described. I anticipate the pleasure of those days not very far distant, and feel a part of it at this moment.[53]

So involved did Mrs. Unwin and he become in the complicated preparations that the month of February, usually so trying to his delicate nerves, seems to have lost, for that year at least, its terrors. He was able to see the comedy in his eager anticipation of her arrival, but he described the difficulties Mrs. Unwin encountered in finding suitable quarters, and the final negotiations for the vicarage with a humor that ill concealed his excitement. As the months went by, Cowper's agitation increased. At least once Lady Hesketh expressed fear for his delicate nervous condition, and certainly she had doubts about what she would find at Olney and Orchard Side.

Her own feelings are not perfectly clear, especially since we can see them only through her cousin's responses. Certainly the fears which she expressed in a letter which he answered on June fourth and fifth must have been genuine, although liberally salted with curiosity and a tactfulness probably intended to disarm his trepidation.

Ah! my cousin, you begin already to fear and quake. What a hero am I, compared with you! I have no fears of *you;* on the contrary am as bold as a lion. I wish that your carriage were even now at the door. But what cause have you for fear? Am I not your cousin, with whom you have wandered in the fields of Freemantle, and at Bevis's Mount?

When Harriet finally arrived later in June, it was his nerves that failed:

Her first appearance was too much for me; my spirits, instead of being greatly raised, as I had inadvertently supposed they would be,
broke down with me under the pressure of too much joy, and left me
flat, or rather melancholy throughout the day, to a degree that was
mortifying to myself, and alarming to her.[54]

But he soon "made amends for this failure," and "in point of
cheerfulness have far exceeded her expectations, for she knew
that sable had been my suit for many years."

Like most of Cowper's friends and relatives, Harriet was pressed
into service to help prepare the way among her friends for the
forthcoming translation of Homer. Like the others, she felt free to
criticize, although in a way befitting a lady, eschewing serious
tone and meticulous effort. Certainly she could not have forgotten
that in one of his first letters to her on the matter, he had written
that "a translation of Homer must be chiefly a lady's book"; [55] a
gentleman read the original.

Having made arrangements with Joseph Johnson, his printer,
for the publication of proposals for his translation, Cowper began
to have fears about the success of his work. To an extent this reaction was the normal one a writer experiences upon realizing that a
goal has been all but achieved and that there is no turning back
from the consequences of that achievement. To this factor was
added, however, the fact that he had set himself up through his
translation as a rival to Alexander Pope. In a letter contributed to
the August, 1785, issue of *The Gentleman's Magazine,* Cowper
had anticipated criticism of his own publication by criticizing
Pope, whose translation, despite its many detractors, continued to
have a high reputation. Not many years earlier Samuel Johnson
had praised it in his *Life of Pope.* To Harriet, Cowper made it
clear that he intended to excel the work of his predecessor. If
Johnson had praised Pope, his argument ran, it was because he
had "talked at random, that either he had never examined it by
Homer's [performance] or never since he was a boy." [56] Cowper
continued with the asperity typical of a poet staking out his claim:
"For I would undertake to produce numberless passages from it,
if need were, not only ill translated, but meanly written."

Aside from his fears for the success of his translation and his
rebellion against Pope's close, compact expression and smooth
numbers, Cowper also blamed his constitutional melancholy for

the depression he experienced. When his cousin William Cowper, now a general, suggested in a note conveyed by Harriet that he publish a specimen of his translation of *The Iliad*, the poet declined, and then assured his cousin that he "should be glad of his advice at all times." [57] Examining his reasons for refusing, he found that his reaction had "proceeded from a principle of shamefacedness at bottom, that had determined me against the counsel of a man whom I knew to be wiser than myself." Partly, this was the voice of a man who did not wish to give offense to a benefactor, but the tone of the letter also indicates his lack of confidence. Although he had written his translation with the intention of publishing it, and although he had already published two volumes of poetry and had discovered that he could bear adverse criticism, he could not convince himself that his work was ready. Indeed, he wrote that the specimen he had sent to his friends "had suffered a little through my too great zeal for amendment" and had reached the stage at which he felt some changes were inferior to original readings.

The most formidable criticism of the specimen eventually published by Cowper was by the irascible Paul Henry Maty. Coming from a man who had become "an oracle in every body's account," these criticisms, which the poet felt to be "unjust" and "in part ill-natured," could have done him mischief.[58] But Maty's strictures faded before information from Harriet attributing them to jealousy,[59] and the praise of his friend of former years, George Colman. Apparently General Cowper, with the same solicitude that had more than once before caused him to adopt a patronizing tone toward his cousin, took it upon himself to comfort the beleaguered translator. From a letter to Harriet it becomes clear that the general's efforts were not at all misconceived:

The frown of a critic freezes my poetical powers, and discourages me to a degree that makes me ashamed of my own weakness. Yet I presently recover my confidence again. The half of what you so kindly say in your last would at any time restore my spirits, and, being said by you, is infallible. I am not ashamed to confess, that having commenced an author, I am most abundantly desirous to succeed as such. I have (what, perhaps, you little suspect me of) in my nature an infinite share of ambition. But with it I have at the same time, as you well know, an equal share of diffidence. To this combination of opposite qualities it has been owing that till lately, I stole through life without undertaking any thing, yet always wishing to distinguish myself.[60]

Whatever his fears, the defense of his "rough lines with a deal of meaning" against the elegant verbosity of decadent Neo-Classicism did not prove arduous. To the end of his days the process of revision continued, usually with indifferent success. For, if Cowper could sense exactly what Homer meant and could find the proper English words, he could not make his translation poetry.

The long-delayed arrival of Harriet in June, 1786, did much to sustain the poet during this difficult time. After the initial depression brought by the unnatural heightening of emotion caused by her arrival, serenity and genial humor returned. Lady Hesketh stayed until November. So successful was her visit, in fact, that rumors spread to John Newton in London about the gay and dissipated life being led by the residents of Orchard Side. This report prompted a letter of inquiry to Mrs. Unwin in which Newton seemed to imply criticism of their conduct. Cowper, who was as unable to regard with humor such petty accusations as Newton's, replied with ill-concealed indignation.[61]

Apparently, Newton had at last taken seriously Cowper's repeated protestations about "God's departure" from him and had feared for Mary's soul as well as for the poet's. Since shortly after the mental breakdown of 1773, Cowper had regarded his estrangement from conventional religion and his knowledge of God's hostility toward him with total lack of feeling. Although he wrote often enough to Newton about his "nightly visitors," the dreams which interrupted his sleep and the voices which often taunted him when awake, Newton seems to have felt that the best way to lessen Cowper's tendency toward hysteria and to hasten his return to true religion was to answer him with polite disbelief and with continual reassurances of the mercy of God to all who seek redemption. He ignored the dreams.[62]

During this phase, however, Cowper's stability seems to have been founded upon a refusal to entertain thoughts which might get out of control and undermine his composure. At meals he sat with knife and fork in hand staring straight ahead, while the others lowered their eyes and clasped hands together to say grace. He did not, I think, intend to be perverse; instead, he feared that the very mechanics connected with prayer might excite him and bring to mind ideas that would upset him. Even then, there were times when he sat in gloomy silence, tormented by anxieties, while those around him continued their polite repartee. Fortunately for him, most of his acquaintances were willing to accept his silence as shyness or reserve, or, perhaps, as the eccentricity of genius.

The moments of unrelieved darkness persisted throughout the 1780's and continued to be at their worst in the winter months. In his letters any professions of hope had a mechanical quality, as if to relieve the reader, usually Newton, of concern. But it is significant that the moods alternated with those of a lighter cast and did not seem to become longer or more intense until the third collapse in 1787.

The day after Lady Hesketh left Olney to return to London, Mrs. Unwin and Cowper moved to a house at Weston owned by the Throckmortons. This residence had been vacant and available to Lady Hesketh, but she had preferred the vicarage, probably because of its proximity to Orchard Side. The house at Weston was larger and situated in more healthful, comfortable surroundings than Orchard Side. Cowper, who thought Weston one of the prettiest villages he had ever seen, particularly liked the "most beautiful" environs and proximity to the Throckmorton's pleasure-ground.[63]

Nevertheless, it was difficult to leave the house in Olney for which he had powerful feelings despite the suffering he had known there. In 1783 he had remarked to Newton that

. . . an invisible, uncontrollable agency, a local attachment, an inclination more forcible than I ever felt, even to the place of my birth, serves me for prison-walls, and for bounds which I cannot pass. In former years I have known sorrow, and before I had ever tasted of spiritual trouble. The effect was an abhorrence of the scene in which I suffered so much, and a weariness of those objects which I had so long looked at with an eye of despondency and dejection. But it is otherwise with me now. The same cause subsisting, and in a much more powerful degree, fails to produce its natural effect. The very stones in the garden-walls are my intimate acquaintance. I should miss almost the minutest object, and be disagreeably affected by its removal, and am persuaded that were it possible I could leave this incommodious nook for a twelve month, I should return to it again

with rapture, and be transported with the sights of objects which to
all the world beside would be at least indifferent; some of them perhaps, such as the ragged thatch and the tottering walls of the neigh-
bouring cottages, disgusting.[64]

When it came time to move to Weston, he discovered that he "not
only had a tenderness for that ruinous abode, because it had once
known me happy in the presence of God, but that even the distress I had suffered for so long a time on account of His absence,
had endeared it to me as much." He "was weary of every object,
had long wished for a change, yet could not take leave without a
pang at parting." His mixed feelings could not, however, suppress
a wry humor:

When God speaks to a chaos, it becomes a scene of order and harmony in a moment; but when His creatures have thrown one house
into confusion by leaving it, and another by tumbling themselves and
their goods into it, not less than many days labour and contrivance is
necessary to give them their proper places.[65]

As winter approached, and with it the usual dejection, Orchard
Side became more and more associated with the miserable side of
Cowper's past.

Once, since we left Olney, I had occasion to call at our old dwelling; and never did I see so forlorn and woeful a spectacle. Deserted
of its inhabitants, it seemed as if it could never be dwelt in for ever.
The coldness of it, the dreariness, and the dirt, made me think it no
inapt resemblance of a soul that God has forsaken. While He dwelt
in it, and manifested Himself there, He could create His own accom-
modations, and give it occasionally the appearance of a palace; but
the moment He withdraws, and takes with Him all the furniture and
embellishment of His graces, it becomes what it was before He entered it—the habitation of vermin, and the image of desolation.[66]

Years later, Olney, taking on even more Satanic qualities, would
become the abode of fiendish tormenters in Cowper's dreams.
    Not long after the move to Weston, Mrs. Unwin received notice
of the death of her son—a particularly severe blow also to Cowper, since Unwin had become one of his most intimate friends.
Not only did he date his acquaintance with the family from the

day at Huntingdon many years earlier when William Unwin had, with the diffidence of youth, introduced himself, but a particularly warm friendship had developed despite their difference in age. Cowper had always felt close enough to Unwin to confide in him without reservation, but they did not speak to each other as equals. The poet was always an elder brother, ready with advice but also with genuine concern and a sense of comradeship. This role itself became more than once a subject for jest: "It is hard upon us striplings who have uncles still living (N.B. I myself have an uncle still alive), that those venerable gentlemen should stand in our way, even when the ladies are in question." [67]

On the whole, the friendship with William Unwin was more formal than the one with Joseph Hill, his friend from the days in London, and also less formal than the one with Newton. It provided Cowper with an opportunity to release his affections and to assert his humor. The passage of the letter to Newton in which he tells of Unwin's death gives us some idea of his anguish and his manful attempts to control his grief:

I will only observe, that the death of so young a man, whom I so lately saw in good health and whose life was desirable on every account, has something in it peculiarly distressing. I cannot think of the widow and the children that he has left, without an heartache that I remember not to have felt before.[68]

The restraint of this passage gives way to a more personal and more moving outburst in a letter to Lady Hesketh: "So farewell, my friend Unwin! The first man for whom I conceived a friendship after my removal from St. Albans, and for whom I cannot but still continue to feel a friendship, though I shall see thee with these eyes no more." [69] When Cowper's friend, the Reverend William Bull, "rode over to smoke a pipe, and sympathize a little with them," he found Cowper and Mrs. Unwin bearing their grief better than he had expected.

The move to Weston—with its attendant difficulties, the problem of adjusting to a more crowded and busier life, and the death of Unwin—exacted full toll from Cowper, and in January, 1787, he again lapsed into insanity. The old symptoms recurred. His belief that he had been damned again became an active tormenter, and he became convinced that God was about to wreak

vengeance upon him. Moods of melancholy withdrawal alternated with violent hysteria. As before, he tried suicide. One attempt was foiled by Mrs. Unwin, another by Bull. The physical
strain upon Mrs. Unwin, now in her mid-sixties, was severe; and
her task was not lightened by the fact that Cowper refused help
from anyone but her.

As before, time was the only corrective. In June the illness
passed, almost as suddenly as it had come; and cheerful spirits
returned. But, if the strain on Mrs. Unwin had been severe, the
collapse also had had profound physical effects upon Cowper
himself. Old ailments, such as a chronic weakness of the eyes,
were aggravated. From then on he complained of headaches and
other maladies which his nervous imbalance undoubtedly helped
prolong.

His recovery was consolidated by a generally pleasant environment. A young man named Samuel Rose, the son of a school-
master at Chiswick, stopped by in January, 1787, to convey the
thanks of professors at the University of Glasgow for Cowper's
poetic efforts; and an immediate friendship, which in some ways
took the place of the one for William Unwin, ensued. Not only did
the poet find an appropriate object for his fatherly affections, but
he also gained a disciple temperamentally suited to him with
whom he could converse for extended periods. To Rose we are
indebted for vivid pictures of life at Weston, its regimen, and its
inhabitants, including guests like Lady Hesketh.

The regimen was made up of walking, talking, writing, and the
usual household chores. As before, the poet took refuge in the
peace and stability produced by the uneventfulness of this life.
When a visitor arrived, often to stay for weeks or months, he was
assimilated into this pattern, although conversation naturally became a more important part of the day. During these years Cowper continued with his translation of Homer, and he also wrote
several poems against slavery, an issue which had for some time
bothered the more enlightened public. Some of these poems reveal an unfortunate willingness to substitute direct, unadorned
statement for a more imaginative mode of expression. As in his
other poetry, these poems often improve when the poet allows his
sense of humor to operate. He could be a poet only when powerful feeling had been recollected and quieted enough to permit
him to devote full attention to the mechanisms of the poem. In

"Sweet Meat Has Sour Sauce, Or, The Slave Trader In The Dumps," the manipulation of rhythm and point of view raise the poem above naked statement. The well-known "The Poplar-Field" was also written during this period.

The role played by Samuel Rose was duplicated by John Johnson, a cousin on the Donne side of the family, who appeared without prior notice at Weston in January, 1790. A student at Caius College, Cambridge, "Johnny of Norfolk," as Cowper eventually called him, more nearly matched in his quizzical humor the poet's own personality than did Rose. Furthermore, Johnson brought news of the Donne family, to whom William felt even a deeper attachment than to the Cowpers, and helped to revive friendships that had lain dormant for twenty years. Johnny's youthful gaiety brightened the world of the poet and stimulated a fatherly concern.[70]

Cowper's recovery had been complete enough so that his young cousin was not even aware of the "scene that was acted" in 1787, nor of the fits of melancholy of which William complained. So enthusiastic were his accounts of life at Weston they elicited an invitation from Anne Bodham, his aunt, for Cowper to visit. It received the usual negative answer.[71]

If new acquaintances and the revival of old ones, as well as the arrival of people almost ideally suited to the task of sustaining the poet's recovery, helped to make the years immediately following the breakdown of 1787 happy and useful, the continued presence of Mary Unwin was certainly the most significant factor. Rose's account of life at Weston pictures Mary in the background of the social and intellectual activities of the household; while Rose himself and his mentor were engaged in the edition of Homer or deep in conversation, perhaps with Lady Hesketh, Mrs. Unwin was employed in many domestic tasks.

Although his picture is certainly incomplete, and although we do not know to what extent his ego and his unfamiliarity with Cowper's usual regimen colored his observation, we can be certain, as the poet himself tells us, that Mary served as a companion on most of his walks and visits; that she was an attentive, though not necessarily critical listener; and that she was a tactful counselor in domestic matters. In short, apart from the private world of the poet, into which no one entered, most of his life was shared by her. Cowper needed seclusion in which to work; he also

needed to be relieved of many of the burdens of everyday life—
and Mary provided both the atmosphere and the condition necessary to his poetic efforts. She also provided the tenderness, affection, and generosity which his peculiar nervous condition required. He could get along (as he had for many years) without
his acquaintances and their conversation, but he could not do
without the solace of the continual dialogue with Mary.

With this significance of Mary's role in mind, we should consider the effects upon the poet of her growing age and infirmity,
especially during the last decade of his life. These years, because
of his advancing age and physical weaknesses, particularly a
chronic ailment of the eyes, would under any conditions have
been difficult; but the growing incapacity of Mary made them
immeasurably worse. Several domestic accidents crippled her for
several months at a time and left a permanent disability. When, in
December, 1791, she suffered a paralytic stroke, the suddenness of
the calamity was probably as disconcerting as the burden it threw
upon Cowper,[72] but he seems to have borne the unaccustomed
responsibility rather well. It might have helped that Lady Hesketh was at his side, although she too was an invalid; and household servants also kept him from having to see to all the details of
her case.

Mary's illness imposed, however, a psychological as well as
physical burden. For a long time Cowper had felt guilty about the
degree to which his own illnesses had imposed upon Mary, and, in
the case of the 1787 collapse, had drained her of health. Now he
had to face the full consequences of his self-imposed sense of
guilt. Tormented as he was by the fear of losing Mary, he suffered
even more exquisitely because he thought that he was responsible
for her condition. He felt divine vengeance would now exact from
him the measure of his guilt by reversing the situation that had
obtained for so many years.

Fortunately Mary recovered rapidly from the first stroke. But in
May, 1792, she suffered another, one far more severe, depriving
her of speech and the ability to move about and use her right arm
and leg—even making it practically impossible for her to open her
eyes. All of the feelings that Cowper had experienced a year earlier were revived, and in a second poem, "To Mary," written in the
autumn of 1793, he lamented her growing infirmity:

. . . .
Such feebleness of limbs thou prov'st,
That now at every step thou mov'st
Upheld by two; yet still thou lov'st,
          My Mary!

And still to love, though prest with ill,
In wintry age to feel no chill,
With me is to be lovely still,
          My Mary!

But ah! by constant heed I know,
How oft the sadness that I show
Transforms thy smiles to looks of woe,
          My Mary!

And should my future lot be cast
With much resemblance of the past,
Thy worn-out heart will break at last,
          My Mary!

It is not hard to detect the depth of his feeling. In fact, feeling sweeps before it all of the qualities, the reserve, taste, and delicacy which characterize Cowper at his best. The sufferings of Mary had so vividly impinged themselves upon his mind that they paralyzed his poetic sensibility. In other stanzas the poem becomes embarrassingly graphic.

At this juncture Providence again intervened, and in a way hardly to be reconciled to Cowper's beliefs in a vengeful God. As he wrote to Harriet, it happened well that, of all men living, the man most qualified to assist and comfort him was there, though until that time he had never seen him and had no expectation that he ever would. The man to whom he referred was William Hayley, a poet and essayist of some prestige but not of very great talent, who was drawn to Cowper because they had a common interest in John Milton. Hayley was engaged in writing a biography, having exhausted his vein of poetry and sentimentality; and Cowper, having successfully completed his Homer, was now involved in getting together an edition of Milton's work which would contain translations of the Latin and Italian poems. Some attempts had been made to excite a rivalry between the two, partially because *The Task*, having replaced Hayley's *The Triumphs of Temper* in public esteem, Hayley had some reason to resent Cowper. Hayley's erratic temperament might have risen to the occasion at a different time, but early in 1792 he chose instead to write a friendly letter and commendatory sonnet to his potential rival. The letter he received in answer assured him that Cowper's work would in no way clash or interfere with his, for it would not contain a life of Milton.

In April, 1792, Hayley visited Weston, where a warm friendship immediately developed between the two poets. Hayley, whose high spirits complemented Cowper's reserve, grew to admire the author of *The Task* as much as he admired his works. Cowper, depending more and more on outside influences to relieve his preoccupation with gloomy thoughts, was probably thankful for Hayley's attention, which in his mind placed his new friend among "that race of heroes, men who resolve to have no interests of their own, till mine are served," upon whom he had "stumbled suddenly." [73] He even seemed to ignore Hayley's irresponsibility to his family and rather unorthodox morality, although his oldest and most intimate friends didn't:

I have heard nothing from Joseph, and having been always used to hear from him in November, am reduced to the dire necessity of supposing with you that he is heinously offended. Being in want of money, however, I wrote to him yesterday, and a letter which ought to produce a friendly answer; but whether it will or not is an affair, at present, of great uncertainty. Walter Bagot is offended too, and wonders that I would have any connection with so bad a man as the author of the Essay on Old Maids must necessarily be: Poor man! he has five sisters, I think, in that predicament, which makes *his* resentment rather excusable. Joseph, by the way, has two and perhaps may be proportionally influenced by that consideration. Should that be the case, I have nothing left to do but to wish them all good husbands, since the reconciliation of my two friends seems closely connected with that contingency.[74]

While returning from a walk with Hayley, Cowper received the news of Mary's second stroke.[75] He became hysterical, but his companion, despite his affection for both Cowper and Mary, restrained his emotion enough to be helpful. With a great degree of selflessness, and a characteristic burst of energy, he threw himself into the task of restoring order. Hayley, who thought highly of his own abilities and who regarded himself as a universal man, naturally had some knowledge of medicine to offer; and, where his own learning ended, there was the advice of his friend, a Dr. Austen in London. The advice of Dr. Austen was supplemented by the ministrations of an electric machine borrowed from a neighbor named Socket.

Whatever the effects of the primitive medicine and therapy, Mary recovered sufficiently for Hayley to suggest that she and Cowper visit him at Eartham during the summer. To a man that had for years refused countless invitations from very close friends of long standing because he considered solitude indispensable to his well-being, the suggestion must have been most disconcerting. But Cowper's concern for Mary outweighed all other considerations, except perhaps the hope that a change in surroundings might also relieve his own melancholy.

The slowness of Mrs. Unwin's recovery delayed the visit to Eartham until the beginning of August. Although the plans for the journey were filled with the pathos of advancing age, Cowper could maintain perspective on the whole operation. He laughed to think "what an important thing it is for me to travel":

Other men steal way from their homes silently, and make no disturbance; but when I move, houses are turned upside down, maids are turned out of their beds, all the counties through which I pass appear to be in an uproar. Surrey greets me by the mouth of the General, and Essex by that of Carwardine. How strange does all this seem to a man who has seen no bustle, and made none, for twenty years together! [76]

The trip was less of a strain than had been expected, and the stay at Hayley's improved the health and morale of both Mrs. Unwin and Cowper. As so often in recent years, new acquaintances and the society of vital people so revived the poet's spirits that—although he maintained his correspondence, even writing during his frequent trips to the seashore from Hayley's—he no longer lived only to write letters. Before leaving Weston, he had sat for a portrait by Abbot; now he sat for Romney. But, above all, the improvement in Mary's condition cheered him.

Although he enjoyed the beauty of his new surroundings, Cowper could not forget the less spectacular but more familiar scenes at Weston. Indeed, he wrote to Lady Hesketh that the more rugged terrain and wilderness which surrounded Eartham would have increased his "natural melancholy" "were it not for the agreeables I find within." [77] As sensitive as he was to the beauty of landscape, "mere change of place" could not invigorate him. A letter to Samuel Teedon even suggests that extreme change in itself was upsetting. He was, he confessed, "a little daunted by the tremendous height of the Sussex hills, in comparison of which all that I had seen elsewhere are dwarfs," as well as by the "forests" and "mountains" of Eartham. He preferred the "snug concealment"—the gentle, familiar terrain of Weston.

Mary and William began the return to Weston on September 17, 1792. The prospect of getting home with Mary partially renewed in health and spirits exhilarated Cowper; and, since the journey to Eartham had been moderately successful, traveling did not arouse much concern. Nevertheless, his spirits labored under a dreadful dejection brought about by his promise to visit General Cowper at Ham, and Rose in London during the journey to Weston. Not only did the unpleasant side of visiting for only a brief time a relative he had not seen for nearly thirty years and would never see again depress him, but he also feared the consequences of going to London. All of the old anxieties about death and a future that was not very promising must have crowded upon his mind and then gained strength from the dread that the emotions which these adventures aroused might overwhelm him. The same impulses that caused him to seek "snug concealment" now made the return trip unsettling in the extreme. But he overcame the struggles with his spirit and left General Cowper's, a visit from which he "would have given the world to be excused," with a "lighter heart than I had known since my departure from Eartham." [78]

The letter which Cowper wrote to Hayley upon his return takes up the theme of the successful struggle in a mock heroic vein which the writer's lack of detachment prevents him from maintaining:

Chaos himself, even the chaos of Milton, is not surrounded with more confusion, nor has a mind more completely in a hubbub, than I experience at the present moment. At our first arrival, after long absence, we find a hundred orders to servants necessary, a thousand things to be restored to their proper places, and an endless variety of minutiae to be adjusted; which, though individually of little importance, are most momentous in the aggregate. . . . I will begin with a remark, in which I am inclined to think you will agree with me, that there is sometimes more true heroism passing in a corner, and on occasions the most illustrious; I hope so at least; for all the heroism I have to boast, and all the opportunities I have of displaying any, are of a private nature.[79]

Aside from providing interesting analogies with Gray's "Elegy" ("full many a flower is born to blush unseen"), with its emphasis on the individual, the ordinary man, Cowper's reserve and composure, necessitating a light style in this letter, symbolize a temporary respite in the internal struggle.

Recovery could not, however, last long. Mary was too old to respond permanently to any kind of treatment. As she became weaker, she depended more upon Cowper. As the poem "To Mary" indicates, she was quite literally a burden; for she insisted, somewhat irritably Lady Hesketh indicates in a letter, that he take her on walks around the garden and into the country. In a state of semiparalysis she refused the service of others and insisted querulously that Cowper himself carry her. His devotion to her received no gratitude, only complaints and more exacting demands.

It is not hard, therefore, to see why Cowper's nerves, never strong, began to fail. The long periods of stability in the 1770's and 1780's had resulted in part from Mary's ability to relieve him of anxiety through her affection, encouragement, and cheerful acceptance of many responsibilities and domestic cares. Now an invalid, she was deprived of all the traits of character which had made her vital to him. But this change was not the most severe shock; for even more tormenting was the fear of losing her completely. The more burdensome she became, the more desperately he clung to her.

As if to make matters worse, the edition of Milton demanded much of Cowper's time; and Joseph Johnson asked him to revise the Homer for another edition. In addition, the household, which he had never been able to manage before, now imposed new burdens. A servant, Hannah, who, Lady Hesketh complained, had always been treated so generously that she had never learned subordination, now became faithless and extravagant. Hayley visited in November, 1793, and April, 1794; and Lady Hesketh came in November, 1793, and stayed until July, 1795; but nothing could keep Cowper from retreating into an almost uninterrupted state of melancholy. Through the efforts of Hayley, a pension of 300 pounds a year was granted by King George III, but it came too late to revive his spirits or even arouse much gratitude.

The letters of this period and the years that followed become increasingly more despondent and often much less reserved. As attention turned inward, neurosis and fantasies replaced social commentary as subject matter. Occasionally writing letters still succeeded in dissipating his gloom. A flash of wit might reveal that he had at least returned to a state in which he could say that he lived to write letters. Of this nature also are passages in which larger concerns, such as the political affairs of the French Revolution, might for a while transcend personal difficulties. In letters to Hayley, with whom reserve was necessary, even though Cowper often referred to him as brother, Cowper manfully strove to suppress his feelings and to maintain a cordial, and even bantering, tone: "Oh! you rogue! what would you give to have such a dream about Milton, as I had about a week since?"

Just as the burdens Cowper was forced to assume at his advancing age and in his weakened physical condition account for his melancholy, so his ability to carry them indicates that, despite growing depression, he had not yet, as some critics allege, fallen back into insanity. But his melancholy had reached a dangerous state. Often he spoke to no one, and he apparently did not hear or understand what others said to him. And he became more and more dependent on the religious ministrations of one Samuel Teedon, an impoverished schoolteacher who in earlier years had been the object of Cowper's charity and humor. Teedon, ridiculous to a happier Cowper because of his pompous manner, now became an emissary between God and the poet.

As we know, Cowper had been tormented for years by nightmares and by what he called "voices," words and phrases that impressed themselves to an unusual degree upon his mind. Once the "voices" had led him to the rapturous state of the convert, and in 1773 they had put a violent end to his evangelical phase. Now, probably because of mounting tensions, they again became too insistent to be ignored or evaded through intellectual occupation. Teedon offered an example of that zeal which had marked Cow-

per's recovery at St. Albans. A desperate longing for that happier
state that he had once known or, failing of that, at least hope for
some relief from the terror which, as in 1773 and 1787, had threat-
ened to engulf him, drew the poet to him. Since Cowper could not
pray, he authorized Teedon to give thanks and implore mercy.
When the enthusiastic schoolteacher reciprocated by having
words of encouragement from the Lord to Cowper, Cowper replied with descriptions of his "nightly visitors" about which he
could only hint to others.

It is hard to know exactly what transpired in the minds of the
two men. Why should Teedon have been deemed able to receive
confidences of a kind which not even the most intimate of the
poet's other friends ever shared? Did Cowper really expect
Teedon to work a miracle? Was he making one last desperate attempt to fend off madness while tottering on the abyss? Or was he
merely offering a half-hearted gesture? Teedon's motives also remain obscure; but, if he really believed in the powers that he
claimed to have, he too must have approached, if not madness, a
zeal verging on hysteria. Although it is also possible that he was a
cynical manipulator, it is much more likely that, in his kind, be-
fuddled way, he became carried away both with his mission of
saving his onetime benefactor and by a not unusual degree of
credulity. Visits and correspondence between the two soon were
on a regular basis; and Cowper, despite his breeding and habitual
reserve, confided to a casual acquaintance for whom he had once
had no respect secrets that had seemed too lurid even for the
sanctified ears of John Newton.

Newton, now rector of St. Mary Wolnoth in London, continued
to offer encouragement; but it could arouse neither kindred feelings nor the sometimes bitter humor that had characterized Cowper's replies in the 1780's. Age, hardship, and mental anguish had
made him indifferent even to Newton's zeal and personal warmth.
A year before the poet's death, he wrote to Newton that, if a book
the rector had sent him "afforded me any amusement, or suggested to me any reflections, they were only such as served to
embitter, if possible, still more the present moment, by a sad ret-
rospect to those days when I thought myself secure of an eternity
to be spent with the spirits of such men as He whose life afforded
the subject of it. But I was little aware of what I had to expect,
and that a storm was at hand which in one terrible moment would

darken, and in another still more terrible blot out that prospect for ever." [80] His total hopelessness is seen in the unrelieved gloom of the short letter, which closes, "Adieu, dear sir, whom in those days I called dear friend, with feelings that justified the appellation."

John Johnson, "Johnny of Norfolk," who in 1790 had so renewed Cowper's spirits, now assumed the task of caring for Mary and the poet. In 1795 Lady Hesketh, none too strong to begin with, became ill as a result of her attempt to maintain some semblance of order at Weston for the previous one and one-half years. After her departure, William's letters to her display an almost unrelieved despair, which must have appeared to her sensible nature much as the Enthusiasm of 1765 had. Because she could never be taken into his confidence, the letters contain a monotonous refrain of the same despondent theme: he will never see her again, he will not live out the year, he can no longer collect his thoughts, Nature is a *universal blank*.[81]

Johnson's own affairs and his desire to improve the condition of Mary and William now prompted him to move them to Norfolk, where all the Donne cousins lived; but not even the proposed move aroused the poet from his lethargy. When it was time to leave Weston, he sensed that another link with the past was being shattered and that he was becoming bound more firmly to his terrible destiny. Agonized, he wrote a farewell on a window shutter:

> Farewell, dear scenes, for ever closed to me,
> Oh, for what sorrows must I now exchange ye!
> Me miserable! how could I escape
> Infinite wrath and infinite despair!
> Whom Death, Earth, Heaven, and Hell consigned to ruin,
> Whose friend was God, but God swore not to aid me! [82]

Outwardly he remained calm, although he later told Johnson that he fully expected his "tormenters" to drag him out of the coach as they passed through Olney "and tear him to pieces."[83]

Johnson's rather foolish attempts to restore the health of the two invalids by an extended journey through Norfolk having failed, in October, 1796, he brought them to his house in East Dereham, where Cowper benefitted slightly from a return to a pattern of existence that faintly recalled Olney. Through various subterfuges Johnson induced him to resume his revision of Homer, but he could incite the poet only to brief periods of industry. When Mrs. Unwin died on December 17, this event, which in prospect had seemed so momentous, barely roused him from apathy. After two brief outbursts—one in which he expressed the fear that she, forced by a vengeful God to share his miserable destiny, would be buried alive—he returned to indifference and never again spoke of her.

He continued in a state of "living death" for four years. Having no hope for anything but greater suffering after death, and unable to find anything to occupy his attention, he clung to his few friends, but slipped farther and farther into the world of his fantasies. His friends did not cease in their devotion, even when their labors had no perceptible effect. Samuel Rose handled his financial affairs, but his efforts annoyed an increasingly cantankerous Lady Hesketh. Johnson and a Miss Perowne, hired to care for the invalid, remained at his side, but much of the benefit of Johnson's personality was undoubtedly negated by such clumsy ventures as his attempts, by making noises through a tube in the bedroom wall, to block out the "voices" which continually tormented the poet. Once, upon hearing a tremendous crash like a hammer falling on the table, he turned to Cowper, whose only comment was "I know what it means." [84]

Hayley, in his usual flamboyant manner, conceived a fantastic plot to bring Cowper out of his depression. He professed to have had a vision in which it was revealed to him that many men of note would write to the poet to tell him of their high regard. Hayley's machinations to back up the dream resulted in a few letters, among them ones from the bishops of London and Llandaff. But the product of his efforts could hardly have done justice to his "vision," either in number or effect. Upon hearing the letter from Dr. Porteus, Bishop of London, Cowper exclaimed, "It was written in derision. I am sure of it."

Convinced that God intended only vengeance, and that any evidence to the contrary was merely a way of intensifying his misery, Cowper spent his last years in "unutterable despair." Although he worked fitfully, he undertook no major projects; nor did he complete the translation of Homer and edition of Milton. Then in March, 1799, intense feeling once again burst forth into poetry. "Montes Glaciales" and "The Castaway," his last two

poems, confronted the predicament from which he had been trying to escape through such menial efforts as translation. In "Montes Glaciales" he identified himself with icebergs doomed to
"Cimmerian darkness" and cut off from their "native coast" to dis-
solve in an uncongenial gulf. In "The Castaway" he compared
himself to a drowning sailor, whose story he had read many years
earlier in Anson's *Voyages*. From his own experience he could
sense the desperation with which the sailor fought off a death he
knew was inevitable, and he could envision the desperate attempts
of the crew to save the castaway, all of them frustrated by a
furious nature, and fears for their own safety. Cowper knew that
the sailor, though not condemning the haste of his friends, felt
bitterness at dying deserted while they were still so close. How
long the few minutes of struggle seemed to the castaway! Yet
how brief when the last moment arrived.

To this tale the poet added two stanzas in which he made the
plight of the castaway an emblem of his own fate. He too had
been "snatch'd from all effectual aid," prevented by a vengeful
God from receiving succour from his friends. He too had known
the anguish of those who, trying to save him, found all of their
efforts frustrated by a nature, within and without, that would permit no hope. He too had known how long is a life struggle, yet
how brief all seems as the moment of dissolution arrives. Indeed,
this was the living death, the burial above ground, of which he
had written in 1763. Now, however, he contemplated it not with a
hysteria born of recent discovery but with the dull melancholy of
exhaustion.

In April, 1800, Cowper was seized with dropsy. Now a total
invalid, he fell further into a state of despair. Weary with suffering, weary with life itself, he lapsed into unconsciousness on the
morning of April 25 and died that afternoon. His last words,
spoken the evening before when Miss Perowne had asked him if
he wanted something to drink, were oddly significant; for he replied wearily, "What does it signify?" But, as he died, his wasted
features relaxed into an expression which John Johnson tells us
was one of "calmness and composure, mingled, as it were with
holy surprise."

Cowper was buried at East Dereham beside Mary Unwin. A
monument erected in the transept of the church bears an epitaph
in blank verse by Hayley.

Cowper died while his fame was at a pinnacle. Resting on his religious zeal and his celebration of retirement in *The Task,* his reputation had made even the small details of his domestic life the object of popular curiosity.[85] His opinions were widely quoted, and his poetic achievements widely discussed. But although Cowper's works would continue to enjoy a wide audience in the nineteenth century, among discriminating readers his reputation soon faded. Hayley could capitalize on Cowper's popularity by publishing a *Life* in 1802, yet that event and the poet's death two years earlier have been eclipsed by two greater events: the second and third editions of *Lyrical Ballads.*

CHAPTER 3

The Task

UNTIL recently it has been fashionable to use the term "Pre-Romantic" to describe *The Task*, Cowper's longest and perhaps most famous poem. The term is an admirable one in some ways, for it calls our attention to what is revolutionary in Cowper's work: his experimentation with forms other than the heroic couplet; his use of personal subject matter; his frequent lack of irony and detachment; and his preference of concrete, local description to panoramic landscapes in the manner of "Windsor Forest" and *The Seasons*. It also points out the direction which the revolt against "urban" values, the more sincere interest in the common man, and the search for a new idiom would take.

But "Pre-Romantic" is clearly pejorative in its implications. It suggests that such poems as *The Task* are only a landmark in the journey to *Tintern Abbey*, and that any true estimate of their value must be made from the perspective of what followed. Aside from belittling Cowper's merit as an artist, the classification obscures such undeniably Neo-Classical tendencies as his emphasis on the moral, typical, and general. Like any accomplished man of the century, Cowper could turn an epigram; for he thought in terms of universals and responded emotionally to them. He was a lover of nature in the Neo-Classical sense, as well as of a poplar field, his garden, or the River Ouse. He respected the genres, thought that poetry should teach lessons, and felt that only a diction and syntax more refined and melodious than that spoken in ordinary conversation could properly communicate the ideas worthy of poetry.

As I have pointed out in previous chapters, the letters show both Romantic and Classical inclinations. There is no wonder then that more "public" performances like *The Task* should reveal the same doubleness, for they demanded greater reserve in discussing personal matters and feelings than the letters, whose privacy and intimacy Cowper carefully guarded. In *The Task,* as in the letters, description of Olney helps to define both Romantic and Neo-Classical tendencies in Cowper's work. Olney is not merely the microcosm or a convenient slice of eighteenth-century life to be examined for its foibles and follies; it is a necessary part of the life of retirement which Cowper eventually decided his masterpiece should justify. To stay within the conventions of eighteenth-century landscape poetry, he would have had to make Olney a metaphor or embodiment of certain generally accepted moral and philosophical principles; but his attitude was too subjective for this. Personal experience, not observation of external nature, gives life to his poem; and, when Cowper looks out at the world around him, it is often to project that which lies within him.

I *The Structure*

The Task came into existence because Lady Austen, in answer to Cowper's complaint that he had no fit subject for a blank-verse poem, told him to write about a sofa. The jest and the subject matter demanded as a reply a poem in the mock-heroic tradition, and Cowper began with a burlesque of *The Aeneid:* "I sing the sofa. I, who lately sang/Truth, Hope, and Charity and touch'd with awe/The solem chords . . .". In choosing mock heroic as his vehicle, Cowper assumed a double perspective on reality, mocking both past and present, but at the same time seeing the shortcomings of one as the strengths of the other. His elevation of a mean object seems unnatural, and the fact that he began with a parody of Virgil implies that an age which can praise only furniture has fallen from the greatness of Augustan Rome.

But Cowper's design is more complex than this attitude implies. If the history of man is to be organized according to the genesis of the devices on which he has sat, the past, which can boast only three-legged stools and crude chairs, must defer to the present. And, although the very fact that Cowper can conceive of history in this way comments on the luxury and triviality of the present, the past, which could not afford the luxury of being trivial, must also admit its limitations. Civilization does not always progress downhill.

Cowper soon realized that mock heroic did not suit his deepest feelings. Unnatural elevation of syntax and diction has to be accompanied by a real concern for the heroic potential in man and his falling away from it; instead, Cowper was more interested in the way improvements in furniture reflected the rise from barbarism to modest refinement and then to luxury. That he made aldermen and priests, two of his favorite subjects of attack, contribute to the growth of instruments of leisure suggests his basically religious motivation. He was more interested in the excesses to which luxury had carried man than in the falling away from a primitive ideal of heroism. Significantly, he would later attack heroes, "whose infirm and baby minds/Are gratified with mischief; and who spoil/Because men suffer it, their toy the world," and affirm the values of civilized, social life.

The sofa, then, becomes a symbol both of civilization and luxury; and the repose it yields invites comparison to various forms of personal and social corruption. Nurse, coachman, curate —all put comfort or security above duty; and, at least in the case of the nurse and curate, such irresponsibility involves others: the patient and the tedious rector (I, 89–96). But however the sofa may remind us of the moral laxity fostered by repose, it also testifies that self-indulgence breeds corruption in the flesh:

> Oh may I live exempted (while I live
> Guiltless of pamper'd appetite obscene)
> From pangs arthritic, that infect the toe
> Of libertine excess.   (I, 103–06)

Obviously mock heroic can no longer govern the progress of thought, and a new structure must take its place.

The structure which replaced mock heroic has a strong personal or subjective bias.[1] In contrast to mock heroic, in which the poet does not intrude, but allows tradition to dictate order, *The Task*, as it evolves, is informed by the "I" who offers his experience of life as an alternative to the images of corruption which cluster around the central figure of the sofa. Hence the long-held truism that *The Task* cannot be enjoyed unless we have a good understanding of Cowper's life has its foundation in the very techniques which the poet chooses. If we are to find a unifying principle in the work, we must explore the mind that produced it. The order is not that of an epic or pastoral or essay, but is organic to the poet's imagination. Psychic tensions, preoccupations, and aspirations become the organizing principle.

Cowper's own writings reveal an ambivalent attitude toward the problem of order. At times, he seems wholly subjective. When, in a letter to William Unwin, he calls the irregularity of *The Task* "not altogether indefensible," we suspect that his atttude like the ones toward religion (a matter of individual conscience and inspiration) and nature (defined in terms of personal experience), rises from the conviction that a more rigid order would have corrupted his vision.[2] In the discursiveness of the poem, we become aware of the poet experiencing ideas and seeing nature directly. Cowper's insistence that he didn't imitate anybody is another indication of the value he placed on being perfectly faithful to the idiosyncrasies of his experience. In a letter to John Newton he continues his defense by showing that the title has a personal, symbolic function:

It is not possible that a book including such a variety of subjects, and in which no particular one is predominant, should find a title adapted to them all. In such a case it seemed almost necessary to accommodate the name to the incident that gave birth to the poem; nor does it appear to me that because I performed more than my task, therefore *The Task* it not a suitable title. A house would still be a house, though the builder of it should make it ten times as big as he first intended. I might indeed, following the example of the Sunday newsmonger, call it the *Olio*. But I should do myself wrong; for though it have much variety, it has, I trust no confusion.[3]

The Task continues to be a suitable title because the poem has not ceased to serve the function for which he originally conceived it.

II *Metaphorical Possibilities*

We are encouraged to explore the metaphorical possibilities of the title by Cowper's further admonition in a letter to Newton to think carefully about the significance of the second book, "The Time-Piece."[4] The garden, which provides the title of the third book, and winter, which occurs in the titles of the last three books, are also metaphors. But to return to "task," it—as well as providing like the sofa a "starting-post" from which Cowper addressed himself "to the long race that I soon conceived a design to run"— became a metaphor of the struggle for salvation, and of Cowper's own battle to impose some rational pattern upon the chaos of impressions from which he drew his poem. The domestic connotation of the title further characterizes the quality of the life being held up as an alternative to "the modern enthusiasm after London life." The poet refers again and again to the tasks which fill his days and turn "rural ease and leisure" into a regimen well suited to "the cause of piety and virtue." Still more personal connotations lie in the idea of God as taskmaster, and in Cowper's relationship with such people as Lady Austen, Mrs. Unwin, and Newton.

On the basis of extensive study of the poet's metaphors, Morris Golden finds that the structure of *The Task* is an affirmation of the poet's stability, and that the act of creation, as an assertion of self, has profound bearing on Cowper's own character.[5] Hence structure can have both subjective and objective dimensions. To the extent that biography must be used to explicate the task metaphor, for example, it is subjective. Interest in it becomes the enjoyment of autobiographical revelation, the idiosyncrasies of a charming eccentric. Unfortunately, criticism has too often been limited to this attitude.

At another level, subjectivity opens out into more general statement. Cowper's relationships with various taskmasters is of interest only to those who want to know about Cowper the man; but Cowper, as a man who is morally bound to tasks as a way of revealing his talent, in the biblical as well as personal sense, is of more general importance. The task, as an affirmation of certain values—domestic, rural, evangelical—is not bound by personal references, and thus is objective, a concrete form of universal truths. Similarly, the garden, as a psychotherapeutic device, is wholly of subjective value. But, when the poet sees in his own experience of it a cure of the ills of the larger world, when it becomes a symbol of man imposing order upon nature as an alternative to the dissipated life of the city, it has been objectified. In a slightly different way the tensions between shyness and assertiveness, isolation and communication, submission to others and self-control rise, by virtue of the fact that they are shared by all men, from the purely biographical to a more general level, which ultimately depicts the struggle between self and antiself.

The very structure which Golden points out in his chapter on *The Task* has several levels of objectivity (or subjectivity). Nothing could be more objective than Cowper's analysis of the perilous balance between barbarism and softness ("The Sofa"), the causes of social imbalance ("The Time-Piece"), the personal solution to tensions ("The Garden"), and this solution in conflict with the world (Books IV, V, VI). The subjectivity of the balance in "The Garden" is itself generalized by the biblical nature of the image. But what could be more subjective than the peculiar frame of reference which lies behind the structure? What could be more subjective than the peculiar conditions of the poet's own struggle for stability, or the perilous balance not between barbarism and excessive culture but between his own hopes and fears? If the garden is a stable point between animality and excessive refinement, it is also the one firm place from which he can ward off despair.

This unique mixture of subjective and objective, of personal revelation and cultural and social commentary, informs almost all of Cowper's work. The stricken deer image, which in *The Task* poignantly reveals the poet's own personal condition, appears in much the same form in *Table Talk* as a description of England. Both are at bay, both "undaunted still, though wearied and perplexed." Both have once been saved—England, by Chatham; Cowper, by religious experience. Even literary theory evolves from his private concerns, such as the tension between freedom and restraint. In "Table Talk" (ll. 384–93), this concern operates in the discussion of "th' inestimable estimate of [Dr. John] Brown," which holds that the fame of an author is to a great degree based on popular whim, yet it is characteristic of writers to think that popularity rises from genius. If the audience allows a writer who understands its passions a measure of freedom, it also exerts restraints upon him and ultimately becomes his master. Conversely, he who thinks that by flattering the public he gains a hold over it soon discovers the limits of his power.

It is typical of Cowper that he should see virtue, whether literary, moral, or otherwise, as the ultimate liberating force. But, of course, virtue must always operate within the framework of human limitations. In his analysis of literary history he again sees the human spirit struggling for both freedom and control. If, for example, the Restoration was characterized by libertinism, it was because feelings long repressed by tyranny eventually had to break their confines. In literary criticism he insists on the poet's freedom to create as his imagination dictates, but he also demands that the vehicle of expression impose restraint. Words themselves restrain as well as liberate.

It is obvious, however, that these pronouncements have more than psychological content. Apart from the poet's own feelings, we can detect the force of tradition and the Neo-Classical impulse toward subject matter of general rather than of personal significance. The idea that words must fit subject matter may be relevant to the poet's conflicting passions for freedom and control, but it also was a generally accepted critical notion founded upon the insistence of Descartes and his successors, especially Locke, on purity of diction, on making words conform to ideas. The whole preoccupation with freedom and control, whatever its personal meanings to Cowper, was at the center of Neo-Classical thought.

A cross section of *The Task* reveals Cowper's personal qualities, personal revelation raised to a comment on man in general, and objective analysis in the Neo-Classical tradition. In the letter to William Unwin to which I have already referred, Cowper suggests that he has created several strata of meaning. He admits, for example, that in some passages "You will observe me very satirical. Writing on such subjects I could not be otherwise." He adds that he could write "nothing without aiming at least at usefulness: it were beneath my years to do it, and still more dishonourable to my religion." It is possible to dismiss these statements lightly as a concession, whether before or after the fact is not clear, to the missionary zeal of Mrs. Unwin and Newton; but they do indicate a level of social concern which lies apart from the purely subjective. Later, in referring to the religious "cast" or "tincture" of many passages, Cowper speaks in more personal terms. He has deliberately put these passages at the end (he probably meant those in which he perceives God behind the "veil of creation" and, as a consequence of the insight vouchsafed to him, sees the world as a manifestation of the divine spirit) as a concession to his readers, most of whom do not, he suspects, share his religious enthusiasm but who might, nevertheless, profit from it.

Audience and conscience present, then, conflicting demands; and satire and "the religious cast" are two of the ways to acknowledge them. That religiosity should have a subjective cast is not at all surprising in the light of what follows in the next paragraph of the letter to Unwin. After having announced that his "descriptions are from nature: not one of them second handed," Cowper asserts that his delineations of the heart "are from my own experience; not one of them borrowed from books, or in the least conjectural."

In emphasizing the personalized quality of his vision, he departs from the usual idea of nature. Nature he defines as "first-handed" experience; it does not include knowledge derived from books. If he does not exactly disagree with the Neo-Classical doctrine that the poet should describe the species and not the individual, the aspects of experience which men have in common instead of the peculiarities of the individual, he violates the corollary belief that the poet should sublimate the eccentricities of his own vision to the general truths of the cultural heritage within which he works.

Other aspects of Cowper's method reveal a tendency for the subjective to merge with the objective as personal values are reinforced by traditional practices. The poet's retirement to Olney and his insistence on viewing humanity from afar have often and justly been related to his mental condition. But retirement is also part of the traditional satiric pose, at least from Horace (the Sabine farm) to Pope (the house at Twickenham). From this point of vantage the satirist traditionally can express his removal from, and immersion in, the human condition.

The well-known "stricken deer" passage is also a good example of tradition merging with personal response:

> I was a stricken deer, that left the herd
> Long since; with many an arrow deep infixt
> My panting side was charg'd, when I withdrew
> To seek a tranquil death in distant shades.
> There was I found by one who had himself
> Been hurt by th' archers. In his side he bore,
> And in his hands and feet, the cruel scars,
> With gentle force soliciting the darts,
> He drew them forth, and heal'd, and bade me live.
> Since then, with few associates, in remote
> And silent woods I wander, far from those
> My former partners of the peopled scene;
> With few associates, and not wishing more.
> Here much I ruminate, as much I may,
> With other views of men and manners now
> Than once, and others of a life to come.
> I see that all are wand'rers, gone astray
> Each in his own delusions; they are lost
> In chase of fancied happiness, still woo'd
> And never won.   (III, 108–27)

Here is the man of conscience, so deeply wounded by human ills that he has had to leave society; yet impelled by his own integrity to point out that his fellow men are lost in delusions which only he, by virtue of his superior position, can penetrate. This conventional pose opens out into biography and other subjective realities. Immediately the poet's own mental breakdown and redemption, both mental and spiritual, come to mind. Both his paranoia and his evangelicalism are reflected in the image of a tender, loving, wounded Jesus and in the compassionate tone of the satire.

Moreover, the hunted deer image, with its biblical associations, implies a wholly different range of attitudes toward society from that of the Augustan satirist. Looking forward to the Romantics, perhaps even Shelley, it emphasizes the suffering which becomes a precondition to wisdom. Truth leads to martyrdom, actually or metaphorically; and the only means of reform is a kind of apocalyptic destruction and resurrection in Christ. When society becomes a persecuter, when the satirist, a gentle Christlike figure himself, needs to be preyed upon in order to be saved, we no longer are in the realm of Neo-Classical satire. And certainly no Augustan would have allowed feeling to confuse his central image by making society both the herd and the hunter.

The mixture of subjective and objective takes many forms. At the end of "The Winter Evening," for example, after talking about desertion of the country by the rich, neglect by magistrates, the militia and recruiting methods, corporate bodies, and the natural love of man for rural objects, Cowper retreats from general statement about social problems to personal feeling. From an attack on ambition, he turns abruptly to the consolation he has discovered in rural life:

> Hail, therefore, patroness of health, and ease,
> And contemplation, heart-consoling joys
> And harmless pleasures, in the throng'd abode
> Of multitudes unknown! hail, rural life!
> Address himself who will to the pursuit
> Of honours, or emolument, or fame;
> I shall not add myself to such a chase,
> Thwart his attempts, or envy his success.
> Some must be great. Great offices will have
> Great talents. And God gives to ev'ry man
> The virtue, temper, understanding, taste,

That lifts him into life; and lets him fall
Just in the niche he was ordained to fill.
To the deliv'rer of an injur'd land
He gives a tongue t'enlarge upon, an heart
To feel, and courage to redress her wrongs;
To monarchs dignity; to judges sense;
To artists ingenuity and skill;
To me an unambitious mind, content
In the low vale of life, that early felt
A wish for ease and leisure, and ere long
Found here that leisure and that ease I wish'd.
                                        (780–801)

Superficially, this conventional praise of rural life balances the
satire of the town. But the shift in tone and argument, from vitu-
peration of man's institutionalized greed to an affirmation that society reflects the divine order of things, is as strikingly unusual as
the conjunction in this passage of the generalization "everything
has its place" with the personalized rejection of ambition. To have
kept his poem consistently on one level would have required making country life or domesticity an antidote to greed and ambition.
Or, looked at another way, if "everything has its place" is to be
accepted as the final view of the book, and if the final lines are
merely an affirmation of any man's right to the way of life to
which his urges have consigned him, then ambition and greed are
also justified. What happens in the final lines is that personal feeling takes the place of moral concern. Exhausted by his attack on
social evils, Cowper figuratively and literally retires to the more
congenial atmosphere of Olney, where he can sublimate larger
moral issues in his keen response to nature.

The end of Book V also contains this fusion of personal response and general moral statement. Having proceeded through a
definition of liberty to a condemnation of Deism and an assertion
of the doctrine of grace, Cowper closes with what begins as a
general statement about the nature of true freedom and happiness, but quickly turns into a record of his own personal religious
experience, and finally into an address to the Creator by the poet
himself:

Thee we reject, unable to abide
Thy purity, till pure as thou art pure,

Made such by thee, we love thee for that cause
For which we shunn'd and hated thee before.
Then we are free. Then liberty, like day,
Breaks on the soul, and by a flash from heav'n
Fires all the faculties with glorious joy.
A voice is heard that mortal ears hear not
Till thou hast touch'd them; 'tis the voice of song—
A loud hosanna sent from all thy works;
Which he that hears it with a shout repeats,
And adds his rapture to the gen'ral praise,
In that blest Moment Nature, throwing wide
Her veil opaque, discloses with a smile
The author of her beauties, who, retir'd
Behind his own creation works unseen
By the impure, and hears his power denied.

Books III through VI are more firmly based on personal experience than are the first two books. While they recall an older mode of viewing the universe through the self as microcosm, they also stress the individualism of the poet. True, the garden obviously symbolizes the order of nature, and seems to reflect the Neo-Classical notion that art should reveal the order inherent in creation. But it is also a way of life peculiar to Cowper. Significantly, the poet turns from contemplation of natural order and domestic happiness in general to details of his own life (his hare, for example) which set him apart from man in general instead of identifying him with the human condition as a whole. His reaction to landscape is strikingly unconventional; his preference for the ordinary, plain, cultivated prospect to the spectacular, sublime one is a good example. Moreover, he insists on describing details with which only he could be familiar, an isolated cottage, a water wheel, a particular trip through the countryside.

Cowper's individualism has in it certain metaphorical qualities which tend to move it to the level of moral generalization. The poet seems genuinely convinced that his experience is a subject fit for poetry just because it is his. At the same time, this conviction merges with and becomes a metaphor of his soundly British feeling that personal liberty is the best condition in which man can work out his temporal and eternal destinies. If he praises the ordinary, he does so both to assert the integrity of his personal vision and to carry out a moral task of revealing God in places where He is not usually found. When he evokes moods, he intends not only to point out his own feelings but also to show that these moods may be a solace to others and a stimulus to moral improvement.

That the fusion of subjective and objective in *The Task* often has artistic merit seems obvious if one considers the way it enriches certain images and the role of the poet himself in most of the passages I have mentioned. But it seems only fair to add that the fusion probably happened more often by accident than by design, and there are many dull passages in which design fails or is utterly lacking. In substituting a discursive organization for the mock heroic, Cowper had a broad notion of the function of each book of *The Task*, and he seems within each book to follow deliberately the loose pattern of conversation (probably for its familiar tone). Because of this structure, attempts to find what makes the poem valid artistically, a task which begins with the search for a structural principle, usually return in some way to biography; for the structure of his life seems in some way to make up for structural failings in the poem.

But, if Cowper has no firm, overall notion of his relationship to tradition, or that of his poem, neither has he given himself enough prominence to raise autobiography to a level at which it can satisfy all the demands of a structure. The poem never achieves the degree of unity that Wordsworth's *The Prelude* does. It is significant that, whenever the poet returns to a traditional form, such as satire or mock heroic, he so loads it with his own feelings and personality that it loses its original shape and becomes something else. Enjoyment of the "stricken deer" passage, for example, does not rise from awareness of what Cowper does with tradition but from the vitality of the poet's reactions.

The discussion of the personal and general in *The Task* leads naturally to an attempt to place Cowper somewhere in the spectrum of attitudes which is limited at one end by Neo-Classicism and at the other by Romanticism. The Horatian model, with its heritage of genial manner, loose and conversational style, and wide-ranging subject matter naturally moves the work in the direction of Augustan art, and not only because Pope so carefully imitated Horace. The sanity and detachment of the Roman poet provided for the eighteenth century both an ideal to be imitated and a symbol of man at his best. However, Cowper's readers quickly realize that his own "warmer" personality transforms Horatianism into something different from the original and its most famous imitations. That *The Task* can turn so easily from genial observation of society to religious enthusiasm, and from assertion of social norms to evocations of a personalized religion, indicates that Cowper stands somewhere between the earlier ideal of the spectator and the later one of the bearer of personal vision.

Earlier in the century Pope naturally fell into the habit of cultivating a Horatianism that applied to self as well as to art. Twickenham became a personal refuge from the turmoil of London as well as a symbol of a better life based on Classical principles. Olney also is a personal refuge, and the garden symbolizes a way to a better life; but there the resemblance ends. Much deeper psychological needs dictated Cowper's removal to Olney, and much of his poem is a justification of a way of life he has no choice but to accept. Out of Cowpers' personal distress comes the cause and a great deal of the matter of his poem, and personal needs constitute its framework. The self continually strives with tradition as shaper of the poem so that the result is neither moral essay, epistle, or satire nor another *Prelude*. Olney, then, serves as a resting place on the journey from Twickenham to Grasmere.

III The Task *and Tradition*

As a landscape poem *The Task* follows a long tradition characterized by such works as John Denham's "Cooper's Hill," Milton's "L'Allegro" and "Il Penseroso," John Dyer's "Grongar Hill," and James Thomson's "Seasons." Of these, the closest in time and influence is "The Seasons" (1726–30). To distinguish most clearly the method and achievement of Cowper, I have arbitrarily chosen the following section from the part of Thomson's poem called "Winter" for comparison:

> The mountain thunders, and its sturdy sons
> Stoop to the bottom of the rocks they shade.
> Lone on the midnight steep and all aghast,
> The dark wayfaring stranger breathless toils,
> And, often falling, climbs against the blast.
> Low waves the rooted forest, vexed, and sheds
> What of its tarnished honors yet remain—
> Dashed down and scattered by the tearing wind's
> Assiduous fury, its gigantic limbs.
> Thus struggling through the dissipated grove,

> The whirling tempest raves along the plain;
> And, on the cottage thatched or lordly roof
> Keen-fastening, shakes them to the solid base.
> Sleep frighted flies; and round the rocking dome,
> For entrance eager, howls the savage blast.
> Then too, they say, through all the burdened air
> Long groans are heard, shrill sounds, and distant sighs
> That, uttered by the demon of the night,
> Warn the devoted wretch of woe and death.
>   Huge uproar lords it wide. The clouds, commixed
> With stars swift-gliding, sweep along the sky.
> All Nature reels. Till Nature's King, who oft
> Amid tempestuous darkness dwells alone,
> And on the wings of the careering wind
> Walks dreadfully serene, commands a calm;
> Then straight air, sea, and earth are hushed at once.
> As yet 'tis midnight deep. The weary clouds,
> Slow-meeting, mingle into solid gloom.
> Now, while the drowsy world lies lost in sleep,
> Let me associate with the serious Night,
> And Contemplation, her sedate compeer;
> Let me shake off th' intrusive cares of day
> And lay the meddling senses all aside. . . .
>   ("Winter," 176–222)

Aside from diction and syntax, subjects to be discussed later, several stylistic traits are noticeable. Thomson's landscapes are most reminiscent of painting, and many of his scenes mix details derived from personal observation with those found in the work of landscape painters. True, various parts of the scene are in motion; but, significantly, no motion is described which cannot be implied through the techniques of the painter. The same impulse that led Thomson to combine direct and indirect experience of nature turns each of his scenes into more than a series of visual images. Sounds are described ("thunder," "howls," "groans," "hushed") and suggested through the usual poetic devices of assonance, consonance, and alliteration. Because the poet does not wish to describe individual parts of the scene with great exactness, he often must state the feelings he wishes to communicate instead of allowing concrete detail to suggest them; such words as "aghast" take the place of more detailed description. Feelings are also aroused by the frequent use of personification. The tempest "raves," sleep "frighted flies," the north is "piercing," the sky "saddens," the blast is eager to gain entrance to the cottage. The whole scene suggests "huge uproar" which "lords it wide."

These active verbs suggest the intensity of the storm, and help to arouse the terror which contemporary psychological theory made the basis of the sublime, but they also imply a range of ideas behind the actualities of the scene itself. Raving and eager winds, piercing north, and "huge uproar"—all images of cruelty, madness, and chaos—create the impression that the only way to find order in nature is to see it not as primary cause but as only a part of the divine plan. Hence it is perfectly natural for Thomson to introduce the well-known scene from the New Testament of Christ calming a storm, for it reveals the order which lies behind the apparent chaos, the "huge uproar." Yet the God who can at any time suspend the laws of nature does not do so; instead, He stands aside, once having set nature in motion, and leaves it to man to adjust himself to, and contemplate the meaning of, the environment He has created. We see the poet doing this in the second verse paragraph, a passage reminiscent of Milton's "Il Penseroso."

Just as the grandiose, sublime, and consciously literary, panorama is typical of *The Seasons*, so emphasis on detail, on local domestic scenes which the narrator knows intimately, is characteristic of *The Task*:

> The verdure of the plain lies buried deep
> Beneath the dazzling deluge; and the bent,
> And coarser grass, upspearing o'er the rest,
> Of late unsightly and unseen, now shine
> Conspicuous, and, in bright apparel clad
> And fledg'd with icy feathers, nod superb.
> The cattle mourn in corners where the fence
> Screens them, and seem half petrified to sleep
> In recumbent sadness. There they wait
> Their wonted fodder; not like hung'ring man,
> Fretful if unsupply'd; but silent, meek,
> And patient of the slow-pac'd swain's delay.
> He from the stack carves out th' accustom'd load,
> Deep-plunging, and again deep-plunging oft,
> His broad keen knife into the solid mass:
> Smooth as a wall the upright remnant stands,

With such undeviating and even force
He severs it away . . .

. . . .
Now from the roost, or from the neighb'ring pale,
Where, diligent to catch the first faint gleam
Of smiling day, they gossip'd side by side,
Come trooping at the housewife's well-known call
The feather'd tribes domestic. Half on wing,
And half on foot, they brush the fleecy flood,
Conscious and fearful of too deep a plunge.
The sparrows peep, and quit the shelt'ring eaves
To seize the fair occasion. Well they eye
The scatter'd grain; and, thievishly resolv'd
T'escape th' impending famine, often scar'd,
As oft return—a pert voracious kind.
Clean riddance quickly made, one only care
Remains to each—the search of a sunny nook,
Or shed impervious to the blast. Resign'd
To sad necessity, the cock foregoes
His wonted strut; and, wading at their head
With well-consider'd steps, seems to resent
His alter'd gait and stateliness retrench'd.
(V, 21–76)

The order of this description is chronological, not spatial. Unlike Thomson, Cowper does not present a panoramic view so that the reader can stand aside and behold the overall effect, but a series of clearly and intimately described details which fit together as if the poet were moving from object to object, focusing only on one thing at a time and excluding all others. He confines the subject matter to that which lies within the capacity of the ordinary inhabitant of the country to observe, and the feelings aroused are not generalized for the purpose of composing an overall impression.

Thomson's descriptive details all promote the general feeling of awe, in itself tantamount to religious experience; and this feeling in turn prepares the reader for the ultimate revelation of the divine pattern. If there is any general impression to be gained from Cowper's description, it centers on the tentatively advanced and never overtly stated conviction that the way of life enjoyed by the poet, which enables him to view the scene in his peculiar manner and from his own perspective, is saner than any other because of the peace and solace it offers. His spiritual repose, combined with intellectual acuity, enables him to see potentialities in the minute which others in their preoccupation with more "important" concerns have overlooked.

What he sees has moral, social, and personal implications; but his concern for the inherent beauty of the thing makes it important in itself, apart from other considerations to which it might be related. The description of the grass, for example, suggests how the "unsightly and unseen," the ugly and obscure, can suddenly be transformed so that, by virtue of their newly found beauty and prominence, they lord it over the landscape ("nod superb"). A whole range of ideas centering on the intrinsic worth of the obscure emerges, but it never allows the reader to forget the beauty of the particular blades of grass which have aroused the poet's sensibilities. Despite the "dazzling deluge," the reader can still see the "icy feathers."

There is also a hint of mock heroic in the haughty ("*superbia*") nod of the grass in its sudden and quickly passing moment of glory, a hint which is strengthened as the word "feather" joins the scene to that of the hens (V, 58–76). Indeed, one of the strongest assertions of the poet's sanity lies in his ability to maintain a balance between intensity of feeling and comic reserve, between the beauty of the scene and its absurdity, between pleasure and pain. It is not long before contemplation of the snowy landscape, of the patience of animal life, of human industry (swain), and sheer animal joy give way to suggestions of the inconvenience which the snow, like any deluge, whether dazzling or not, must impose. This line of thought culminates in the comic portrait of gossiping hens and their rather indecorous haste. If their attempts to avoid the indignity of "too deep a plunge" are amusing, much more so is the self-importance of the cock, who must forego his "wonted strut" to wade at their head. To this comic portrait are added the pranks of the sparrows, whose thievishness can amuse because it is devoid of malice.

In an earlier passage Cowper attains greater eloquence through a somewhat conventional apostrophe to winter, only to balance the effect with praise of the "intimate delights" of the fireside. The terrors of winter suggest also its joys, as the impressive, tyrannical, Jovelike figure of Winter appears riding a sleigh, and the poet announces that he loves the season, unlovely as it seems. Instead

of the exhilaration of facing the sublime, we find the enjoyment of
a world secure and comfortable (because of its smallness and intimacy) existing against a backdrop of terrors which are implied
but consciously excluded:

> Oh Winter, ruler of th' inverted year,
> Thy scatter'd hair with sleet like ashes fill'd,
> Thy breath congeal'd upon thy lips, thy cheeks
> Fring'd with a beard made white with other snows
> Than those of age, thy forehead wrapt in clouds,
> A leafless branch thy sceptre, and thy throne
> A sliding car, indebted to no wheels,
> But urg'd by storms along its slipp'ry way,
> I love thee, all unlovely as thou seem'st,
> And dreaded as thou art! Thou hold'st the sun
> A pris'ner in the yet undawning east,
> Short'ning his journey between morn and noon,
> And hurrying him, impatient of his stay,
> Down to the rosy west; but kindly still
> Compensating his loss with added hours
> Of social converse and instructive ease,
> And gath'ring, at short notice, in one group
> The family dispers'd and fixing thought,
> Not less dispers'd by day-light and its cares.
> I crown thee king of intimate delights,
> Fire-side enjoyments, home-born happiness,
> And all the comforts that the lowly roof
> Of undisturb'd retirement, and the hours
> Of long uninterrupted ev'ning, know.
>   (IV, 120–43)

The play on words in "love thee; all unlovely as thou seem'st,"
like that in "unsightly and unseen," reveals a complexity of meaning which draws upon the Platonic tradition that love is the response to beauty. Cowper, again moving away from Thomson,
implies that standards of beauty are subjective. If the generality
of man cannot love winter, seeing in it only "unloveliness," then
Cowper, by insisting that he can love, asserts the independence of
his own way of looking at things. The sublime, Burke (and
others) taught, was opposed to the beautiful; and Thomson's descriptions of the terrors of winter are based upon this commonly
held notion. Cowper's love of the season, then, indicates a rejec-

tion of the sublime, which takes form in his emphasis on domestic pleasures and observation of the minute. More violent emotions and subject matter are pushed into the background. Cowper does not deny that this side of experience has reality, but he does insist that his own view accords more fully with his ideals of stability and order.

To return to *The Seasons*, Thomson, after dwelling on the enormous variety both of nature and of the feelings excited by the contemplation of winter, concludes with a Deistic injunction to man to appreciate the orderly pattern which rationalizes both suffering and happiness:

'Tis done! Dread Winter spreads his latent glooms
And reigns tremendous o'er the conquered year.
How dead the vegetable kingdom lies!
How dumb the tuneful! Horror wide extends
His desolate domain. Behold, fond man!
See here thy pictured life; pass some few years,
Thy flowering Spring, thy Summer's ardent strength,
Thy sober Autumn fading into age,
And pale concluding Winter comes at last
And shuts the scene. Ah! wither now are fled
Those dreams of greatness? those unsolid hopes
Of happiness? those longings after fame?
Those restless cares? those busy bustling days?
Those gay-spent festive nights? those veering thoughts,
Lost between good and ill, that share thy life?
All now are vanished! Virtue sole survives,
Immortal, never-failing friend of man,
His guide to happiness on high. And see!
'Tis come, the glorious morn! the second birth
Of heaven and earth! awakening Nature hears
The new-creating Word, and starts to life
In every heightened form, from pain and death
Forever free. The great eternal scheme,
Involving all and in a perfect whole
Uniting, as the prospect wider spreads,
To reason's eye refined clears up apace.
Ye vainly wise! ye blind presumptuous! now,
Confounded in the dust, adore that Power
And Wisdom oft arraigned: see now the cause
Why unassuming worth in secret lived
And died neglected; why the good man's share

> In life was gall and bitterness of soul;
> Why the lone widow and her orphans pined
> In starving solitude, while Luxury
> In palaces lay straining her low thought
> To form unreal wants; . . .
>
> ("Winter," 1024–89)

If the peasant must suffer, reason tells us that suffering well endured has a moral value and that it provides valuable instruction for the nonsufferer. The misery of the peasant, to an extent the product of luxury, enjoins others to moderate their wants, to exercise compassion, and to know the vanity of the flesh. If this peaceful conclusion after the wild exhibitions of the violence of nature and amidst the joys of returning spring seems anticlimactic and even incongruous, it is because the vision of order is not the central experience of the poem. More important are the emotions themselves which nature arouses, especially the feelings of pity and terror which mid-century critics like Warton considered the wellsprings of true poetry. At its best, the sublime has almost a religious quality; and we cannot help feeling that enjoyment of it provided a substitute for those elements of religious experience that Deism excluded.

To an evangelical like Cowper, however, Deist beliefs approached blasphemy; for they put too much of the divine pattern within the grasp of reason. By reducing the importance of faith, they narrowed the awesome gulf between God and man which orthodox Christianity has always envisioned. True religious experience, we feel sure Cowper would say, rises not from a pretentious desire to behold God's plan but for man's recognition that he can never begin to account for the injustices he beholds. This attitude goes to the heart of the experience of *The Task*.

Unlike Thomson, who seems to consider emotional response to nature tantamount to religious experience so that it becomes a way of beholding divinity, Cowper, because of his evangelicalism, carefully separates response to nature from religious feeling. Moreover, Cowper exhibits less of the smugness and complacency in the face of human misery which too often ran along with the Deistic conviction that the rightness of the ways of God can be apprehended by man. Although religious belief and social class caused him to end his long passage about the wagoner lost in the snow with what to some appears a rather unsuitable lecture on the evils of sloth, he seems to share the humanitarian impulses of such critics as Samuel Johnson. The conditions under which he lived in Olney probably account for his sensibility.

To apprehend God, Cowper implies, the emotions must be sublimated in a Christian pattern of thought. *The Task* attacks the person who ruminates like an animal upon the landscape, or, resting "content/With what he views" and not reading "his wonders, in whose thought the world,/Fair as it is, existed ere it was." The soul that has the grace necessary to see God, that has either received new faculties of observation or learned to use more properly his old powers, soon detaches itself from emotional response and turns to religious truths. Praising nature becomes the threshold to praising God. What emotion is involved in the latter experience is refined of its earthly manifestations and turns about the contemplation of divinity. Once the feelings are aroused, they cast a ray of light upon "all forms/Terrestrial in the vast and minute." And they allow man to see everywhere "the unambiguous footsteps of . . . God." It is significant that the ray "gilds" all forms, for it is only the mind of the "elect" that can project its notion of divinity upon the lower world. If a man can perceive the glory of God behind all creation, then each created thing becomes endowed with that glory; and man responds with equal fervor to "an insect's wing" and "the rolling worlds." Reason shares in this attitude. The idea of divine wisdom, for example, gives a new "lustre" to creation by causing man to see in all of its parts signs of divine genius.

There is, then, nothing like the Hartleian scale of mechanistic advancement from raw emotional stimulation to theopathy. Without divine grace, man cannot proceed beyond emotional response. With grace, response to landscape becomes only a way of activating an otherwise sluggish nature to contemplate ideas which lie dormant and which are essentially separated from response to nature.

Science was in part responsible for this emphasis on grace. Besides dwelling on man's animal nature, it had shown the universe to be much larger than people had previously thought. Instead of comforting Cowper with the vision of an orderly universe, it filled him with a sense of the loneliness of a world in which man is so insignificant. This response is usually expressed in highly particularized imagery which gives form not to the idea of the universe as a divine mechanism, but to a highly personal longing for communion with God. For example, gazing at the stars (in V, 822–49) leads to a moralistic concern with the need for a loftier perspective from which to view man's condition. The brightness of the stars reminds the poet that Heaven is infinitely brighter; their distance, that man on earth is woefully separated from God; their position in the skies, that Heaven is infinitely more lofty a conception than the physical world can contain.

In the passage the celestial landscape cannot be complete until Cowper's imagination, animated by religious truths, has supplied a distant shore beyond it, and has turned his own point of vantage from a hilltop to a ship returning home after a long voyage. It is not the beauty of the stars that excites him so much as the idea of returning home; love is kindled not by the sublimity of the scene but by the notion that the stars, as beacons, are symbols of God's desire that the poet be saved.

Characteristically, Cowper in these lines gives personal meaning to landscape, both as natural phenomenon and symbol. The poet himself enters the landscape spiritually and emotionally, actually and figuratively. He relates the landscape of the poem to himself, not as a representative of man in general nor with the generalized responses of the *persona*, or depersonalized narrator. In this passage we are aware of the progress of the poet's own experience. If there is drama, it is the one of his own feelings as he moves from contemplation of the stars to his own situation. From one viewpoint, the description of the shore merely acts as a transition from the address to the stars to an outburst of personal feeling. But another dimension is given by the fact that the form of the passage is that of the poet's own experience. In this context the outburst of love assumes a highly autobiographical importance, for by it the poet implies that he recognizes, or at least has recognized, within him the gift of grace which allows him to see divine goodness throughout Creation. The expression of love is for the ability to supply the shore behind the stars and to turn them into beacons lighting the way.

Cowper's insistence that the only way to praise creation is by praising the Creator, and his practice of sublimating response to landscape in conventional moral and religious thought are based upon the dualism of his Calvinistic heritage. His use of animal imagery to describe the state of those who cannot see God behind nature has a religious orientation; for it signifies immersion in the flesh. Just as needs of the body motivate the animal, so the unsaintly, lacking the stimulus of grace, act from physical impulse. That the "saint" owes his superior insight either to "new faculties" or to the ability to learn how to use his powers to better advantage seems to indicate that Cowper could not decide whether grace added a new quality to the mind (in addition to reason, fancy, etc.) or consisted of the ability to use these qualities properly. Whatever the means by which grace works in the psyche, it alone provides, however, the ability to rise out of the prison of the flesh. On his own, man cannot find his way out of the maze of error which nature presents to the unredeemed. Christianity has always had a cabalistic tendency, and in Cowper's work it is intensified by evangelicalism with its central doctrine of conversion. The parables, for example, were intended to reveal truth to the initiated while excluding the unworthy who see but do not perceive, hear but do not understand. To Cowper, nature was like a parable of divine goodness. To the "converted" it is

> His t' enjoy
> With a propriety that none can feel,
> But who, with filial confidence inspir'd,
> Can lift to heaven an unpresumptuous eye,
> And smiling say—My Father made them all!
> (V, 743ff)

What could be more like Cowper than this longing for filial confidence, which allows the meek and gentle soul to lift its eyes to the Father, the ultimate symbol of authority and protectiveness? But we must place due emphasis on the *can* in "Can lift to heaven," for it again implies "election." The pun on "propriety," also typical of Cowper's thought and style, implies that election comes through God and must be acknowledged by one's own sense of being converted. Only God can make the individual his proprietor; and, without the sense of propriety and proprietorship which comes through religious conversion, man cannot feel at one with God and Creation. Overwhelmed by knowledge of his election, the "saint" looks upon the world with gratitude, joy, and even pride, boasting in the goodness of the God of Whom he feels himself so intimately a part. His emotion colors all things and intensifies the beauties he could only dimly perceive before.

The outsider does not share this intimate sense of communion with God and Creation. To him the beauty with which nature is "cloth'd" conceals rather than reveals the mind of God. Only when man is freed from the bonds of flesh through divine grace does nature "throwing wide/Her veil opaque" disclose

> . . . with a smile
> The author of her beauties, who, retir'd
> Behind his own creation, works unseen
> By the impure, and hears his power denied.
>
>   (V, 892–95)

The poet has almost a religious mission, then, to put readers who have the capacity of knowing God in the proper frame of mind to receive religious truth. As an imitator of nature, he helps to draw back the veil. Part of this mission is the obligation to revive in the minds of men a sense of the miraculous quality of the universe. Even the saved have a tendency in the monotony of daily life to forget that "all we behold is miracle" (VI, 132). If Cowper spends a disproportionately large amount of space in *The Task* on winter, it is partly because from the perspective provided by contemplation of this season that man can appreciate the miracle of life itself. The death of winter inspires a poignant reminiscence of the life of summer:

> Where now the vital energy that mov'd
> While summer, was, the pure and subtle lymph
> Through th' imperceptible meand'ring veins
> Of leaf and flow'r? It sleeps; and th' icey touch
> Of unprolific winter has impress'd
> A cold stagnation on th' intestine tide . . .
>
>   (VI, 134–39)

It is also from the perspective of winter that man can most clearly see the meaning of the recurring pattern of nature:

> From dearth to plenty, and from death to life,
> Is Nature's progress when she lectures man
> In heav'nly truth; evincing, as she makes
> The grand transition, that there lives and works
> A soul in all things, and that soul is God.
>
>   (VI, 178–85)

Nature lectures those who will attend her by exciting feeling and by affirming in her endurance through constant change the exist- ence of the Creator. But only the mind illuminated by Revelation can see in the pattern of life to death and of death to life an indi- cation that the death of a human will be followed by eternal life. Intuition will not suffice.

The praise of domestic life in *The Task*, as opposed to Thom- son's celebration of the grandeur of nature, must in part derive from this same religious inspiration. Motivated by the desire to show the goodness of God everywhere, Cowper could respond to his relatively narrow range of domestic activities and restricted geographical area. In talking about the pleasures of domestic life, he reveals the ray of heavenly light gilding the minute as well as the vast. In accordance with the doctrine of plenitude, which held that divine goodness revealed itself through the enormous variety of creation and the perfection with which even the least element of life was endowed, he shows how a moral life and Christian truths can dignify the most insignificant person. Though superfi- cially similar to Deistic admiration of the mechanical perfection of minute things as a sign of divine order and goodness, Cowper's reaction differs profoundly in his lack of detachment, or, more appropriately, deep involvement, his enjoyment rather than won- der.

But, aside from asserting the beauty of Christian life, Cowper exhibits a fascinated concern for the damned and for their efforts to give meaning to their lives. He sees the lost soul asserting itself in many ways, but primarily by constructing false notions of the universe. Its situation is described by the ambiguous statement that the world is "cloth'd with beauty for rebellious man" (V, 754), which on the surface seems to emphasize God's goodness to man, but also indicates that God allows the beauty of nature to turn one's attention from Him to it. Far from knowing God or being able to know God, the rebellious man sees only the beauty of nature but cannot penetrate the veil. Closed off from God by the veil of nature, the mind teaches itself to worship idols and profane truth instead of serving it (VI, 231–37) by glorifying Cre- ation (Pan, Flora), not the Creator.

Obviously Thomson's Deism has no place in a poetry that ulti- mately derives its strength from an "inner light." Cowper's attacks on philosophers or scientists (synonymous terms in the eighteenth century) are part of his critique of the Deistic position, which, by overstressing reason as a guide to truth, tended to make God in man's image.

> Full often, too,
> Our wayward intellect, the more we learn
> Of nature, overlooks her author more;
> From instrumental causes proud to draw
> Conclusions retrograde, and made mistake.
> (III, 146–47)

In his attacks on social evils, Cowper also reveals his religious bias. Unlike Thomson, who regarded a vice like wastefulness as primarily a violation of reason and Shaftesburian benevolence, Cowper saw it in more orthodox Christian terms as a result of sin, as a kind of paganism which deifies the body. Thus materialists offer their wealth on "fortune's velvet altar," and fortune itself is a goddess "costlier far/Than all that held their routs in Juno's heav'n." Clearly the worship of fortune is a form of self-worship, a praise of man's earthbound impulses; and, like all other false religions, it is self-destructive. The self is immolated not in order to achieve communion with God but in a paradoxical attempt at aggrandizement.

Another crucial difference between Cowper and Thomson lies in Cowper's retreat, metaphorically and physically, from a society of corrupt men to the innocence of country life, both human and animal. Thomson, putting faith in human reason, could end "Winter" with an appeal to man's better nature; but, as the stricken-deer image shows, Cowper thought that a much more fundamental change, even a "conversion," must occur. The new, innocent man is of a different order of being than the old:

> The innocent are gay—the lark is gay,
> That dries his feather, saturate with dew,
> Beneath the rosy cloud, while yet the beams
> Of day-spring overshoot his humble rest.
> The peasant too, a witness of his song,
> Himself a songster, is as gay as he.
> (I, 493–98)

Aside from the evangelical joyfulness of the blessed, which is not necessarily characteristic of Thomson's benevolent rational man, the removal from worldliness implied by the images establishes a wholly different range of experience. But it would be wrong to say that Cowper advocates a "return to nature" as the way to purity. What he values is a way of life that will turn man's energies to some useful purpose. Greed, lust, jealousy, and cruelty exist because man strives for pleasures that he can anticipate but never know. If he were like the lark which is perfectly content to perform the function that God has assigned it, he could find peace and contentment. Having adjusted to their conditions, the lark and peasant by singing a joyful song reveal their lack of frustration.

The country, then, reminds us of the "state of innocence." By providing amply for the needs of man, but with less possibility of luxury and competition, and by making one more dependent on his own resources, country life relieves one of the "fleshly" distraction of the city. But, if the country is the state of innocence, the story of the conscripted peasant in Book IV is a repetition of the not-so-fortunate Fall. The peasant gains refinement but loses that simplicity which before permitted him to adjust to his permanent station in life.

In Cowper's preference for country life we can see personal feeling highly colored by religious belief aspiring to the level of general moral statement. His "God made the country, and man made the town" has the epigrammatic ring with which general truths or "nature" are usually expressed in Neo-Classical poetry. But the sometimes enthusiastic and colorful description of London which precedes this aphorism outbalances the more sincere but pedestrian praise of the country which follows:

> There, touch'd by Reynolds, a dull blank becomes
> A lucid mirror, in which Nature sees
> All her reflected features. Bacon there
> Gives more than female beauty to a stone,
> And Chatham's eloquence to marble lips.
> Nor does the chissel occupy alone
> The pow'rs of sculpture, but the style as much;
> Each province of her art her equal care.
> With nice incision of her guided steel
> She ploughs a brazen field, and clothes a soil
> So sterile with what charms soe'er she will,
> The richest scen'ry and the loveliest forms.

Where finds philosophy her eagle eye,
With which she calculates, computes, and scans,
All distance, motion, magnitude, and now
Measures an atom, and now girds a world?
In London. Where has commerce such a mart,
So rich, so throng'd, so drain'd, and so supplied,
As London—opulent, enlarg'd, and still
Increasing, London? Babylon of old
Not more the glory of the earth than she,
A more accomplish'd world's chief glory now.

. . . .
    God made the country, and man made the town.
What wonder then that health and virtue, gifts
That can alone make sweet the bitter draught
That life holds out to all, should most abound
And least be threaten'd in the fields and groves?
                      (I, 700-53)

This common-sense realization that everything has its place—that the city, though it can foster vice, attracts a great many worthy people—keeps Cowper from indulging in primitivism or identifying too closely with the pastoral tradition. If he prefers the spiritual environment of his rural retreat, he refuses to eschew the improvements which a highly developed culture provide. The newspaper, for example, is as important to him in his own way as it is to those who figure in the events which it records. Because he enjoys these events from a distance, he can gain the proper moral perspective upon them. They provide ample subject matter for innocent amusement or enlightening conversation, and the newspaper itself serves as a means of information which connects him to the larger world without destroying the peace of the life he has chosen.

Convinced that uncivilized man amounts to little more than an animal, Cowper goes to considerable pains in *The Task* to answer those who hold that institutions, not man himself, could be blamed for the corruption of the age. If society has imperfections, they result from human imperfection. Man created society; how could he create something worse than himself? When society fails to call man to his true destiny but instead offers him false attractions, it does so not because it is the work of the devil but because, in creating a system to control his own disorderly impulses, man cannot hope to find a panacea for all of his problems. That the very system by which he exercises discipline should be the instrument of temptation for man is a paradox created by his own imperfect ability to give form to his will.

That the need to defend social life against its detractors engaged Cowper's deepest feelings is seen in the complete lack of wit or humor with which he attacks the heroic ethic. Instead of a travesty or mock heroic, he writes a sermon. "Nations would do well," he suggests, "t'extort their truncheons from the puny hands/Of heroes, whose infirm and baby minds are gratified with mischief" (V, 188–91). The heroic ideal might have had some place in a chaotic environment in which personal strength was needed to quench the "seeds of murder in the breast of man" (V, 210). But a strong society, resting upon a well-developed system of laws and sanctions, no longer needs a hero to subdue the passionate.

This state of society does not indicate that man has improved in nature, that he has evolved to a state above his primitive origins. As a result of original sin, he will always find that "in ev'ry heart/Are sown the sparks that kindle firy war;/Occasion needs but fan them, and they blaze." (V, 205–08) But, if a strong social system is necessary to discipline unruly urgings in the body politic, it must, to function properly, be purified of the remainders of egocentricity and the older system of order.

The attack on corporations in Book IV is another manifestation of Cowper's basic notion of social order based on Christian brotherhood. If society, through discipline and order, provides the only environment in which man can reach full maturity and turn his talents to use, corporations, representing a throwback to a primitive ethic based on acquisition, constitute a threat to social order and, through it, to freedom and productivity. Individual dignity fades when sublimated in the anonymous personality of the corporation, and all that remains is the gratification of selfish desires which have caused the members to band together. The only proper motives for incorporating are social order and religious truth; anything else results in a public plague:

> . . . burghers, men immaculate perhaps
> In all their private functions, once combin'd,
> Become a loathsome body, only fit
> For dissolution, hurtful to the main.

> Hence merchants, unimpeachable of sin
> Against the charities of domestic life,
> Incorporated, seem at once to lose
> Their nature; and, disclaiming all regard
> For mercy and the common rights of man,
> Build factories with blood, conducting trade
> At the sword's point, and dyeing the white robe
> Of innocent commercial justice red.
>
> (IV, 671–83)

The attack on merchants distinguishes Cowper from writers who held that private vice (enlightened self-interest) worked to the advantage of the public. But, on the other hand, the pride and selfishness which lie behind laissez-faire capitalism, having their roots in man's sinful nature, cannot be eradicated. Whatever social change Cowper might envision must occur within the framework of immutable human deficiencies. He was not a revolutionary.

In ranging widely over the matter and method of *The Task*, we can see that Cowper occupies a significant place as a delineator of many important currents in the history of ideas. He is very much a poet of the wondrously exciting world bequeathed to eighteenth-century man by the philosophers and scientists of the seventeenth and eighteenth centuries. For him, it is still an orderly world in which science and speculation, when properly used, subserve religious truth.

But order is coming under attack more and more by those who do not preserve a "proper" frame of reference, and the shrillness of the poet's indictment of them might well hint at a vague uneasiness which they inspire. Both Renaissance man and the Augustans gloried in the spacious universe which their minds had opened to them. Contrary to expectations, the shift from an anthropocentric to a solar universe did not necessarily destroy belief in human dignity. Even when man came to be but a link in the chain of being, he was capable of making himself into the image of a rational God. Cowper shares this faith in man which provides the rationale for the satiric tradition of which *The Task* is in some ways a part. But his attitudes are profoundly altered by their Calvinistic and evangelical context. He does not believe in Hobbesian man, hardly more than an animal, fighting for self-protection and aggrandizement; nor does he have much faith that private urges

or vices can be turned to public good. Certainly he does not believe in the doctrine of benevolence. If his universe is a spacious
one, man too often gets lost in its vast reaches. For, although his
universe is Christocentric, the Creator is not an immanent Being.
The significance of the great extent of the universe is that it shows
the separation between man and the True Center.

In the seventeenth century, it had been easy to see the apparent
biological connections between man and lower animal forms as
evidence of man's fallen, depraved nature. The eighteenth century reacted to this interpenetration of the new science and Calvinism by stressing the primacy of reason. By raising man above
the animal and by diminishing evil, reason turns the world into a
tidy, orderly, functioning mechanism. In Cowper's evangelical rejection of this form of rationalism, he restores the more ample
universe of the seventeenth century. The dichotomy between
"elect" and "damned" takes on, at least as metaphor, the notion of
man's animal nature, and evil again becomes not a cloud nor a
partial eclipse but an all-encompassing, impenetrable darkness.
However, if Cowper's universe differs from the Augustans' in this
respect, it certainly bears little resemblance to what will follow,
the egocentric universe of the romantics.

IV *Style in* The Task

Cowper's response to the ideas I have mentioned differs from
what we expect of a philosopher, historian, or social scientist. Although we might well be impressed by the amount of didactic
material in *The Task*, and by the fairly abstract level on which the
argument generally proceeds, the poem is more than a "verse
essay," a work in which the poet decorates prose statement to
make it more palatable to the reader. Always statement results
from, and gives form to, sensibility; it does not adhere to the requirements of scientific analysis. Cowper's purpose is to reveal,
not the facts nor the laws of nature, but its texture: the way it
"feels."

In choosing a style for *The Task*, Cowper had to consider that
his poem, which began as a poem about a sofa, had by its nature
to be mock heroic. But the variety of subject matter necessitated a
variety of styles. Sometimes Cowper works in the tradition of the
"moral essay," sometimes in that of the sermon, and sometimes he
affects the manner of polite conversation. At other times he tries

satire of a generalized sort which does not single out particular
evildoers, as does Pope's, but nevertheless has an asperity which
makes it unlike most of the satire of Dr. Johnson. In still other
passages Cowper expresses in lyrical form his enjoyment of nature. To give some semblance of unity to his treatment of this
variety of materials, he creates a blank verse which, like all eighteenth-century blank verse, recalls Milton; but in diction and syntax, and often in cadence, it is influenced by Pope and other couplet writers.

Cowper rarely tries to raise his ideas to the sublime by using the
majestic harmonies and full tones of Miltonic diction. Words of
Latin origin are mixed with Germanic words in a ratio which
more closely approximates spoken English than does *Paradise
Lost*. A catalogue of flowers in Book VI includes such names as
Laburnum, Hypericum, Althaea, Jasmine, Nezerion, but also
Broom, and common, though musical names, such as *Lilac.* Furthermore, though the description of the flowers includes such
phrases as "purple spikes pyramidal," "copious of flow'rs," "never-
cloying odours," "thick beset/With blushing wreaths, investing
ev'ry spray," the passage closes with the observation that "from
dearth to plenty, and from death to life/Is Nature's progress." [6]
There is a hint of epic style in the introduction to the catalogue:
"Then, each in its peculiar honours clad,/Shall publish, even to
the distant eye,/Its family and tribe" (VI, 177–79). But the idea
of family and tribe is lost by the end: "And all this uniform un-
coulour'd scene,/Shall be dismantled of its fleecy load,/And flush
into variety again" (VI, 178–79). If he limits resonance, he also
strives for a flexibility which allows for a greater variety of local
effects. We cannot say that sound creates a uniform quality.

At times sound adds another dimension to the visual imagery of
a passage. If words themselves evoke a scene, the sound of those
words allows us to appreciate details which the eye alone cannot
capture:

> How soft the music of those village bells,
> Falling at intervals upon the ear
> In cadence sweet, now dying all away,
> Now pealing loud again, and louder still,
> Clear and sonorous, as the gale comes on!
> (I, 6–10)

or

> Tall spire, from which the sound of cheerful bells
> Just undulates upon the list'ning ear.
>   (I, 174–75)

The sound is often as detailed as the scenes themselves. "Village
bells . . . falling at intervals," "cadence sweet," and "dying all
away" have a softer quality than "cheerful bells" or "pealing loud
again." And "clear and sonorous" has the full effect that the gale
gives as it augments the sound of the bells. "Undulates upon the
list'ning ear" preserves the vividness of sound but softens the
harshness that proximity would create ("cheerful"). The relaxing
quality of liquid sounds can also be used for a quite different purpose: "how much the hand/Of lubbard labour needs his watchful
eye,/Oft loit'ring lazily." Or in the following passage the tentative
"peeping" of the sun separates the harsher sounds and scene from
the gentler:

> He, therefore, timely warn'd, himself supplies
> Her want of care, screening and keeping warm
> The plenteous bloom, that no rough blast may sweep
> His garlands from the boughs. Again, as oft
> As the sun peeps and vernal airs breathe mild,
> The fence withdrawn, he gives them ev'ry beam,
> And spreads his hopes before the blaze of day.
>   (III, 439–45)

Sound can also be used to emphasize the mock heroic, as when
Cowper lavishes his most Miltonic diction upon a manure heap:
"The stable yields a stercoraceous heap;/Impregnated with quick
fermenting salts,/And potent to resist the freezing blast . . ."
(III, 463–65). Or it can emphasize the terror-evoking qualities of
the face which the "sage" affects to keep control over his critics:
"Terribly arch'd and acquiline his nose,/And overbuilt with most
impending brows" (III, 192–93). Or a ponderous line might be a
way of helping to perceive the quality of an image. Concern for
the poor and the cruel toil they must endure comes to a point in
the following description of a cart moving through the snow:

> Ill fares the trav'ller now, and he that stalks
> In pond'rous boots besides his reeking team.

> The wain goes heavily, impeded sore
> By congregated loads adhering close
> To the clogg'd wheels; and in this sluggish pace,
> Noiseless, appears a moving hill of snow.
>   (IV, 341–46)

The subject, a peasant and his car, and the theme, "the poor work hard," seem to justify the style.

In sentence form Cowper also mediates between Milton and more colloquial practice. Effects are local and particularized, but usually the sentences are fairly long and their pace is from moderate to slow. Periodic and loose structures are mixed:

> His slanting ray
> Slides ineffectual down the snowy vale,
> And, tinging all with his own rosy hue,
> From ev'ry herb and ev'ry spiry blade
> Stretches a length of shadow o'er the field:
> Mine, spindling into longitude immense,
> In spite of gravity, and sage remark
> That I myself am but a fleeting shade,
> Provokes me to a smile.
>   (V, 6–14)

Full periods give emphasis to metaphorical qualities of the scene, but, at the same time, seem a bit out of harmony with the scene itself. "Spindling into longitude immense" has the impressive quality consistent with the "sage remark," but its resonance is limited by the images of the rays sliding ineffectually, tinging (but not penetrating), and playfully stretching "a length of shadow" from each object. If Cowper's shadow "spindles," it does so not only because it represents to him the "thread of life" but also because the sun has so lightheartedly unwound the thread of his shadow. "Length of shadow," "longitude immense," and "gravity" refer both to Newtonian physics and the poet's state of mind. Significantly, "in spite of gravity" hovers between "spindling into longitude immense" (physical gravity) and "sage remark" (spiritual).

Book III, "The Garden," begins with a long, periodic sentence:

> As one who, long in thickets and in brakes
> Entangled, winds now this way and now that

His devious course uncertain, seeking home;
Or having long in miry ways been foil'd
And sore discomfited, from slough to slough
Plunging, and half despairing escape;
If chance at length he find a greensward smooth
And faithful to the foot his spirits rise,
He chirrups brisk his ear-erecting steed,
And winds his way with pleasure and with ease;
So I, designing other themes, and call'd
T'adorn the Sofa with eulogium due,
To tell its slumbers, and to paint its dreams,
Have rambled wide.

                                            (III, 1–14)

Again suggestions of Milton in the Latinate syntax and diction
("devious"), in ellipsis ("long" instead of "for a long time"), and
perhaps in heroic jargon ("sore discomfited") enable Cowper to
enforce a delicate system of balances: between the two dimensions of mock heroic (things as they are and things as they should
be), between mock heroic and moral essay, between chaos and
order both in Cowper's thought and in the contrast between the
thicket of error and the peace of his garden. The very structure of
the sentence seems to dramatize the movement away from chaos
and emotional stress to control and repose. From the floundering
meter and syntax of the beginning issue the more orderly syntax
and meter of the main clause. This movement is confirmed by the
final sentence of the verse paragraph: "I feel myself at large,/
Courageous, and refresh'd for future toil,/If toil await me, or if
dangers new."

A similar use of the periodic sentence is found in Book VI,
when Cowper describes his encounter with a squirrel. The long
introductory phrase throws emphasis upon the quick, abrupt motions of the squirrel as it emerges from its nest:

Drawn from his refuge in some lonely elm
That age or injury has hollow'd deep,
Where, on his bed of wool and matted leaves,
He has outslept the winter, ventures forth
To frisk awhile, and bask in the warm sun,
The squirrel, flippant, pert, and full of play:
He sees me, and at once, swift as a bird,
Ascends the neighb'ring beach; there whisks his brush,

> And perks his ear, and stamps and cries aloud,
> With all the prettiness of feign'd alarm,
> And anger insignificantly fierce.
>
> (VI, 310–20)

But throughout *The Task* Cowper was much influenced by the cadence and rhetoric of the heroic couplet. At times the two modes clash rather violently, as in the following passage in which balanced, coordinate phraseology seems to demand the couplet:

> The paralytic, who can hold her cards,
> But cannot play them, borrows a friend's hand
> To deal and shuffle, to divide and sort
> Her mingled suits and sequences; and sits,
> Spectatress both and spectacle, a sad
> And silent cypher, while her proxy plays.
>
> (I, 472–77)

Often there are simply too many words to fit into the couplet:

> 'Tis pitiful
> To court a grin, when you should woo a soul;
> To break a jest, when pity would inspire
> Pathetic exhortation . . .
>
> (II, 466–69)

> 'Twas transient in its nature, as in show
> 'Twas durable: as worthless, as it seem'd
> Intrinsically precious . . .
>
> (V, 173–75)

As was the practice in the couplet, the expectation raised by one line is often cancelled in some way by the next: "He comes, the herald of a noisy world,/With spatter'd boots, strapp'd waist, and frozen locks" (IV, 5–6). Frequently a line stands out as if it belonged in a couplet: "Retrench a sword-blade, or displace a patch" (II, 318). Always we are aware of the influence of the aphoristic style of the Augustans, but often this influence is modified or unbalanced by verse form:

> God made the country and man made the town.
>
> (I, 749)

> The fairest capital of the world,
> By riot and incontinence the worst.
>   (I, 698–99)

>   . . . giving laws
> To distant worlds and trifling in their own.
>   (III, 165–66)

>   the cups
> That cheer but not inebriate, wait on each . . .
>   (IV, 40)

>   Knowledge dwells
> In heads replete with thoughts of other men;
> Wisdom in minds attentive to their own.
>   (VI, 89–91)

In *The Task,* then, we see antithesis in thought, imagery, rhetoric, and levels of diction, all of which subserve the ends of the critic or analyst, side by side with remnants of the evocative, sublime style of Milton, which seems fit for a different order of imagination. Yet each extreme colors the other, for Cowper is never wholly Miltonic or wholly the Neo-Classical man of wit. Together, his styles allow him to combine a social criticism, which is often weighted with subjective values, with a sometimes intense personal vision, one lying outside the realm of criticism, that always contains traces of wit. The mixture of styles might also be seen as a function of Cowper's discursive method. As he "rov'd far" and "gather'd much fruit," he selected styles within the range of blank verse appropriate to the particular passages, whether they be elegiac, pastoral, or satiric. But always he was careful to subdue eloquence, primarily on moral grounds: " 'Tis not in artful measures, in the chime/And idle tinkling of a minstrel's lyre,/To charm his ear, whose eye is on the heart . . ." (VI, 1020–22).

In this respect, Cowper probably thought of his style in much the same terms that he used to describe good preaching: "in language plain,/And plain in manner; decent, solemn, chaste,/And natural in gesture" (II, 400–02). Eloquence belongs to the politician, that phenomenon of the city, who exists by using words to deceive, to insinuate, and to intimidate (IV, 64–73).

V *Structure*

If Cowper avoids eloquence, he also rejects excesses of wit in which, as was the practice of the time, he saw a distortion of wisdom (I, 728). Like eloquence, which conceals truth behind a veil of attractive sounds and connotations, wit, which sacrifices "nature" to gain fantastic twists and perspectives, cannot belong in Cowper's highly moral poem. When images are used, for example, they do not constitute the primary way of expressing ideas. Being only one of the devices at the disposal of the poet, they take their place as a means of amplifying statement. Although they are at the heart of the meaning of the poem and of Cowper's way of looking at the universe, they do not have the more exclusive position that they demand in the works of a metaphysical poet or of a contemporary like Collins. We are never surprised to see an image in the context in which it appears in *The Task*; we accept immediately the correspondence between the image and the thing it describes. Nor do we look to image patterns to find the central principle of unity and coherence in the poem.

Nevertheless, in Cowper's many references to his method can be found a deviation from the Neo-Classical ideal of emotion balanced by reason, fancy balanced by judgment—of the poem as a highly finished, well-ordered whole. The following passage is typical:

> But truce with censure. Roving as I rove,
> Where shall I find an end, or how proceed?
> As he that travels far oft turns aside,
> To view some rugged rock or mould'ring tow'r,
> Which, seen, delights him not; then, coming home,
> Describes and prints it, that the world may know
> How far he went for what was nothing worth;
> So I, with brush in hand and pallet spread,
> With colours mix'd for a far diff'rent use,
> Paint cards and dolls, and ev'ry idle thing
> That fancy finds in her excursive flights.
>
> (IV, 232–42)

If Cowper really intended, as he suggests, to prove that fanciful excursions are vain, that they lead the poet to objects unworthy of concern and can gain worth only by showing the emptiness of the search for value in the material universe, the objective is self-defeating: he uses chaos to describe chaos. Nevertheless, it is difficult to think of *The Task* as a whole because of its "excursiveness"; we tend not to see the whole poem for its variety of local effects, and these suffer because they are entangled "in thickets and brakes" (III, 1–2) where they can easily be overlooked. Certainly the fact that the poem benefits when some of the brambles are cut away does it no credit; nor does the realization that even when individual sections are thus exposed for closer attention, the poem does not achieve the higher unity of the well-designed garden, which seems to be a metaphor of the work as a whole.

To appreciate *The Task* fully, we must adopt Cowper's frame of mind and delight in seeing experience recorded with no other purpose than to follow the moment-to-moment, day-to-day ramblings of the mind. Truth to nature in this poem seems to mean fidelity to the movement of what might with some justification be called a "stream of consciousness." The record extends even to the times in which the mind is vacant:

> Nor less amus'd have I quiescent watch'd
> The sooty films that play upon the bars,
> Pendulous and forboding, in the view
> Of superstition, and prophesying still,
> Though still deceiv'd, some stranger's near approach.
> 'Tis thus the understanding takes repose
> In indolent vacuity of thought,
> And sleeps and is refresh'd.
>
> > (IV, 291–98)

Although poetic sensibility in *The Task* seems at times divorced from understanding at its most profound levels, recurrent ideas and images establish a pattern of implication which often takes the place of design. These patterns were at best dimly apprehended, if they were conscious at all; and they emerge tentatively and only with a tenuous claim to effectiveness. Indeed, I suspect that they exist primarily because of the intrinsic consistency of Cowper's thought.

The apparent discursiveness of *The Task* conceals such organizing principles as the theme of finding stability and spiritual repose, which generates much of the imagery of the poem. Out of

Cowper's claustrophobia (which I have mentioned in the previous chapters) emerges a preoccupation with both the smallness of the poet's world and the spaciousness of the universe. Since the sequestered life of Olney had saved Cowper from the abyss of despair and madness, it is not surprising that images like the garden and fireside should figure so largely. But snugness and security represent only one side of the poet's quest for order and stability. If he finds peace amidst his domestic concerns, he also longs for the freer atmosphere of the open countryside. Looking at the stars liberates him, for he can see them floating in an endless, tranquil sea of space. Similarly, nature, although it may free him from the narrow confines of his life in Olney, can excite his feeling of guilt and his claustrophobia. Closed in by the material universe, he can feel comfortable only when God draws back the veil of phenomena to reveal His infinity.

The paradox of a mind which seeks security in a confined domestic environment, yet longs for the freedom of endless space, is captured by such metaphors as "heart's dark chambers." The relative freedom of Cowper's life until 1763, it may be recalled, had left him with the feeling of being "buried above ground" in a "fleshly tomb." From this predicament the orderly life of the Unwin household had freed him. But the superficial tranquility of the Unwin regimen in Huntingdon and Olney could not protect Cowper from his deep-seated moral and psychological difficulties, the "thickets" and "dark chambers" of *The Task*. Rays of light piercing the dark abyss, stars or beacons shining from afar, prisoners languishing in the Bastille, all are images of the paradox of security/unrest which is central to the poem. So is Cowper's concern with heroic and mock heroic. Even his sense of humor has symbolic properties, for it ridicules the smallness and tidiness of his world while sheltering his mind from more agonizing concerns. Perhaps the tension in his style between the openness of blank verse and conciseness of the couplet is still another metaphor of this basic conflict.

Theme and image serve as structure when they link together various kinds of subject matter. As unpoetic as Cowper's denunciation of scientists and politicians sometimes seems, they are joined imaginatively to his basic concern with order and stability. In contemporary science and the materialistic temper of his time he sees a concern with surfaces or "veils" as fraught with danger as the

superficial stability of his life in the 1750's. His abusive, canting
tone shows the depth of his feeling. Satire and wit, which elsewhere he can manage with a light, deft touch, fail him when he
functions as an Elijah, for wit cannot do justice to the gravity of
his subject matter or the depth of his feelings.

Nevertheless, the imagery of the passages concerned with science, politics, and other public matters is the same as that of the
wittier or more personal sections; in every context it possesses another structural quality unique to *The Task*. Many of Cowper's
metaphors are drawn from the Bible (e.g. "the sempiternal source/
Of light divine," "pure fountain of eternal love," "road of wisdom"). Viewed with a Calvinistic bias, these Biblical figures of
speech link personal conflicts with those Cowper observes in the
world around him. They also show that for Cowper Biblical metaphors had unique vitality. To him "source" and "light" and "darkness" were not clichés but often painful reminders of the remoteness of God, the spaciousness of the universe, and the insignifi-
cance of man, hence the irony of the scientist trying to comprehend the universe with his "philosophic tube," or telescope, and
confusing physical light (phenomena) with "light divine." The
scientist's search for knowledge seems impure, because the
draughts he draws from the "crystal stream" are always polluted
by his materialistic motives. But in words like "delirium" and "in-
toxication," the drinking metaphor becomes more than an attack
on human conceit or intellectual pride. It goes to the heart of
Cowper's own Biblically oriented myth of life, death, and regeneration. We cannot help but think of the "fountain filled with
blood" in his famous hymn, or the images of drought and thirst in
"R.S.S. Written in a Fit of Illness."

As with Cowper's life, too much emphasis on the poet's seriousness and the fact that imagery and structure are rooted in personal experience obscures the sense of order and stability that
continually asserts itself through comedy and comic detachment.
Since changes in tone are as essential to the discursive poem
as variety of subject matter, it is not surprising that Cowper
ranges from lyric, to invective, to good-humored satire. But
humor has other functions which might also be considered structural. It extends the basic themes and images into the small, domestic world of Olney, the poet's refuge and his alternative to the
corruption of London. Just as the snugness of his fireside and the

order of his garden remind us of his paradoxical attitudes toward freedom and constraint, so the warmth and security of his world has to evoke mixed feelings; irony must balance lyrical celebration.

Cowper's humor is always turned as much against himself as against the particular object of description in *The Task*. In the beginning of Book V, he is one of the comic figures populating the winter landscape. His shadow, "spindling into longitude immense,/In spite of gravity, and sage remark/That I myself am but a fleeting shade," helps to ridicule his perpetual melancholy. In Book IV the arrival of his newspaper establishes an ironic connection between the larger world and his own. The poet fairly dances with excitement as he sees and hears the stage arrive. To him the "twanging horn" is "heart-shaking music" and the length of the bridge over which the stage passes is "wearisome," since it delays the arrival for a few moments. Burning with desire to open his newspaper, he rushes home, and after frenzied preparations settles down to "welcome peaceful ev'ning in." He undercuts his enthusiasm through anticlimax: the "wearisome" bridge is also "needful"; the cups of tea "cheer but not inebriate"; all of the activity results in nothing more than a peaceful evening. Contrasted with the activity which the post brings to Cowper's world are the manifold activities of the "noisy" world of the newspaper; and contrasted with both is the peace that lies above all, symbolized by the unwrinkled face of the moon.

Cowper's self-effacing humor is another indication of the subjectivism of his work. Like his imagery it never entirely frees itself from personal associations or becomes wholly externalized, as, for example, does the wit of Pope or Swift. To appreciate Cowper's humor, we must see it in the context of his insecurity, his sense of personal unworthiness and separation from God, and his fear of the coldness and deadness of spirit which followed his period of Enthusiasm. These personal concerns also tell us more about such images as "heart's dark chambers," "stricken deer," "thicket," and "with rapture tastes his style" than we can discover by examining the popular consciousness upon which Neo-Classical theories of "nature" and "true wit" depend. Personal associations, then, serve as an organizing principle, for they arrange images and ideas in patterns, or to use Cowper's own metaphor, "chords," which move in harmony with the poet's feelings and reveal various levels in his

responses. Darkness, disorder, and death; thickets and orderly
gardens; light, streams of water, and stars are connected in his
mind by his personal myth of death and regeneration. From this
nucleus radiates his concern with such disparate subjects as scientific research, politics, life in Olney, landscape, and gardens.

VI *Minor Discursive Poems*

Cowper's other long poems, most of which are verse essays, are
not of much interest as poetry; for they lack imaginative order as
well as firmly structured arguments. We might use Cowper's own
standards to judge his performance:

> Fervency, freedom, fluency of thought,
> Harmony, strength, words exquisitely sought,
> Fancy, that from the bow that spans the sky
> Brings colours, dipt in heav'n, that never die;
> A soul exalted above earth, a mind
> Skill'd in the characters that form mankind;
> And, as the sun in rising beauty dress'd,
> Looks to the westward from the dappled east,
> And marks, whatever clouds may interpose,
> Ere yet his race begins, its glorious close;
> And eye like his to catch the distant goal,
> Or ere the wheels of verse begin to roll;
> Like his to shed illuminating rays
> On ev'ry scene and subject it surveys:
> Thus grac'd, the man asserts a poet's name,
> And the world cheerful admits the claim.
>   ("Table Talk," ll. 700–15)

Certainly Cowper possessed a fervent commitment to his ideas,
but fervency has to reveal itself through "fancy," "harmony," and
"words exquisitely sought." In these areas such poems as "Table
Talk," "Truth," "Hope," and "The Progress of Error" fail to rise
above prose. That fancy should bring colors "dipt in heav'n" indicates the religious bent of Cowper's imagination, but exalted spirit
and sublime figures must be in harmony with language and structure if they are to inspire the reader with a similar zeal.

A good example of what I mean is Cowper's use of the heroic
couplet, which is the verse form of all the poems. Although *Bart-
lett's Familiar Quotations* contains many citations from Cowper's

long poems, individual lines and couplets have neither the brilliance, conciseness, and proportion of their Augustan predecessors nor the fuller harmonies of a more open form. Essentially, the poet has failed "to catch the distant goal" or to shed his illuminating rays "ere the wheels of verse begin to roll"; he has not considered carefully the relationship of each aspect of the poem (diction, meter, rhyme, rhetoric) to the others and to the whole.

In the other category, skill "in the characters that form mankind," the poems are somewhat better. The passages that stand out in "The Progress of Error" and "Hope" are often "characters" in the seventeenth- and eighteenth-century definition of the word. But even these cannot match the verbal brilliance, the well-turned phraseology, the point, the concision of the best works in the tradition; nor do they reach a greater psychological depth:

> Gorgonius sits, abdominous and wan,
> Like a fat squab upon a Chinese fan:
> He snuffs far off th' anticipated joy;
> Turtle and ven'son all his thoughts employ;
> Prepares for meals as jockies take a sweat,
> Oh, nauseous!—an emetic for a whet!
> ("The Progress Of Error," ll. 217–22)

Often the tone has a sneering quality which cannot rise either to the malice or the indignation that more personalized attacks often had:

> That poor JONQUIL, with almost ev'ry breath,
> Sighs for his exit, vulgarly call'd death:
> For he, with all his follies, has a mind
> Not yet so blank, or fashionably blind. . . .
> ("Hope," ll. 89–92)

At times, amidst the heavy moralizing, there is a refreshing use of the couplet and the comedy of situation:

> Adieu, Vinoso cries, ere yet he sips
> The purple bumper, trembling at his lips,
> Adieu to morality—if grace
> Makes works a vain ingredient in the case!
> The Christian hope is—Waiter, draw the cork—

If I mistake not—Blockhead! with a fork!—
Without good works, whatever some may boast,
Mere folly and delusion—Sir, your toast!—
My firm persuasion is, at least sometimes
That heav'n will weigh man's virtues and his crimes
With nice attention, in a righteous scale,
And save or damn as these or those prevail.
                                    ("Hope," ll. 357–68)

But Cowper cannot sustain the comic situation nor his ludicrous imitation of individual styles through the long conversation that ensues among Vinoso, a colonel, an ensign, and Sir Smug, a priest.

What most clearly distinguishes poems like "Hope" or "The Progress of Error" from *The Task*, however, is Cowper's failure to reveal in them his own good-natured personality upon which so much of the humor of *The Task* depends. Without good nature, pointed wit, or rhetorical brilliance, the moral essays, or conversations as he seemed to think of them, become either tedious or uncomfortably like a ranting sermon. Cowper knew that others might find in the poems a tendency to overstate in the manner of a rant; but, instead of restraining himself, he accused his readers of not being sober enough to take to heart the truth of what he was saying:

No wild enthusiast ever yet could rest
Till half mankind were like himself possess'd.
Philosophers, who darken and put out
Eternal truth by everlasting doubt;
Church quacks, with passions under no command,
Who fill the world with doctrines contraband.
Discov'rers of they know not what, confin'd
Within no bounds—the blind that lead the blind;
To streams of popular opinion drawn,
Deposit in those shallows all their spawn.
The wriggling fry soon fill the creeks around,
Pois'ning the waters where their swarms abound.
Scorn'd by the nobler tenants of the flood,
Minnows and gudgeons gorge th' unwholesome food.
The propagated myriads spread so fast,
E'en Leuwenhoeck himself would stand aghast,
Employ'd to calculate th' enormous sum
And own his crab-computing pow'rs overcome.

> Is this hyperbole? The world well known,
> Your sober thoughts will hardly find it one.
> ("The Progress of Error," ll. 479–89)

At the end of "Retirement" Cowper admits that his moral poems are feeble and vain efforts, but he then says that his most important role, that of "monitor," or conscience, has been fulfilled. "Monitor," as he points out in *The Task*, is an ironic term since it also means a device to improve physical, not spiritual, appearance. As a "monitor" of the inner self, concerned not with superficial appearances but with ideal forms, Cowper turns his poems into a collection of ideas, some of them commonplaces, which were subjects of controversy in his time.

In "Table Talk" Cowper attacks ambition and desire for recognition. As loyal Englishman and Whig, he warns against the dangers of concentrating too much power in the king; but he is careful to point out the awesome difficulties of kingship. If he shows proper respect for the royal establishment, he also evinces concern that Parliament remain able to correct the errors the king might make in discharging his almost superhuman duties. He also contrasts the liberty of England with the oppression of France, warns that selfishness will lead to the decline of England, and then turns to a discussion of poetry which contains the popular, somewhat Neo-Platonic notion that it has declined from its original, we might say "ideal," form. He ends with praise of Thomas Sternhold and John Hopkins' psalms, favorite objects of Augustan wit, because they put truth before art.

In "The Progress of Error" Cowper condemns those who put flesh before the spirit. After asserting that free will implies a choice between earth and spirit and that temptation is thus necessary, he proceeds to show that virtue brings peace, but that pleasure results in pain. But material pleasures are not in themselves evil; they become so only when they are an end in themselves and cause suffering and boredom. Again, in a passage reminiscent of the Dissenters' attacks on the stage in the seventeenth and early eighteenth centuries, art is distinguished from truth as an earthly pleasure which puts enjoyment of intellectual powers before the higher objective of intellect—to know and serve God. Both artists and scholars suffer from pride of intellect. In a long passage centering on travel as a metaphor of the progressive immersion in

error, the Grand Tour is attacked as an institution for propagating
love of the world.

In "Truth" Cowper turns to the failure of people to accept the
truths of Christianity because they are easy to understand. He
avers that man insists on complicating religion because his mind
seeks earthly satisfactions that simplicity cannot provide. Clearly,
he places himself in opposition to the tendency in "the Establishment" to emphasize intellectual aspects of religion at the expense
of inspiration and emotional satisfaction. The attack on excessive
intellectualism leads naturally to a condemnation of the pride of
the rationalists, especially Voltaire, which in turn is followed by
praise for the simple cottager, who, even though she lacks understanding and wit, has a clear knowledge of truth:

> Oh, happy peasant! Oh, unhappy bard!
> His the mere tinsel, her's the rich reward;
> He prais'd, perhaps, for ages yet to come;
> She never heard of half a mile from home;
> He, lost in errors, his vain heart prefers;
> She, safe in the simplicity of her's.
>   ("Truth," ll. 331–36)

The passage recalls the Augustan vision of a perfectly orderly
world, where everything has its place. Neither poverty nor wealth
can in themselves lead to salvation, but poverty, which diminishes
responsibility, makes salvation easier; wealth, which creates responsibility, makes salvation more difficult to attain. Similarly,
lack of intelligence is compensated by the ease with which it
makes possible the apprehension of truth, while great wit and
understanding, as well as creating responsibility, increase the possibility of falling into error.

In "Expostulation," Cowper, like Dryden before him, attacks
corruption in England by comparing it to difficulties encountered
by a former Chosen People, the Jews. The fall of Israel should
serve as a warning to England that favoritism shown to it in its
prosperity and civil order might soon be taken away because of its
crimes: profusion, debasement of religion, enslavement of India.
In a brief history of England, Cowper reveals a pride in his na-
tional heritage typical of his time, which cannot lead to an equally
typical complacency because of the sin he sees around him. His

love of order, his anti-Catholicism, and his Whiggish distrust of authority are seen in the particular signs of divine favor that he lists: salvation from the Spanish Armada, from the Stuarts, and from religious persecution.

Another interesting development is Cowper's attack on excessive oathtaking and on the use of acts of religious conformity as requirements for holding office. In a passage replete with allusions he argues that to take communion or to swear loyalty as a requisite to political preferment is not only to turn these actions into meaningless routine but also to deprive them of their symbolic value. When an oath becomes a political gesture and when every job requires the taking of oaths, there ceases to be any sanctity in the act:

> And hast thou sworn, on ev'ry slight pretence,
> Till perjuries are common as bad pence,
> While thousands, careless of the damning sin,
> Kiss the book's outside who ne'er look within?
>   (ll. 386–89)

In "Charity" Cowper relates Christian doctrine to economic theory, and he offers in the process a glimpse at some of the humanitarian impulses of the times. Charity is the tie that binds together humanity. Commerce manifests this tie, for in the beautifully ordered world that the poet envisions, trade has the function of moving the surpluses of one individual or area to supply the deficiencies of another. Each deficiency has a corresponding surplus, and only the idle can upset the system. The only form of trade that Cowper will not countenance is traffic in slaves. Of course, humanity must always transcend the material concerns with which trade is involved. Cowper also attacks the practice of imprisoning for debt.

"Tirocinium," an attack on public school education, differs from the previous poems in the extent to which the poet gives play to his feelings. What begins as a typical satire turns into a recollection of both the pleasant and unpleasant experiences of the poet's youth. Cowper's attacks on the evils of the system are as subjective as his celebration of youth in the poem. The low quality of the education offered by public schools interests him less than his memories of the loneliness and insecurity of life away from home, and the brutality of the schools seems less important than the fact that living away from home weakens the bond between father and son. If Cowper recalls with deep feeling the embarrassment of returning "shy and strange" from school to a home where he could no longer take "with fearless ease/His fav'rite stand between his father's knees" (ll. 569–70), he also seems to understand the desire of fathers to relive through their sons the rough and tumble life of the schools. This vicarious enjoyment he thought a cruel imposition on a sensitive boy, who must discover to his sorrow that "Great schools suit best the sturdy and rough."

Obviously "Tirocinium" is less an attempt to arouse the *sensus communis* or popular conscience than a testament to the poet's own feelings of insecurity. It is unfortunate that the task of cutting the bonds between parent and child often fell to the schools, and it is probably true that the process occurred at too early an age. But these considerations should not be allowed to obscure the fact that all boys must eventually leave their "fav'rite stand between [their] father's knees." Cowper's ideal of a son who retains his innocence under the tutelage of a father who is friend as well as teacher may have had emotional validity to the poet but would in most cases have been unworkable.

Cowper's characterization of the father as a friend, not an authority figure, expresses the gentleness of the poet's temperament as well as his insecurity. In "Expostulation" this gentleness takes another form when Cowper refuses to indulge in satire which pillories individuals. Recognizing that vehemence has its place, he, nevertheless, fears that to ridicule a particular person might be to injure him unjustly:

> Far be the thought from any verse of mine,
> And farther still the form'd and fix'd design,
> To thrust the charge of deeds that I detest
> Against an innocent unconscious breast:
> The man that dares traduce, because he can
> With safety to himself, is not a man:
> An individual is a sacred mark,
> Not to be pierc'd in play, or in the dark;
> But public censure speaks a public foe,
> Unless a zeal for virtue guide the blow.
>   (ll. 428–37)

If the mildness of Cowper's satire is connected with his fear of being cruel, it also appears to be connected with his religious convictions. In "Hope" Cowper implies that man's most important concerns transcend satire. The poet performs his most valuable service not in attacking evils but in pointing the way to peace and happiness. He must arouse the public conscience by reminding it of its moral values, but he also must reconcile his readers to a world in which evil will always exist:

> For lift thy palsied head, shake off the gloom
> That overhangs the borders of thy tomb,
> See nature, gay as when she first began,
> With smiles alluring her admirer man;
> She spreads the morning over eastern hills;
> Earth glitters with the drops the night distils;
> The sun, obedient, at her call appears
> To fling his glories o'er the robe she wears;
> Banks clothed with flow'rs, groves fill'd with sprightly sounds,
> The yellow tilth, green meads, rocks, rising grounds,
> Streams edg'd with osiers, fatt'ning ev'ry field
> Wher'er they flow, now seen and now conceal'd. . . .
> (ll. 37–48)

But Cowper's impulse to comfort as well as chastise does not fully express the personality of his satire. How could he comfort the afflicted when he himself had been instructed by God to abandon hope? Because of his sense of propriety, he can never state his predicament. Nevertheless, to anyone acquainted with his biography, his poems have a particular poignance. For example, in "Hope" we can see more in the description of the saved man than appears on the surface:

> As when a felon, whom his country's laws
> Have justly doom'd for some atrocious cause,
> Expects, in darkness and heart-chilling fears,
> The shameful close of all his misspent years;
> If chance, on heavy pinions slowly born,
> A tempest usher in the dreaded morn,
> Upon his dungeon walls the lightning play,
> The thunder seems to summon him away,
> The warder at the door his key applies,

Shoots back the bolt, and all his courage dies:
If then, just then, all thoughts of mercy lost,
When hope, long ling'ring, at last yields the ghost,
The sound of pardon pierce his startled ear,
He drops at once his fetters and his fear;
A transport glows in all he looks and speaks,
And the first thankful tears bedew his cheeks.
Joy, far superior joy, that much outweighs
The comfort of a few poor added days,
Invades, possesses, and o'erwhelms, the soul
Of him, whom hope has with a touch made whole.

(ll. 712–31)

The details of this description are reminiscent of two dreams that Cowper recounted in the letters to Samuel Teedon ten years later. In one, Cowper is the felon who "in a state of the most insupportable misery . . . looked through the window of a strange room being all alone, and saw preparations making for my execution. That it was but about four days distant, and that then I was destined to suffer everlasting martyrdom in the fire, my body being prepared for the purpose and my dissolution made a thing impossible." In the other he "seemed to be taking a final leave of my dwelling, and every object with which I have been most familiar on the evening before my execution. I felt the tenderest regret at the separation, and looked about for something durable to carry with me as a memorial. The iron hasp of the garden-door presenting itself, I was on the point of taking that, but recollecting that the heat of the fire in which I was going to be tormented would fuse the metal, and that it would therefore only serve to increase my insupportable misery, I left it." [7]

Two long poems are of interest as precursors of *The Task*. "Conversation" discusses the pleasures of quiet intercourse devoid of asperity and pretentious debate. Conversations should inform and amuse, and the main hindrance to success is defects in personality, such as bashfulness or assertiveness, and such unpleasant habits as smoking and wearing perfume. Its ultimate model is the discourse on the road to Emmaus. "Retirement" further defines the tranquil atmosphere which in "Conversation" is a precondition to talk. The poet indicates that although everyone seeks retirement at one time or another, few have the maturity and repose of spirit to enjoy it for a long period of time. He points out that much love of the country is in reality only a longing for an impossibly idyllic life such as that found in pastorals. True retirement is a state in which freedom from the restraints of the city and a balanced schedule of intellectual and physical activities provide the opportunity for spiritual development. This life is the basis of his poetry, in which he converses on moral subjects with his readers.

CHAPTER 4

Short Poems, Lyric and Comic

A T THE end of the fourth book of *The Task*, Cowper, after
referring to the placidness of his life at Olney, hails rural
life, the "patroness of health and ease/And contemplation," and
resolves never to add himself "to the pursuit/Of honors, or emolu-
ment, or fame." "Great offices," he continues,

> will have
> Great talents. And God gives to every man
> The virtue, temper, understanding, taste,
> That lifts him into life, and lets him fall
> Just in the niche he was ordained to fill.
> To the deliverer of an injured land
> He gives a tongue t'enlarge upon, an heart
> To feel, and courage to redress her wrongs;
> To monarchs dignity, to judges sense,
> To artists ingenuity and skill;
> To me an unambitious mind, content
> In the low vale of life, that early felt
> A wish for ease and leisure, and ere long
> Found here that leisure and that ease I wished.

Two tendencies should be observed in this passage. One, which
might be labelled "Pre-Romantic," is not so much indicated by
Cowper's love of life in the country as by his insistence on the
individuality of his way of life. There is no attempt to overrate
Olney, to pretend that it is "sweet Auburn," to make it into the
pastoral ideal. Nor, continuing in this vein, is there any sign that
Olney symbolizes the need for all men to seek retirement from the
city. Life there is the "low vale," satisfying only to Cowper, and
then only because of his own psychological needs. If elsewhere
the garden, a paradigm of life in the country, does seem an Eden
when compared to the depraved life of the city, this symbolic

meaning is lost for a moment in our contemplation of it as the place where Cowper's personal regeneration occurred.

But, however Romantic may seem the impulse to build a way of life which is, if not unique, at least individual, in the above passage it is almost lost amid assertions of the old truisms "everything has its place" and "whatever is, is right." The assumption that underlies praise of life in Olney is the same notion of order in variety which Pope and Adam Smith, among others, celebrate in different ways. Although retirement distinguishes the poet from others, it "has its place"; it fits in the spectrum of social and moral attitudes which constitute the whole of eighteenth-century civilization. Had he known what direction poetry would take in the generation following his, Cowper undoubtedly would have given even greater emphasis to his notion that true social harmony can exist only when each person seeks his enlightened self-interest.

The tendency to anticipate what was to come while looking backward exists in Cowper's shorter poems as well as in *The Task*. Although a relatively small number of these poems are concerned with life in Olney, they exhibit the same impulses toward individualism and conventionalism in idea and form which are seen in the Olney-centered parts of *The Task*. If Cowper uses "Boadicea," "Verses Supposed to be Written by Alexander Selkirk," and "On the Loss of the Royal George" as platforms for expressing sentiments which are peculiarly English, he also has the capacity for strikingly original statements about his personal condition, most notably in "Lines Written During a Period of Insanity" and most artistically in "The Castaway." And if in "The Castaway" feelings seem to triumph over form, or at least form seems not to contribute crucially to the development of feeling, in the mock odes and elegies form is used with the subtlety of the Augustan masters.

The distinction between Cowper and the Romantics seems clear when we compare his poems on the slave issue with those of Blake. Cowper appeals to humanitarian values in a not very novel, or interesting, way; Blake, transcending satire and the issue itself, makes his "Little Black Boy" another revelation of his personal myth of innocence. Cowper's "Sweet Meat Has Sour Sauce or, the Slave-Trader in the Dumps" and "Pity for Poor Africans" do not stand apart from many other poems on the same subject which flooded periodicals in their use of modified ballad stanzas,

in their irony, and in their exhortations to the public to acknowledge its selfishness and hypocrisy:

> I pity them greatly, but I must be mum,
> For how could we do without sugar and rum?
> Especially sugar, so needful we see?
> What? give up our desserts, our coffee, and tea!

Blake's use of form and irony and his assertion of moral values
are much less conventional than Cowper's. First of all, Blake
writes from the Negro's point of view and makes no direct appeal
to the English public. But more important are the innocence and
compassion with which his little boy responds to his plight and
that of his civilized white "brother." As a child and primitive, he is
superior to his white brother, but not because of the favorite
eighteenth-century myth of the "noble savage" nor because
Blake's humanitarianism dictates that he should be, but because
suffering has taught him compassion, and the abjectness of his
state has ground into him a sense of his personal unworthiness.
The sweetness and purity of the boy's voice as it speaks through
ballad stanza and the profundity of Blake's irony and moral make
Cowper's conventionalism seem hollow and trivial.

But, if the distinction between Cowper and the Romantics
seems clear in this case, it is not so in others. The author of "Lines
Written During a Period of Insanity," which is as close to "spontaneous overflow of powerful feelings" as poetry ever comes, seems
remote to the cool satirist or polemicist on the slave issue, as does
the poet who in "The Castaway" projects his own feeling of aban-
donment into the story of a drowning sailor.

The essential quality which distinguishes Cowper's lyrics and
satires can be defined by such words as "gentleness," "modesty,"
and "restraint." Such terms as "restraint" remind us of the Augustan manner of viewing a subject with the irony and detachment
necessary to gain proper perspective, or to put the subject in its
place. Yet in Cowper's best poems personality counts as heavily as
wit. In "Epitaph on a Hare," for example, satire of Tiny's pre-
tences gives way to poignant revelation of the poet's gentle and
humane personality. This same impulse to turn away from satire
to personal revelation can also be detected in *The Task*, and we
suspect that the tendency to moralize in that poem has the same

origin. Certainly the major defects of *The Task*, prolixity and lack of point, can be laid to the fact that satire inhibited Cowper's sensibility. The best parts of *The Task* and the best short poems are those in which his personality can find fuller expression.

Cowper's best poems are not those like "Boadicea" or "On the Loss of the Royal George" which gained immediate fame because they appealed to popular sentiment or because they serve as fine pieces for declamation. Nor are they those which show the effect of the vogue for sentimentalism, as "On the Receipt of My Mother's Picture from Norfolk." They are, to use the division into Romantic and Neo-Classical with which I began this chapter, those which capture in a new and unforgettable way the peculiarities of the poet's psychological condition and those in which comic reserve interacts with personality to freshen literary convention while providing a glimpse of the poet and his life, as "Epitaph on a Hare" and "On the Death of Mrs. Throckmorton's Bulfinch." One way of isolating these peculiar excellences for examination is to look at some poems in which he did not completely succeed.

"On the Loss of the Royal George" was inspired by a calamity which occurred in 1782. We must assume that Cowper's humanitarian and patriotic feelings were aroused as deeply as anyone's by the event; but, as is so often true of poets writing on occasions of state, particularly the laureates, great distress did not result in great poetry. It must be admitted that Cowper labored under restrictions arbitrarily placed upon him: Lady Austen had wanted words to the march in *Scipio*. It seems clear, however, that not the form but the subject matter raised the greatest difficulties. Indeed, the best lines in the poem, those with which it begins, gain their majestic tolling quality and their sense of finality because of the form to which Cowper had to set his words. Cowper seems not to have been able to conceive of his subject matter except in terms of trivialities and moral clichés. Instead of memorializing "the brave that are no more," as he resolves in the first stanza, he records details of the accident, none of which justify his declamatory style. How can the information that "Eight hundred of the brave/ Whose courage well was tried,/ Had made the vessel heel" be arranged in the traditional rhetorical patterns of parallelism, repetition, and climax? The following stanza illustrates Cowper's predicament:

It was not in the battle,
No tempest gave them shock,
She sprang no fatal leak,
She ran upon no rock;
His sword was in the sheath,
His fingers held the pen,
When Kampenfelt went down
With twice four hundred men.

After this stanza the poem goes down under a mass of clichés and commonplaces and the wholly irrelevant promise that the boat will be raised to "float again,/Full charg'd with England's thunder,/And plough the distant main." After this impressive assurance it seems hardly proper that we should be reminded that Kampenfelt "is gone" and the eight hundred crewmen "must plough the wave no more."

If "On the Loss of the Royal George" were unique in its failure to achieve pathos, we might blame an unfortunate rhetoric, one more suitable for other occasions, and turn our attention to other matters. But to do so would be to ignore the fact that Cowper is not much more fortunate in many other poems for which he is still remembered. Not only the poems of state or of patriotic sentiment but such personal lyrics as "The Poplar-Field" exhibit a falling away from emotional intensity and eloquent expression. The first stanza of "The Poplar-Field" is unforgettable for the way sound and meter evoke a scene and set a mood:

The poplars are fell'd, farewell to the shade
And the whispering sound of the cool colonnade,
The winds play no longer, and sing in the leaves,
Nor Ouse on his bosom their image receives

Rhythm, sound patterns, and images in succeeding stanzas do not live up to the expectations created by the first four lines. If sound beautifully supports sense in the first stanza, the singsong of the rest of the poem seems appropriate to its clichés, platitudes, and trite sentimentalities:

My fugitive years are all hasting away,
And I must ere long lie as lowly as they,
With a turf on my breast, and a stone at my head,

Ere another such grove shall arise in its stead.
'Tis a sight to engage me, if anything can,
To muse on the perishing pleasures of man;
Though his life be a dream, his enjoyments, I see,
Have a being less durable even than he.

"On the Receipt of My Mother's Picture out of Norfolk," another of Cowper's well-known lyrics, presents the same problem. The poet suggests an interesting theme, the timelessness of art: "Blest be the art that can immortalize,/The art that baffles time's tyrannic claim/To quench it . . . ." He next introduces the paradox that art renews grief while solacing it, but nothing is made of either idea. The structure of the poem, a loosely connected and fanciful excursion through his memories, in a way gives form to the basic ideas. Art achieves its timelessness in its ability to inspire the poet's thought; the memories cause grief but offer respite from other kinds of misery. But the repose which the poet gains by thinking of his mother's goodness is poorly founded on the most trivial sentiments and hackneyed images:

> Thou, as a gallant bark from Albion's coast
> (The storms all weather'd and the ocean cross'd)
> Shoots into port at some well-haven'd isle
> Where spices breathe and brighter seasons smile . . .
> And thy lov'd consort on the dang'rous tide
> Of life, long since, has anchor'd at thy side.

It may be that one of the reasons for the insufficiency of the poem is that, to use Cowper's own image, it describes a love that never rises above a "constant flow" and knows no "cataracts and brakes." As a result, the attempts at pathos seems excessive; and when Cowper, striving for greater poignancy on which to found his eloquence, introduces the theme that love can be selfish and cruel, he can do so only in the most bathetic way:

> Could those few pleasant hours again appear,
> Might one wish bring them, would I wish them here?
> I would not trust my heart,—the dear delight
> Seems so to be desir'd, perhaps I might—
> But no—what here we call our life is such,
> So little to be lov'd and thou so much,

That I should ill requite thee to constrain
Thy unbound spirit into bonds again.

Those who particularly admire this poem usually rely on an argument familiar to readers of *The Task*: it is moving because of
its autobiographical content. According to this line of thought,
when we remember the effect on the poet of the loss of his
mother, we are more willing to accept a certain lack of control
and to abandon ourselves to the intensity of feeling which obviously lies behind the poem. Of course, such arguments only turn
our attention from what is inartistic; they do not justify the poem
as art.

Like "On the Receipt of My Mother's Picture," the second poem
"To Mary" is little more than bald statement of fact and feeling.
What ostensibly is a poem to Mrs. Unwin becomes unsuitable as
an address to her because it reflects on the most unpleasant aspects of her illness and on the wasting away of qualities that formerly distinguished her. When Cowper does turn to the more appropriate theme of the abiding nature of his love, he does so in a
way characteristic of the rest of the poem. His assurance that she
remains the sustaining force in his life merely accentuates the
burden that has been forced upon her and which she can no
longer carry.

It can be observed in these poems that strong feeling often stul-
tified Cowper's imagination. Instead of giving new and interesting
form to statement, his emotions turned him down the easy path of
moralism, of platitude, and of sentimental cliché. In satiric poetry,
which presents a different kind of challenge, Cowper was more
often successful. Satire did not force him to confront his own
deepest and darkest feelings but focused his attention outward on
the world around him. Hence, though it may at first seem damn-
ing to admit that poetry for Cowper was a mental exercise and a
kind of therapy, ultimately such nonartistic motives, by detaching
him from his materials and allowing his wit and fancy to play
more fully and easily, account for his success.

The danger that inheres in poetry shaped by a need for relief
from anxiety is that it will be merely facetious or clever. Admittedly, many of Cowper's burlesque poems fall in this category.
The "Ode to Apollo" and "The Colubriad" are examples picked at
random. Yet while noting this tendency, we must remember that

comic masterpieces like "Epitaph on a Hare" and "On the Death of Mrs. Throckmorton's Bulfinch" have the same source. As I have pointed out in the previous chapter, Cowper's satire was always relaxed and gentle; he was incapable of the kinds of intensity that are variously revealed in the satiric works of Pope, Swift, Fielding, and Sterne. Cowper did have wit, a sense of humor, and generous impulses. He apparently had no desire to take upon himself the responsibilities of a gadfly; consequently, his satire touches in only a glancing manner on serious problems and seldom gives pain.

If Cowper's best satire did not spring from indignation, an aroused moral sense, or hatred of human folly and was not inspired by occasions of great moment nor of universal significance, it still made an original contribution and breathed vitality into the genre. His contribution consists of a peculiar interaction of personality with forms that had been in use since classical times. Unlike the Augustans who vented their indignation on follies in which they did not participate, Cowper involves himself in the absurdities which he ridicules. There is no persona, no Gulliver, Scriblerus, Cibber, Theobald, nor "Modest Proposer" to stand between author and subject and to present a point of view which, through its imperfections, implies the values of the author. In the satire of Swift and Pope, folly is usually distributed evenly between the subject and speaker (for example, between the Irish in "A Modest Proposal" and the scientist who would solve their problem); through understanding the defects in both, and in particular the incompetence with which the persona handles his subject, we arrive at the author's point of view.

When Cowper uses the first person in satire, it is not to trick the reader into accepting a point of view which he must ultimately reject. As in *The Task*, the "I" conveys the poet's own attitudes. Moreover, even when he uses the third person, Cowper finds a way to involve himself in the poem. Either he shares in the follies satirized, as in "Epitaph on a Hare," or in some other way manages to make the reader conscious of the role his feelings play in a particular situation.

"Vice" and "ridicule," the two words most frequently used to describe the object and intent of satire, are too harsh to be employed in a discussion of Cowper's short poems. Since the follies against which the poet directs his wit rarely are of great importance, the prevailing attitude of the satire must necessarily be mild and humorous, not slashing and acerbic. Yet this lack of seriousness does not seem to justify the charge that the satire is trivial. As a group, Cowper's witty poems leave the same impression as Pope's classic mock heroic, "The Rape of the Lock": that, among people in an advanced state of civilization, problems often seem more serious than they really are. Moreover, Cowper seems to imply that undeniably serious problems demand a generous or pathetic response instead of invective. Harsher satire belongs in a more heroic environment, where vice or folly are of greater moment; and it presupposes a more heroic temperament, one that is rigid, unbending, filled with a sense of its own dignity and lacking in charity. If Cowper's subject matter is usually domestic, perhaps the reason is that domestic matters are closer to the center of civilized life.

The world of Cowper's satire, then, is enclosed by its domestic concerns. Within its narrow dimensions, it reflects in a diminished way larger concerns, but always with the assumption that, for most people, the world is a fairly tight and secure place. The frame of mind which results is one skeptical of pretenses, yet able to see value in details of life beneath the attention of "greater" men. Unable to conceive of the truly heroic or tragic, this mind feels at ease in the ordinary or pathetic. Here lies another difference between Pope's mock heroic and Cowper's.

In "The Rape of the Lock," the beauty of Belinda's world can be seen behind its absurdity; and, in "The Dunciad," true literary values can be perceived behind the falseness and pretentiousness of Cibber. By contrast, a poem like "On the Death of Mrs. Throckmorton's Bulfinch" does not use Classical myth to symbolize a better world than the present. Behind the absurdity of Mrs. Throckmorton's behavior lie no serious allusions to a more noble pattern of behavior in the past. Instead of exhorting Maria to greater heroism, Cowper does no more than offer her his compassion. His generous, compassionate nature shapes the world of the poem, not the Greek and Roman values against which Pope's mock heroics are projected. Hence it can be seen that Cowper's personality becomes an important aspect of the form of his poem, for it serves as the framework in which the values, and even the structure, of the poem develop.

"On the Death of Mrs. Throckmorton's Bulfinch" makes use of

parody in a two-handed manner. It attacks Mrs. Throckmorton's sentimentalism, and it makes fun of the usual rhetoric of elegiac poetry. In describing the birthplace of the finch, it recalls the traditional reliance of the elegy on mythical allusion: "Where Rhenus strays his vines among,/The egg was laid from which he sprung. . . ." The use of Classical analogy to elevate the dignity of the subject is parodied in the comparison of the bird's beak (all that was left after Bully had been eaten by a rat) to the head of Orpheus:

> Maria weeps—The Muses mourn—
> So, when by Bacchanalians torn,
>   On Thracian Hebrus' side
> The tree-enchanter Orpheus fell;
> His head alone remained to tell
>   The cruel death he died.

Following convention, Cowper calls upon the nymphs to bewail the loss of the finch, invokes the muses, and personifies nature.

The use of Classical machinery seems to be justified when the subject of a poem is the cruelty of nature to a Damon or a Lycidas, a Clough or a Hallam, or when a poem pays tribute to ordinary men in general, as in Gray's "Elegy." But to commemorate a bird in this way is another matter. Like the metamorphosis of an inkdrop into a part of the rainbow in the "Ode to Apollo," allusion does not seem to be warranted by intensity of emotion. Maria is seen to be guilty of misplacing values, and at the same time literary conventions are given a ludicrous turn.

As a mock elegy, Cowper's poem portrays not the spacious world of the heroic but the much diminished one of the eighteenth-century gentleman's household. As the poem proceeds, its focus steadily narrows from the world to the household, to the study, to the cage in which Bully suffered. Dawn, instead of splendidly coloring the sky, is reflected in the dimensions of a finch's bosom; and the piping winds of early morning are reduced to a bird's whistle, reminiscent of flageolet or flute:

> And though by nature mute,
> Or only with a whistle blest,
> Well-taught, he all the sounds express'd
>   Of flageolet or flute. . . .

His bosom of the hue
With which Aurora decks the skies,
When piping winds shall soon arise
To seep up all the dew.
(ll. 9–12, 15–18)

Small as it is, the domestic world in which the finch's destiny plays itself out faintly reflects the greater world of Classical tragedy. Bully is, the poem makes clear, the victim of the good intentions of those humans who control his environment. Trying to protect him from cats, they made him vulnerable to rats. In an attempt to protect his feathers, they smoothed the grate of his cage until it no longer could keep out his enemies. Had the Throckmortons been more willing to trust fortune, he probably would have died of old age (and been a somewhat less worthy subject for poetry).

So far, nothing has been said to indicate how Cowper's poem differs from a number of mock elegies (like Gray's "On the Death of a Favorite Cat"), all testifying to the enduring popularity of a form which had flourished in Classical Rome. Unlike most writers of mock elegy, Cowper is less interested in lamenting the dead than in commiserating with the living. Had Bully occupied the center of focus, undoubtedly Cowper would have treated him as Gray did Walpole's cat, the vain and fatuous Selima. Once Bully has been mocked, however, and once the poet has pointed out with tongue in cheek that fate, the Throckmortons, the rat, and, of course, Bully all share responsibility for the "tragedy" that has occurred, there remains the need to sympathize with the bereaved, even if Maria's loss is not as great as her grief would seem to make it. In choosing to make Maria and not the finch the true subject of his poem, Cowper brings into balance wit and feeling. As well as humorously chiding her—"ridiculing" would be too strong a word—he is performing an act of friendship.

If Cowper's poem can give pleasure to a larger audience than the one for whom it was originally intended, it is because of the skill with which he manages his role as critic and sympathizer, as mock elegiast and friend. While cleverly dissociating himself from the sentimentality that the situation demands of him, he must also hint delicately that Maria's distress has aroused his own feelings. Of the two tasks, the first is much the easier. To accomplish it, Cowper skillfully blends parody and bathos. The poem begins its steady progress toward anticlimax with the entrance of the rat, and reaches its high point when the cage is assaulted and when the poet bewails the finch's beak, all that remains after the attack:

> Just then, by adverse fate impressed,
> A dream disturbed poor Bully's rest;
>   In sleep he seemed to view
> A rat, fast-clinging to the cage,
> And, screaming at the sad presage,
>   Awoke and found it true.

> For, aided both by ear and scent
> Right to his mark the monster went—
>   Ah Muse! forbear to speak
> Minute the horrors that ensued;
> His teeth were strong, the cage was wood—
>   He left poor Bully's beak.

> He left it, but he should have ta'en
> That beak, whence issued many a strain
>   Of such mellifluous tone
> Might have repaid him well, I wote,
> For silencing so sweet a throat,
>   Fast set within his own.

The persona assumed by Cowper suits his basically comic purpose. Presumably like Maria herself, the writer of the poem becomes so strongly moved that he cannot utter what occurred during that pregnant pause between the assault and the retreat. Cowper's technique is not unlike that of Chaucer in the *Canterbury Tales,* who, by playing the role of pilgrim and drawing attention to his own absurdity, whether real or feigned, serves as a mirror of his audience. But, unlike other satirists, Cowper cannot allow his persona to become separated from his own character and personality. Only through demonstrating his affection can he achieve his purpose: to make her laugh at her folly. He must not laugh *at* her but *with* her.

The word "minute" in the above passage best describes the nature and scope of Bully's calamity. Hovering between adjective and adverb, it forbids the muse to describe the catastrophe in detail while hinting that the horrors implied were not of great proportion. With this double meaning, it might well have been used to describe another of Cowper's best satires, "Epitaph on a Hare," where the world of Tiney, the dead rabbit, has the dimensions of the poet's living room carpet. Here again pretense and presumption are the satirist's target. Tiney conceives of himself as an Oriental potentate. In his arrogance he learns to deny the existence of the natural enemies from which the poet protects him. He shows no gratitude for the protection which he seems to think is owed him.

Ostensibly the "epitaph" is closer to Gray's elegy on the death of Walpole's cat that is "On the Death of Mrs. Throckmorton's Bulfinch." The mood comes closer to ridicule; the folly of Tiney seems less capable of inspiring pathos. But the poem reflects Cowper's personality even more clearly than "On the Death of Mrs. Throckmorton's Bulfinch." Tiney's ingratitude causes gentle —and fond—amusement. When Cowper tells us that he kept the rabbit for "his humour's sake," two senses of the word "humour" are involved: it refers to the animal's malevolent disposition as well as to the enjoyment which the poet derived from that temperament. Tiney's antics turned Cowper's attention from thoughts that gave him pain. Hence, the surly hare is not seen in the context of moral, ethical values but in the context of the poet's psychological response.

As in the mock elegy on Mrs. Throckmorton's bullfinch, there is irony in the relationship between the author's personality, which frames the poem, and the situation described within. In the elegy, irony took the form of a contrast between Cowper's sentiment and Mrs. Throckmorton's sentimentality. In the epitaph, the contrast is between the poet's self-possession and the hare's. If Tiney was possessed by a sense of his own worth, however, the poet is too much involved in thoughts of a different cast. Cowper's introversion is as passive as Tiney's is savage and egocentric. The mock heroic nature of the poem helps to define both kinds of self-possession, reducing Tiney's arrogance to its proper size and revealing the mild and gentle personality of the poet. One of the most amusing aspects of the poem is the way the diction undercuts Tiney. His "lawn" is a carpet; his "juicy salads" are twigs and peels; sand is necessary to "scour his maw." In such a context Cowper's own sorrows cannot become the agonies of a romantic hero but must stay within the range of his timid, retiring nature.

To say that Cowper's main innovation is the way he injects his own feelings into mock heroic is to ignore his skill with the traditional resources of the form. Just as the absurdity of using the Orpheus myth to lionize a bullfinch has little to do with the poet's personality, so the violent contrast between the first and second stanzas of the "Epitaph" creates a kind of humor which betrays nothing of Cowper's feelings:

> Here lies, whom hound did ne'er pursue,
> Nor swifter greyhound follow,
> Whose foot ne'er tainted morning dew,
> Nor ear heard huntsman's hallo',
>
> Old Tiney, surliest of his kind,
> Who, nurs'd with tender care,
> And to domestic bounds confin'd,
> Was still a wild Jack-hare.

The description of Tiney is always lively and amusing, and the interplay between the tamed and untamed, the sentimental and unsentimental, show skill in managing form. Cowper has succeeded in the poem, as in the "Elegy," because he can distance himself from his feelings and make them part of the structure.

Unlike the "Elegy" and "Epitaph," "The Diverting History of John Gilpin" did not grow out of a situation in which Cowper had directly participated. Since the poet set out to write merely an amusing ballad founded on a story he had heard, the poem succeeds in a way different from the other two. Cowper's personality plays a less important role, and formal considerations a correspondingly more important one. Gilpin himself is a burlesque figure in the tradition of Chaucer's Sir Thopas. Both are anachronisms: solid middle-class men in a romantic world. The main difference, of course, is that Chaucer's humor is turned against himself, or at least against the persona he has adopted for *The Canterbury Tales*; for, as an egregious bourgeois, he pretends to be unable to tell a chivalric tale. Like Thopas, Gilpin epitomizes middle-class responsibility and respectability. He is a train-band captain (a soldier drawn from the populace to supplement the regular forces) and a hard-working linen dealer, whose relationships are confined to his family and business. He stands for such solid moral values as frugality, prudence, circumspection, and modesty. Living in a commercial area, he spends his time in mundane pursuits, the everyday details of "getting and spending." Even when enjoying his first day of vacation in twenty years of marriage, he must put business before pleasure, must be concerned with making the best use of his leisure, and must be careful not to let it appear that he is enjoying himself too much.

Cowper's narrator, like Chaucer's, is a man of mediocre social station. He speaks the language of the Gilpins and, as I have already pointed out, is overimpressed with their wit and prestige. He has difficulties making English syntax and pronunciation fit in the confines of ballad measure, and he resorts to clichés and line padding. Unfortunately, the cadence of his lines and the arrangement of words do not always emphasize the most important words and ideas:

> John Gilpin's spouse said to her dear—
>   Though wedded we have been
> These twice ten tedious years, yet we
>   No holiday have seen.
>
> To-morrow is our wedding-day,
>   And we will then repair
> Unto the Bell at Edmonton
>   All in a chaise and pair.
>
> My sister, and my sister's child,
>   Myself, and children three,
> Will fill the chaise; so you must ride
>   On horseback after we.
>
> He soon replied—I do admire
>   Of womankind but one,
> And you are she, my dearest dear,
>   Therefore it shall be done.

Sometimes the narrator runs out of ideas before the stanza is complete:

> So like an arrow swift he flew,
>   Shot by an archer strong;
> So did he fly—which brings me to
>   The middle of my song.

When it comes to diction and figures of speech, the narrator is almost always unfortunate. Early in the poem the "six precious souls" of Gilpin's family are "all agog/To dash through thick and thin"; then Gilpin proceeds on his adventure "with caution and good heed." The snorting beast next begins to trot and "gall'd him in the seat." There is some justification in the heroic tradition for Gilpin's "reeking" head, but certainly not for the flanks of the horse to smoke "as they had basted been"! A reference to the Wash at Edmonton "so gay" introduces a string of laundry images which also increases the hero's indignity.

To further discomfit Gilpin and the narrator, Cowper, as in "On the Death of Mrs. Throckmorton's Bulfinch," introduces variations in a stanza form which in this case seems naturally to rise to moments of highest tension in the second and fourth lines. The effect is resoundingly anticlimactic:

> John Gilpin at his horse's side
> Seiz'd fast the flowing mane,
> And up he got, in haste to ride,
> But soon came down again.

> What news? what news? your tidings tell;
> Tell me you must and shall—
> Say why bare-headed you are come,
> Or why you come at all?

Moreover, the language which casts Gilpin as a knight, "nimble steed," "snorting beast," "smoking flanks"; the omen that anticipates his downfall; the rumors of his heroic behavior—all are ridiculously inappropriate to his situation.

The success of "John Gilpin," then, is a triumph of form. Parody of ballad conventions blends perfectly with mock heroic. The galloping rhythms and the understatement of the ballad stanza sustain the tone of the poem and advance the characterization of both the narrator and Gilpin. Nevertheless, Cowper's personality lends a quality to his poem which separates it from other eighteenth-century satires. In the rollicking humor, so well conveyed by ballad rhythm, can be seen the poet's own good nature. His attitude is benevolent, and he joins with the speaker at the end to sing of the hero's exploits:

> Now let us sing—long live the king,
> And Gilpin long live he;
> And, when he next doth ride abroad,
> May I be there to see!

His good nature carries over into the characterization of Gilpin as a man who can accept his condition in "a merry guise":

> Now Gilpin had a pleasant wit,
> And lov'd a timely joke;
> And thus unto the calender
> In merry guise he spoke:—
>
> I came because your horse would come;
> And if I will forbode,
> My hat and wig will soon be here—
> They are upon the road.

From the title, which tells us that Gilpin (perhaps like Odysseus) "went farther than he intended, and came safe home again," rhythm and rhetoric maintain the buoyancy of the narrator's spirits and the author's humor.

It seems clear that Cowper usually had greater success with small subjects which allowed him sufficient detachment to give play to his imagination and to project his good nature into the structure of his poetry. Form itself became more complicated and more interesting in the work of lighter moments. Against the bombastic stanzas of "On the Loss of the Royal George," or the monotonous banalities of "The Poplar-Field," we might measure the more supple stanzas of "On the Death of Mrs. Throckmorton's Bulfinch." Pauses are varied, creating many different cadences and sentence rhythms.

A few of Cowper's best-known, most successful poems do not benefit from comic detachment; indeed, they seem to be exceptions to the generalization that powerful emotion tended to block his imagination. Foremost among these is "The Castaway," which, for intensity of feeling and control, stands out as Cowper's most impressive poem. As I have already pointed out, it is of biographical interest that Cowper wrote the poem at the end of his life. But biographical interest alone cannot make the poem succeed as art.

The success of "The Castaway" depends upon its ability to convey the poet's despair, loneliness, and exhaustion.

The tone of "The Castaway" can be most accurately defined by comparing the poem with "Lines Written During a Period of Insanity," composed in 1763. The violence of the earlier poem is spent by the time of the later. Despair has so exhausted the poet's spirit that he no longer conceives of his predicament in extravagant language like "hatred and vengeance/ . . . Wait, with impatient readiness to size my/Soul in a moment," "Damn'd below Judas: more abhorr'd than he was," or "*Him* the vindictive rod of angry justice/Sent quick and howling to the center headlong,/*I*, fed with judgment in a fleshly tomb, am/Buried above ground." In "The Castaway" his diction is subdued:

> No voice divine the storm allay'd.
> No light propitious shone;
> When snatch'd from all effectual aid,
> We perish'd, each alone:
> But I beneath a rougher sea,
> And whelm'd in deeper gulphs than he.

Moreover, the complicated six-line stanzas of "The Castaway" do not tumble forth as the tormented sapphics of the earlier "Lines." And the imagery of "The Castaway" does not have the striking originality of the imagery in the "Lines." In the 1763 poem, for example, the conventional image of the bolted door, used to signify the closing off of divine mercy, becomes the "bolted mouth" of Hell. This metaphor carries over into the last stanza where it helps to convey a sense of utter desolation, of being completely without hope yet totally unfulfilled; but it also climaxes the grand irony of Cowper's situation: his angry God, an embodiment of the cold outside world, was a projection of his personal sense of failure. The image is juxtaposed with the apocalyptic destruction of Abiram. Instead of being destroyed, and thus completed or fulfilled, Cowper is "fed with judgment" so that his burial in the flesh may continue. If the "Lines" reveals the poet's claustrophobia, "The Castaway" shows his sense of being abandoned in a world too large for him.

In "The Castaway" Cowper views the world with greater charity than in the "Lines"; for, although no one had been able to relieve his distress, some had had the courage to try. Formerly, he thought in terms of paradox: "living death" and "buried above ground." Now irony turns on the recognition that in everything lies a potential for good and evil: the wind which carries the sailor's voice to the ship also carries the ship away from him. It is no longer a demented universe in which the poet lives, but it nevertheless is one which has rejected him. Cowper gives us the impression that he accepts the popular eighteenth-century religious myth of a watchmaker God who sets creation in motion and then stands aside to let it operate. The poet himself, who has been caught among the cogs and wheels, knows only that the functioning of the whole seems to have little regard for his personal needs. His God is as remote as the Deistic God; but, with his basically Calvinistic overview, Cowper could not take solace in the Deistic belief that the mechanism of the material universe operates for the good of all.

If the watchmaker God comforted the Deist, allowing him to regard the world as a fairly efficient machine, for Cowper the remoteness implied that God had turned the machine against him, that he was damned. This almost paranoid feeling accounts for the difference between pathos in "The Castaway" and pathos in much of the rest of eighteenth-century poetry. In Cowper, feeling springs not from a general benevolence toward mankind or from social impulses but from a deep sense of personal involvement. He experiences intense emotion because he cannot separate himself from the predicament of the drowning sailor. Lacking detachment, he employs irony not to stress order through exposing incongruities and absurdities, as in comedy, but to emphasize disorder and lack of proportion, as in tragedy. Looking at the plight of the castaway, he discovers himself. Hence form becomes highly personal, representing a discovery on the part of the speaker (who is not a persona but the poet himself) of his own condition and expressing the feelings generated by his personal predicament.

In "The Castaway" Cowper shows that he has grasped, although unconsciously, the paradox stated by Wordsworth in the 1800 preface to Lyrical Ballads that poetry is both the spontaneous overflow of powerful feeling and feeling recollected in tranquility. We have only to compare "The Castaway" with "Verses Supposed to be Written by Alexander Selkirk" to see that he speaks from the heart instead of mouthing platitudes, but, at the same time, the poem is free of the maudlin sentimentality which spoils his other poems expressing deep feeling. Narrative seems to have provided the kind of detachment that he needed to ponder fully his own situation.

It is interesting, of course, that "The Castaway," one of Cowper's greatest and most Romantic poems, appeared so shortly after *Lyrical Ballads* and so close to the publication of the famous preface in which Wordsworth articulated his theory of poetry. However, there are no signs that Cowper was influenced by what history declares to be the major literary events of the time. "The Castaway" was not the product of a theory; it was solely a reflection of the poet's psychological state, and the only work of its kind that Cowper wrote. For a more "typical" performance we might turn to a poem like "Yardley Oak."

"Yardley Oak" is Romantic in the same way that certain passages of *The Task* are. It reveals a feeling for nature, not as seen in landscape or generality, but as observed in specific things. Just as Cowper, when writing of the country around Olney, did not present a composite picture, as was the standard practice, but fixed his attention on the actual scene before him, so he makes Yardley Oak not a generic tree but a particular one individualized by its decayed condition and capable of exciting in the poet's imagination certain feelings about his own life. Yet the poem is more ambitious than "The Castaway." Personal response is not enough; the poet must strive to balance his own feelings and particularized description with general truth.

"Yardley Oak" satisfies the Neo-Classical insistence on justness of sentiment, imagery, and ideas that spring naturally from the subject contemplated and accord with the cultural heritage. Because of the enormous size and age of the tree, it seems naturally to symbolize both a life longer than that which men can know and "mutability in all/That we account most durable below." As in most eighteenth-century nature poetry, it is not the tree but the truths about nature of which the tree reminds the poet that are the subject of the poem. Also in the Neo-Classical tradition are the moral reflections which the tree sets in motion. The impressive size of the oak draws forth a Calvinistic reflection on man's fallen nature, here symbolized by the Druid rite which the poet speculates had once been carried on under the protection of the tree.

Moreover, the tree reminds Cowper of the myth of Castor and Pollux, who also sprang from a "bauble," an "embryo vastness," and were eventually metamorphosed to stars. Also in keeping with tradition is the view of nature as both giver and taker, its act of giving the acorn life balanced by its slow destruction of the tree.

The theme of the vanity of human wishes, then, is coupled with close observation of the image as the central factor of the poem. Like many eighteenth-century predecessors, "Yardley Oak" presents a panoramic view of history to substantiate its theme. It is also characteristic of the century that the tree, as well as symbolizing the ravages of time, should cause the poet to dwell on the social implications of his subject; each link in the chain of being reflects the others:

> So stands a kingdom, whose foundations yet
> Fail not, in virtue and in wisdom laid,
> Though all the superstructure, by the tooth
> Pulveriz'd of venality, a shell
> Stands now, and semblance only of itself.

Yet there still remains the tendency to particularize which sets "Yardley Oak" off from Neo-Classical poetry and points in the direction of the Romantics. Not only has Cowper found in the oak a vehicle for personal or subjective statement, but the tree and the experience of seeing it are too vividly portrayed just to remind us of trees in general or of "natural" truths. Sentiments like those concerning the growth of the tree and the enormous potential of an acorn are conventional enough, but Cowper's vision of the tree as a "huge throat calling to the clouds for drink" evokes feelings beyond the scope of most social and moral poetry in the eighteenth-century. Likewise, the history of the tree, although providing an opportunity for moral reflection, seems to set the tree apart instead of identifying it with the grand scheme of things. Even in personifying the oak, Cowper seems to be giving a unique turn to convention; for the figure of speech seems to focus attention on the particular properties of Yardley Oak.

In setting the tree off as an individual, Cowper not only reflects a tendency apparent in Romanticism but also mirrors his practice in "The Castaway" of abandoning generalized statement for a

more particular revelation of his feelings. The feeling akin to idol-
atry which he feels on looking at the oak bears a clear relationship
to his own longing for security and stability, a "closer walk with
God." His personification of the tree makes it appear that in it he
has found a kindred spirit, another being shattered by experience.
This identification was made easier by the fact that the oak was
"survivor sole, and hardly such, of all/That once liv'd here thy
bretheren, at my birth." It is even possible that Cowper's reference to the worthlessness of the tree as lumber, despite the "sincerity" of its roots, has autobiographical meaning.

In "Yardley Oak" Cowper had the kind of subject matter to
which he could respond with eloquence. Like landscape in *The
Task*, the tree engaged his feelings at just the proper level. He
could avoid the sentimentality which attended stronger feeling;
but, at the same time, he could feel deeply enough about his
subject matter to rise above frigid generalization. Like "The Castaway," "Yardley Oak" exhibits Cowper's need for objective subject matter that would allow him to recollect strong feelings in
tranquility. Unable to confront his deepest feelings in a more
direct manner or to give them imaginative form, he had to seek
subjects external to himself with which he would feel a kindred
spirit. In his lyric as in his comic verse, control is, therefore, the
key to excellence.

CHAPTER 5

Hymns

BECAUSE a hymn is a public rather than a personal poem, the hymn writer must sublimate any spontaneous outburst in ideas and imagery which are close to the experience of the public. This requirement accounts for the fairly narrow resources of words and figures which Samuel Johnson in his "Life of Isaac Watts" noted as a characteristic of religious poetry. The hymn writer stays close to the modes of expression sanctioned by the Bible and by popular religious discourse; he cannot explore metaphysical complexities, and he must avoid rhetorical subtlety. Moreover, he can draw from personal experience only that which will not prove embarrassing, obscure, or unorthodox to a congregation. Early in the century Isaac Watts pointed out that even the Old Testament contained images and themes which were inappropriate to modern devotion:

When we are just entering into an evangelic frame, by some of the glories of the gospel presented in the brightest figures of judaism, yet the very next line perhaps which the clerk parcels out unto us, hath something in it so extremely jewish and cloudly, that it darkens our sight of God the Saviour. Thus by keeping too close to David in the house of God, the veil of Moses is thrown over our hearts. While we are kindling into divine love by the meditations of the *loving kindness of God,* and the *multitude* of his tender mercies: within a few verses, some dreadful curse against men is proposed to our lips; that *God would add iniquity unto their iniquity, nor let them come into his righteousness, but blot them out of the book of the living,* Psalm lxix 27, 28, which is so contrary to the new commandment of *loving our enemies;* and even under the Old Testament is best accounted for by referring it to the spirit of prophetic vengeance.[1]

Both Watts and Cowper chafed under the restrictions of the hymn, but they solved the problem in characteristically different ways. Watts, who was much less a poet, merely set aside all works which might be considered inappropriate and published them as religious lyrics. Cowper turned to other, more attractive subjects and forms. To both men the task of writing hymns seems to have become an annoying exercise instead of a means of releasing powerful feelings.

As an evangelical with Calvinist leanings, Cowper, like Watts and Charles Wesley, opposed Deistic tendencies found in such poems as Addison's "The Spacious Firmament On High" in which the poet, expanding on a verse from Psalm 19, "The Heavens Declare The Glory Of God," argued that the perfect mechanism of the universe proves the existence of God. Addison saw the universe as a perfectly orderly structure in which each part and each function could be reconciled to divine goodness and omniscience. Throughout the poem he emphasized through imagery, "spacious firmament," "unwearied sun," and rolling planets, the grandeur of the God, who is omnipotent, and His goodness, which should be evident to the rational observer.

Addison's central image of nature as messenger, which is authorized by the verb "declare" in Psalm 19, establishes a hierarchical relationship between God and man, with nature serving as intermediary. Man is to praise God and admire nature in a way which is analogous to that in which he expresses regard for a king whose machinery of government runs smoothly. Man, who has direct knowledge of God through reason and the senses, can see the marvelous order with which planets roll and night succeeds day. And he can perceive a correspondence between the various elements of Creation. If the planets roll in harmony, then their motion must in some ways resemble the harmony of speech or music. (Behind this notion lies the Platonic idea of the music of the spheres, which the verb "declare" also suggests to Addison.) If the universe functions, as Newtonian science tells us, in an orderly manner, the Creator must also embody order.

To an Enthusiast or an evangelical, the Addisonian view seemed too tidy, too much within the grasp of human reason to account for many of the aspects of experience with which religion must deal. The urbane couplets of "The Spacious Firmament" are supposed to proclaim the "great Original," as does the "shining frame" that they celebrate. Within their polished and balanced phraseology, they depict the contrasting extremes which compose the order and unity of nature: sun, moon; king, messenger; day, night; firmament, earth; reason, senses; physical, spiritual; God, man. As the figure "pole to pole" implies, these extremes, as well as distinguishing the various limits in the great chain of being from each other, reflect one another. The universe mirrors God, just as the moon mirrors the sun. Addison was not troubled by the metaphysical profundities which caused poets of an earlier period to build their poems around a rhetoric of paradox. That death should be life, and life death, or that freedom should exist only in accepting certain forms of bondage are notions which seem far removed from his poem, which rises not from distress or rapture but from a well-bred notion that man should realize his place in the universe and act accordingly. His way of defining this place is typically through comparison: man is not the firmament, not the Creator, not completely physical. He must realize the justice of his position and glorify the God who put him in it. It is not surprizing that Addison should have offered several of his Psalm paraphrases as a demonstration of the ease with which Hebrew idiom and rhetoric blend with the usual speech of an early eighteenth-century gentleman.

The world of Cowper's hymns differs from that of Addison's. In some ways Cowper's God resembles the Old Testament deity, who insists that no man may know Him or the working of His mind. According to Cowper, man can perceive only signs of the existence of God through His "footsteps," the ambiguous working of nature. God's "unfathomable," "mysterious" will is not to be judged by "feeble sense" nor discovered by scanning His work. Faith is necessary because "God is his own interpreter." It is to this God that the Christian must turn in times of distress and confusion. The comfort that he receives does not rest on rational deduction of the mercy of God from the order of nature:

> In vain by reason and by rule,
>   We try to bend the will;
> For none, but in the Saviour's school,
>   Can learn the heav'nly skill. . . .
>   .   .   .   .

If man will simply avoid trying to justify God or himself, if he will admit the limitations on his reason and trust in divine goodness, he will have the happiness that he seeks. The simple message of

Christianity emphasizes that, no matter how difficult man's problems, they could be worse. They cannot approach the sufferings of Christ or of the damned, and faith can make them vanish.

Both Addison's and Cowper's poems express contentment, and both derive that contentment from faith. But Addison's faith has its foundation in belief in the power of reason, encouraged by the Bible, to draw the proper inferences from nature; Cowper's faith rises directly from revealed truth. Something like this contrast exists in the old dispute over natural religion and Revelation, in which one side held that reason alone could bring man to God while the other averred that without the Bible no one could be saved. In Cowper's hymn the school in which man learns contentment is the "Saviour's school of grace," to which, of course, only the Elect can gain admission. Addison's school is a more open kind in which moral development leads to election.

In keeping with this difference, the Olney Hymns place much greater emphasis on biblical proofs or, to use Cowper's own figure, on tracing the footsteps of the Lord. When Cowper expresses confidence, he does so not on the basis of his experience nor because he perceives an analogy between the order of nature and divine goodness, but because the New Testament offers sufficient examples of the mercy of God. In "Jehova-Jesus" (Hymn 25), he firmly bases his notion of God as "without beginning or decline" on faith, not sense. He begins by insisting on his right, authorized by the Bible, to give the name of "Saviour" to "the great Supreme, the mighty God"; and then he shows that this right is consistent with the conception of Jesus as God/man. If Genesis tends to overemphasize the "supreme" and "mighty," the New Testament assures us that the same God in his mercy could become man in order to pity human distress. Even the name *Emmanuel*, "God with us," assures us of divine protection. Nevertheless, there is a sense of the enormous condescension of God in the wonderment with which Cowper asserts his right to pronounce the name of Saviour.

Religious zeal follows from consideration of the signs of divine favor in the Bible. Confidence leads to joy, which in turn creates zeal. But confidence is not based on an intuition of divine immanence in the world. Cowper's footsteps image, which has approximately the same meaning as St. Paul's "now we see through a glass darkly, but then face to face," indicates that nature manifests

God but does not embody Him. Storms and movements of the sea might indicate the way in which divine Will operates, but they conceal its motives or darken its light. Even the Old Testament reveals only darkly the will of God. Paschal sacrifices, scapegoats, images of lambs and doves, although they foreshadow Christ, do not reveal His merciful, compassionate nature.

Cowper's imagery hints that an awesome gulf exists between man and God. This gulf was broadened by his conviction that philosophical enquiry or study of the natural universe was futile and deceptive. Only through a spontaneous act of faith and profession of hope can man achieve communion with God. Those who lack the grace necessary to faith must find it impossible to penetrate the "veil," to know God and repose confidently in divine mercy. Calvinistic beliefs like this one led to rapturous celebration of grace. As I have shown in the first chapter, "A Song Of Mercy And Judgment" (1764) reveals the extent to which Cowper, recovering from insanity, considered spiritual revival a basic requirement of religious experience. In its refrains the poem emphasizes the joy which must accompany faith in one's election: "Grace Divine, how sweet the sound,/Sweet the grace that I have found." The refrains demonstrate Cowper's inability because of religious excitement to do much more than pronounce the words "grace" and "sweet." His constant returning to them has somewhat the same hypnotic, incantatory effect as the repetition in Christopher Smart's "*Jubilate Agno.*"

Springing from the peculiar nature of the evangelical religious experience, "A Song Of Mercy And Judgment" shows that once the spirit has been revived, its rapture, to use a figure from *The Task*, gilds the universe. As a converted sinner, the poet can recognize the "cheerful" nature of morning sunlight; he can discuss his insanity as if it were only a bad dream; bathed in the light of day, he can forget the gloom that enveloped him the night before. Cowper's rapture should not be seen, therefore, as an outgrowth of his mental instability so much as a rather violent extension of the usual form which evangelicalism takes. If his former state appeared dark, it was not hopeless; for his profound "dismay" reveals a sensibility which is a precondition to revival. As well as providing autobiographical insights, the description of his insanity in "A Song" also serves as a metaphor of the state of the graceless. Without grace he can take no pleasure in "the cheerful beams of morning." Physically "bound and watched" in the asylum, he recalls the state of the damned.

The picture of the poet physically bound and wasting away in body symbolizes the doctrines that only the truth can free and that freedom strikes the passions abruptly and apocalyptically. Needless to say, truth is not perceived through rational process or even through devoted reading of the Bible: "Visionary scenes and voices,/Flames of Hell and screams of woe" only increased his misery until "Grace Divine" manifested itself in a complete overturn of feeling and outlook. Transitions from verse to refrain and repetition in "A Song" indicate that the poem itself, in its violent changes and ecstatic formulations, rejects the usual ideas of form and substitutes for them a more subjective order based on the structure of personal experience.

In Cowper's religious poems and hymns the state of grace is seen as a salvation in itself from a personal Hell. The poet, "bound and watch'd," strikingly resembles the figure often used in parables of the evil man bound and cast into the outer darkness. In "The Valley Of The Shadow Of Death" the experience of the unsaved is portrayed with terrifying clarity:

> My soul is sad and much dismay'd;
> See, Lord, what legions of my foes,
> With fierce Apollyon at their head,
> My heav'nly pilgrimage opposed!
>
> See, from the ever-burning lake
> How like a smoky cloud they rise!
> With horrid blasts my soul they shake,
> With storms of blasphemies and lies.
>
> Their fiery arrows reach the mark,
> My throbbing heart with anguish tear;
> Each lights upon a kindred spark,
> And finds abundant fuel there.

We may contrast this portrayal with Addison's restrained, deliberately pallid and considerably more general treatment of the same Psalm:

> Though in the paths of death I tread,
> With gloomy horrors overspread,
> My steadfast heart shall fear no ill. . . .

Cowper's hymns probe a range of experience and psychological intensity which Addison shunned because of religious beliefs and disposition.

Inevitably a religious experience which contains at its center a great emotional upheaval cannot endure in its early state. In the *Olney Hymns* the falling away from enthusiasm is recorded in a characteristically personal way. There is, for example, the longing of the first hymn, "Walking With God."

> Oh! for a closer walk with GOD,
> A calm and heav'nly frame;
> A light to shine upon the road
> That leads me to the Lamb!
>
> Where is the blessedness I knew
> When first I saw the LORD?
> Where is the soul-refreshing view
> Of JESUS, and his word?
>
> What peaceful hours I once enjoy'd!
> How sweet their mem'ry still!
> But they have left an aching void,
> The world can never fill.
>
> (I, iii) [2]

Just as visions of Hell served as a background for a sensibility of grace, so loss of serenity and intimacy lies behind the renewal of despair and fear. The hymn is almost entirely lacking in theological and moral content, so devoted is it to describing the feelings (calm, peace, sweetness, rest), the disappearance of which has left an "aching void."

Cowper most often uses light imagery to convey his notion of the state of the blessed. In "The Light And Glory Of The Word," "light" expresses the ability of precepts and promises to sanctify, but in this case the words have much more than the conventional meaning of truth, which is derived ultimately from the Gospel of St. John. In the words of the hymn, "a glory gilds the sacred page,/Majestic like the sun"; the divine word has the ability to fill the blessed with emotional gratification as well as moral and ethical truth.[3] For this gratification the evangelical should give thanks, for "it makes a world of darkness shine/With beams of

heav'nly day." But, if the "bright display," which banishes the
fears and apparitions of night inspires the Christian with confi-
dent joy, it is but a flickering beam compared to the full glory that
will break upon the view "in brighter worlds above." Ecstasy is a
central part of Cowper's religious experience and, therefore, of his
hymns.

In another hymn, "The Shining Light," the "beam of day"
stands for faith, hope, truth, and joy, none of which can exist
without the others.[4] Cowper makes clear that he has imitated the
sixth verse of Psalm 130—"My soul waiteth for the Lord,/More
than they that watch for the morning:/I say, more than they that
watch for the morning"—but, unlike the psalm, the hymn makes a
deeply personal thing of the image. The beam "shines for me,/To
save me from despair." In the last stanza light imagery merges
with St. Paul's metaphor of the foot race. The beam is the goal
toward which the Christian runs.

As the title of "Light Shining Out Of Darkness" suggests, the
metaphor that lies behind that hymn is sunshine breaking through
clouds.[5] It reveals itself by implied analogy in lines like "Behind a
frowning providence./He hides a smiling face." The "footsteps"
which God plants on earth possess two kinds of darkness. Storms
and the turbulence of the sea, for example, illustrate the harshness
with which a "frowning providence" manifests itself. But, at the
same time, the difficulty of understanding the motives of providence makes them dark in a different sense. Cowper's vivid apprehension of the harshness and inscrutability of divine justice
turns his conventional language into a vigorously imaginative medium. Metaphors inherent in words like "mysterious," "unfathomable," "bright," "blind," and "plain" become vital when, together,
they establish a pattern of meaning which itself is in conjunction
with the central image of sun and clouds.

It is not, of course, unusual for writers to speak of providence as
"mysterious," "unfathomable" or "smiling." But these adjectives in
Cowper's hymn manage to convey a feeling of the enormity, the
remoteness, and the glory of God, which is opposed to man's
"feeble sense." If the "bright designs" escape our understanding,
they do so because we cannot comprehend the unfathomable. But,
if the unfathomable manifests the gulf between man and God, it
also gives hope that what infinitely surpasses "feeble sense" will
ultimately transcend human notions of justice. The great mistake

is to assume that, because the sun is concealed by clouds, it doesn't exist.

The idea of the hymn is enveloped in an irony which rises from ambiguities in the title. "Light shining out of darkness," besides being the sun shining through clouds, suggests that light comes from the darkness itself. To the believer, one kind of darkness— the "unfathomable" nature of Providence—turns the other kind, misfortune, into proof of the necessity for man to seek something beyond the covering of clouds. Misfortune becomes light when it results in *contemptus mundi*. We are reminded, therefore, of the letters Cowper wrote following his first attack of insanity in which he regarded his sufferings in just this way.

Clearly, then, Cowper realized the imaginative possibilities in his vision of the universe, and he could give form to them while employing a conventional language suitable to hymn. But the subtlety of "Light Shining Out Of Darkness" is less characteristic of the hymns than the strongly personal qualities hinted at in the consistent preoccupation with light and dark. In autobiographical hymns like "Walking With God," "The Shining Light," and "The Valley Of The Shadow Of Death," imagery succeeds in demonstrating the intensely passionate nature of Cowper's religious experience.[6] "Darkness" means more than divine wrath or incomprehensibility; it also signifies the Hellish legions rising in a smoky cloud to lay siege to his heart and turn it into a battleground; the "storms of blasphemies and lies" which give form to the spiritual battle that convulses him; and, most horrible of all, the fiery arrows that tear his heart and, instead of destroying it, create even greater ability to suffer. "Light," by contrast, indicates the intense joy that bursts upon the individual when he is praying or singing a hymn: "Sometimes a light surprizes/The Christian while he sings." It also suggests the cheerfulness of day driving away the "shades" or fears of night, or the calmness and serenity which he possessed at times, but which seemed a Paradise lost to him during much of his adult life.

Was the darkness inside or outside of him? The evangelical answer to this question goes to the heart of Cowper's revelations of self in the hymns and, it will be recalled, in *The Task*. The light shining in the darkness to which the poet runs and which draws him toward an apocalyptic communion with God here and in the afterlife enkindles a light within that projects itself upon his environment. To the saint, divine words are gilded with glory because the light of faith is projected upon them. When in "The Light And Glory Of The Word" Cowper says that "the Spirit breathes upon the word,/And brings the truth to sight," he means that, through grace or the spirit of God in him, he has the ability to see the truth in Biblical precepts and promises.[7] When he loses the feeling of divine presence, he can no longer project light upon his environment and upon the divine word. His heart becomes the valley of the shadow of death, an internal Hell projecting its gloom upon the world. Whatever he does strikes him as being polluted; he has no confidence in his own goodness, nor does he any longer feel that God intends him to be saved.

For Cowper the chief sign of this loss of communion with God was the existence of turmoil instead of rapture. In "Jehovah Our Righteousness" this loss appears in the form of a split in the unity of faith/hope, grace/desire, spirit/body, God/self.[8] When in the state of darkness the poet would "speak what thou hast done/ To save me from sin," he could not whole-heartedly attribute all to divine grace: "I cannot make thy mercies known/But self applause creeps in." Desire, colored by fleshly needs and by selfishness, becomes impatience. The heart only feels personal anxieties and longs for earthly attractions.

Acts of faith, hope, and love are necessary to revive the spirit; but it is characteristic of Cowper's theology that these can come about not through personal effort but through grace. If the solution to the problems stated in "Jehovah Our Righteousness" consists, as the last stanza indicates, of trusting in God and in refusing to justify the self, this solution lies outside the grasp of all but the "saved." One must have faith, but faith is a gift and is not self-created.

Faith, as Cowper describes it in his hymns, descends from his Calvinistic belief in the division of humanity into elect and damned. In *The Task* this dichotomy influenced his motives for writing, his imagery, and his conception of nature. In the hymns it is inextricably involved with the light-dark imagery and with the themes of unity/disunity and communion/separation. In "Praise For The Fountain Opened," it is faith that allows him to see the blood drawn from Emmanuel's veins, and dictates that the name Emmanuel, "God with us," should be the metaphorical and actual source of his praise. But, in terms of poetic practice, the most significant outgrowth of his notion of faith is his unblushing use of imagery and expressions that seem indecorous to the non-Enthusiast. A good example is the "fountain fill'd with blood/ Drawn from Emmanuel's veins" where "sinners, plung'd beneath that flood,/Lose all their guilty stains." Or, in "Welcome To The Table," the feast metaphor is incongruously applied to Holy Communion: in phrases like "royal dainties" and "costlier treat." [9] In "Jesus Hasting To Suffer" the crucifixion almost becomes an act of masochism;[10] Jesus "longs to be baptiz'd with blood" and "pants to reach the cross."

Such extravagant outbursts hint at a deeper psychological unrest than hymns might be expected to reveal. The fountain filled with blood in one sense is no more than a metaphorical expression of the Christian paradox that death is life and life, death; and baptism of blood is an orthodox enough notion, but the longing for this kind of baptism and the emotional implications of the fountain metaphor bespeak the burning zeal of a Crashaw or the erotic preaching of Swift's Aeolists. It was not unusual for evangelicals to express themselves in rather violent language, but even then Cowper's hymns often seem to reach out of the evangelical context to a more personal reality. Lingering in the fountain image is the imprint of a mind that considered itself "a fountain of vile thoughts" and sought death in preference to the agony of being "buried above ground," a mind that considered the anguish of Hell more bearable than the terror of uncertainty. This mind conceives religious experience in terms of violent, destructive joy and is tormented at times by its lack of security and by fantasies growing out of its fears and its lack of fulfillment. In "Jehovah Our Righteousness," Cowper describes himself as a spring of polluted water. If Jesus pours out his merits in a fountain filled with blood, Cowper reveals his sinfulness in one overflowing with filth. Gushing to the surface is self, which floats like a scum. The polluted heart is opposed to the fountain of blood, which cleanses or baptizes. Clearly, the idea of Christ's sacrifice had a greater emotional significance for Cowper than it had for the less Enthusiastic and for most people in the twentieth century. When reading "Praise For The Fountain Opened," we suddenly feel that Cowper was in some ways closer to the Old Testament tradition of sacrifice and scapegoat than to us.

Because of the violence of such images, the conclusions of many

hymns seem anticlimactic and superficial. They may bring an end
to the hymn, but they fail to lay to rest all of the feelings excited
during its course. The excessiveness of "Jesus Hasting To Suffer,"
for example, seems to have no bearing on the message of the
hymn:

> And while thy bleeding glories here
> Engage our wond'ring eyes;
> We learn our lighter cross to bear,
> And hasten to the skies.

Having offered a glimpse of his private world, Cowper submerges
it beneath conventional, often banal expressions.

Many Enthusiast divines in the eighteenth century wrote
hymns to revive in their congregations a religious sensibility.
Their efforts were based upon the idea that the passions are, as
Isaac Watts put it, "the most effective allurements or spurs to duty
in this present animal state." Without the passions to fix in the
mind and give vitality to the ideas received by reason, religion
would, they thought, vanish quickly and be lost in darkness.
Watts wrote: "Notions of religion in the understanding, without
any touch upon the passions, have been compared to the stars in a
winter midnight, bright and shining but ever cold; or rather to the
meteor which is called a shooting-star, which vanishes quickly,
and is lost in darkness." [11]

Watts's argument is interesting for two reasons. Its imagery
demonstrates the universal emotional appeal of dark/light imagery to the religious; at the same time, it distinguishes between
religious truth and passion. The "motions of religion in the understanding" are the light in the darkness, but they can have little
efficacy without the warmth of passion. Although man may be
convinced through reason of the justice of God, he must "feel" or
experience this conviction through the emotions. And without a
strong emotional impression reason might prove capricious: it will
either turn away from its convictions, or it will fail to serve as a
strong and enduring motive.

Cowper agreed with Watts on the need to engage the passions,
but to Cowper this necessity lay at the very center of his religious
experience. Faith itself has emotional qualities; it comes to the
"convert" in a rush of joy and is intuitive rather than rational.

Hope follows in feelings of contentment, peace, serenity, and childlike confidence, as the image of a "closer walk with God" implies.

Perhaps I can make the distinction clearer by comparing a few of Watts's hymns with Cowper's. Watts's "God Invisible" has the same basic concern as "Light Shining Out Of Darkness"; both talk about the incomprehensibility of God. Like Cowper's hymn, Watts's is ultimately based on the Biblical notion that man, because of his fleshly nature, cannot conceive of God. Unlike the gentiles, who worshipped gods in the form of animals or of men, the Chosen People worshipped a deity who refused them permission even to make graven images of him. In "Light Shining Out Of Darkness" this idea results in a dichotomy between "feeble" sense, "blind" unbelief, "mysterious" ways, and "unfathomable" mines. In "God Invisible" the dichotomy is between "blind" and "bright," between man's inability to "glance a thought half way to God" and the infinite distance beyond the sky where "the Great Eternal reigns alone." Both Watts and Cowper use paradox to express the way in which Providence is felt on earth. In Watts's hymn God creates "substantial beams," evidence which, while obscuring the nature of deity, do reveal the existence of God. Cowper approximates this with his footsteps image, and immaterial sign of the existence of God, and with the paradox of light shining from darkness. Both Watts and Cowper play upon abstract and metaphorical levels in words to express dualism. "God Invisible" uses "blind," "mortals," "behold," "beyond," "glance" to describe both physical and spiritual acts. In "Light Shining Out Of Darkness" the list is somewhat longer: "light," "dark," "unfathomable," "bright," "feeble," "smiling," "frowning," "blind," "clouds," "providence."

But the interplay between abstraction and metaphor has different purposes in each hymn. In "Light Shining Out Of Darkness" it reveals the emotional state of the blessed, but also indicates the dichotomy between spirit and flesh, God and man. It also projects many of the internal tensions which informed Cowper's religious experience. Watts's hymn, simpler and less profound psychologically and emotionally, has, however, more wit. Rhetoric emphasizes the inability of the physical to comprehend the invisible in such phrases as "where neither Wings nor Souls can fly" and "Beyond our Praise thy Grandeur flies." Together these phrases create an image of the soul engaged, with adoration and love, in hot but futile pursuit of divine grandeur. The "Substantial Beams of gloomy Night" which the Lord "lays beneath his sacred Feet" embrace both the physical and spiritual. In one sense they are floor beams separating the insufferably bright throne room from the world. In another, they are "darkness visible," emanations in the form but not the nature of light. Unlike beams of sunlight, a conventional image for expressing the glory of God, these are "substantial," the dark, material form in which Providence often makes itself felt.

In "The Vanity Of Creatures" one of Watts's major concerns is again to develop ironic patterns of images instead of using them to project his own feelings: man's "vast desires" are ironically opposed to his vanity. Other ironies exist in man's attempt to find some "solid" good (as opposed to spiritual) to "fill the Mind," as if it were a material thing. But, besides playing on vanity as "emptiness," Watts explores another meaning, "futility" or "restlessness." Like a "raging Fever," desires cause "vicious thirst"; the tormented man shifts "from side to side by turns" but can gain little relief.

All of the preceding indicates that in contrast with Cowper —who tends to internalize conventional imagery and to use it as an extension of his own spiritual condition—Watts tends to externalize the spiritual by finding analogies with it in the outer world. In contrast to the hymn in which Watts plays upon the word "beam" and the notion that man, because of his physical nature, can harbor no idea of God, Cowper in "Walking With God" turns the conventional image of the path or walk into an expression of his longing for a restoration of the feeling of closeness, filial confidence. Not surprisingly Cowper continues his hymn as a dramatization of self by referring to the peaceful hours he once knew when he was "walking with God" and the "aching void" he now feels on having lost this relationship. And it is equally as characteristic that Watts should stress the moral and ethical implications of his image: that an inability to conceive of God should not deter man's impulses toward love and adoration. Similarly, Watts's fever imagery does not bear the mark of personal experience as do Cowper's images of fountains and thirst.

Just as the walk becomes an image of the self, so "light shining out of darkness" and "the valley of the shadow of death" have profound subjective meanings in Cowper's hymns. The tension between light and darkness reveals a tension within the self between fear and confidence, despair and rapture. "Light shining out of darkness," like "sometimes a light surprizes," indicates that faith is intuitive and that religious confidence comes not from reason but inspiration. "Light shining out of darkness" and "the valley of the shadow of death" together reveal that the transition from joy to despair, peace to turmoil, is not controlled by reason.

The difference, then, is between self finding expression in images and ideas finding definition in imagery. In the following hymn, for example, Watts, revealing his Lockeian beliefs that ideas have their foundation in sense reaction and that images should clarify ideas, uses a candle and a rustling leaf to explain how religious ideas can cause earthly preoccupations to fade away:[12]

> Had I a Glance of thee, my God,
> Kingdoms and Men would vanish soon,
> Vanish as tho' I saw 'em not,
> As a dim Candle dies at Noon.
>
> Then they might fight, and rage, and rave,
> I should perceive the Noise no more
> Then we can hear a shaking Leaf
> While rattling Thunders round us roar.

The hymn merely draws an analogy between spiritual or abstract, between physical or concrete. The same thing is true of the image of the sick man in "The Vanity Of Creatures." In "There Is A Land Of Pure Delight" the method differs only in that the analogy is to biblical history, not to material reality. Again Watts purposes to define spiritual longings in terms of concrete experience.

Of course Watts's images do more than clarify ideas. Certainly the contrast between candlelight and sunlight, rustling leaf and thunder, inspires a feeling of the awesome gulf between Creator and Creation and the ludicrous nature of human pretensions. "The land of pure delight" arouses the emotions to accept the belief that a better world exists and that it is separated from the present only by the thin Stygian channel of death or the equally thin veil of the flesh. The image of the sick man also provides an emotional basis for contempt of the world. But these emotions might with some justice be called "public" or "universal" responses to truths that exist on the level of generality.

The other of the great eighteenth-century hymn writers, Charles Wesley, in some ways mediates between Watts and Cowper. Like Cowper's, Wesley's hymns are highly personalized; for they rise from a passionate rather than philosophical Christianity: "I'll wait 'till Thou appear *within*,/And plant thy Heaven of Love in me" [13] ("Waiting for Christ"). Wesley's emphasis on feeling goes far beyond Watts's notion that passion is necessary primarily to fix religious ideas in the mind and to afford motives to virtuous conduct. Wesley approximates Cowper's belief that religious conviction must involve a feeling of confidence, or, certainly, a sense of having been converted. Consequently, his imagery, like Cowper's, internalizes the exterior. In "For The Anniversary Day Of One's Conversion," the "glorious Sun of Righteousness" shines "on my benighted Soul" [14] giving repose from "legal strife." From this emotional experience springs faith. For Wesley, as for Cowper, light and dark are more than projections of moral and ethical values; they are revelations of emotional states. In "A Morning Hymn," Wesley cannot stop at making an analogy between the glory of God and the rising sun.[15] He must draw the imagery of day and night into the self until the dawn becomes an "inward" light and the majesty of the sun triumphs over an interior night. Instead of remaining exclusively an image of God, light becomes a "radiancy divine," a joy within which must be contrasted not only with the darkness of judgment and wrath but with the "gloom" of sin, grief, and doubt. To Watts, light piercing darkness meant the kingdom of God asserting its power over the legions of Satan; but to Wesley and Cowper, it meant evangelical joy renewing a spirit of joyful confidence. The "gloom of sin and grief" to Watts meant the terrors of Hell or the long history of mankind struggling in error; the same words to Wesley and Cowper connoted a state of mind, a loss of spiritual repose, a Hell within.

When Wesley pleads with Jesus, as "lover of my Soul," to protect him, he does not seek refuge from the minions of Hell or from a material environment, which can condition the human mind to desire it instead of higher objectives, but a haven from the storm of tensions which threaten to destroy him:

> Hide me, O my Saviour, hide,
>   'Till the Storm of Life is past:
> Safe into the Haven guide;
>   O receive my Soul at last.
>
> . . . .
>
> Wilt Thou not regard my Call?
>   Wilt Thou not accept my Prayer?
> Lo! I sink, I faint, I fall—
>   Lo! on Thee I cast my Care:
> Reach me out thy gracious Hand!
>   While I of thy Strength receive,
> Hoping against Hope I stand,
>   Dying, and behold I live!
>
> ("In Temptation")

The agony of suspense with which Wesley awaits a sign of divine favor recalls the storm which raged within Cowper.

The chief enemies of religion to Wesley and Cowper are casuistry and legalism which demonstrate the victory of reason over soundness of spirit, but to Watts the enemy is the fleshly nature of mind which subverts reason by insisting that all knowledge comes from sense impulses. Watts in his hymns constantly places man against a cosmic background or against the long continuum of history, and continually urges him to raise his spirit to God, for Lockeian philosophy and his Calvinistic heritage told him that, shorn of distinct ideas of God, man needed incentives of this nature to condition him to proper notions of himself. Far from being intended to serve as conditioners of reason, Wesley's and Cowper's hymns focus on emotional experience.

Cowper's hymns illuminate in an interesting manner his relationship to the dichotomy between Classical and Romantic in the eighteenth century. His tendency to regard the hymn not so much as a vehicle for public expression but as a way of giving form to internal realities seems to point ahead to the Romantics. So also does his use of imagery to define personal religious experience instead of abstract truths, a philosophical or moral system. Like the Classicist, Cowper as a hymn writer worked with received forms and a fully developed background of images and ideas. But his way of using this tradition is somewhat unclassical. He does not attempt to bring it to bear upon contemporary problems, but uses it instead as a means of expressing personal feelings. As a result, imagery, although it retains enough of its original meaning to be readily apprehensible to a congregation, becomes so filled with Cowper's own psychological tensions that it loses much of its original form. Cowper's best-known hymns, unlike Watts's but somewhat like Wesley's, are those in which he succeeds best in dramatizing the self and in communicating his own experience in such a way as to establish a common bond with his readers.

Conclusion

FROM a reading of Cowper's poetry we might conclude that "Post-Augustan" is a more useful term for literary history than the more popular "Pre-Romantic." Cowper's work is rooted in the past. It shows respect for the genres and carefully exploits the possibilities of various stanza forms. Even in departing from the couplet, a practice which was not so daring as some literary historians seem to imply, Cowper could not forget the harmonies and cadences of Pope and Dryden. Moreover, like other Neo-Classical poets, he wrote satires and landscape poems, and in them he typically conceived of art as the imitation of nature. But nature to Cowper was more than the laws according to which human character and other phenomena operate. In his rejection of the composite landscapes of the past in favor of more particularized description of the world of the Ouse and Olney, he rebelled against objective description in the Neo-Classical manner and moved toward the subjective, personal outpourings sanctioned by Romantic critical theory.

When Cowper bothered to defend his poetic practices, we see him reacting against the past, not anticipating the future. Feeling that Augustan satire lacked charity, he did not disavow the genre but resolved to behave in a more humane manner, one which accorded with his sense of uncertainty and guilt. Because he lacked faith in himself, he could not thrive on controversy nor take it upon himself to write a new *Dunciad*. In rejecting the closed couplet, the form most widely used by the Augustans, he shows his respect for the past; for his feeling that the balanced phraseology, antitheses, and anticlimaxes of the couplet could not properly express his own sentiments weighed less heavily than his belief that no contemporary poet, including himself, could improve on the form that Pope had mastered.

Cowper's criticism of Pope also flowed from his conviction that form must not triumph over personality. In *The Task* and in some of his shorter poems, he discovered that he could use blank verse and ballad stanza to reveal his enthusiasm for nature and retirement and to express his distinctive sense of humor. Whether consciously or not, he also invested his imagery with personal meanings of a kind unfamiliar to the reader of Augustan poetry. Being of the eighteenth century and a gentleman, he could not give free rein to his imagination and impulses, for not only did propriety restrict him but also Neo-Classical strictures against fancy and novelty. But if his reticence may have stifled Romantic tendencies in his poems, consigning some of his most penetrating and poignant insights and revelations of character to letters, it left him enough latitude to express the sense of alienation, uncertainty, and guilt which tormented him during much of his adult life. Through patterns of imagery in *The Task* and tone in satire, as well as through sapphics in "Lines Written During a Period of Insanity" and narrative in "The Castaway," he turned personal distress into poetry.

It is a curiosity of literary history that many of the eighteenth-century poets who have been called Pre-Romantic share the theme of alienation. It appears in such diverse forms as Peter Grimes's separation from his father and society in George Crabbe's *The Borough,* Burns's satiric thrusts at Holy Willie and the rest of the Scotch Presbyterian establishment, and Cowper's terrifying dreams, the residue of which may be detected in his poems and hymns. Indeed, Grimes's anguished cry, "Fathers should pity," "Father . . . have mercy," might well be taken as a description of the theme of Cowper's religious poetry. Historically, we might say that Cowper, Burns, and Crabbe together show the eighteenth-century consensus disintegrating. In Cowper we perhaps feel most poignantly the psychological impact of this disintegration, for in Cowper it becomes less a social problem than a personal concern.

Modern psychological theory holds that dreams are often a defense against deep-seated anxieties. As frightening as Cowper's dreams about his impending damnation were, they may well have protected him from an even more painful sense of personal failure. Paradoxically, Cowper defended himself against feelings of inadequacy which sprang from the Calvinist doctrine that the Elect must have material proof of their election, by tormenting himself with a Calvinistically oriented notion of the vengeance God intended to exact from him. As a result, feelings of guilt and inadequacy underlie his most memorable short poems and the best passages from *The Task*. They lead to the humor and pathos of "Epitaph on a Hare," the diffident praise of life in Olney, and to many vivid images, like "stricken deer."

Cowper's reticence may not have allowed his imagination to work freely upon his feelings, but undoubtedly it was also responsible for many qualities which have made his poems endure. It redeemed his work from sentimentality, shaped the sense of humor with which he placed his personal mark on the Neo-Classical tradition, and infused the world of Olney with a warmth that make both *The Task* and Cowper's letters so appealing.

Notes and References

Chapter One

1. "On The Receipt Of My Mother's Picture Out Of Norfolk," ll. 3–10, 58–67. *Complete Poetical Works of William Cowper*, ed. H. S. Milford. Fourth Edition. (London: Oxford University Press, 1934), pp. 394–95. This edition hereafter listed as *Works*.

2. *Memoir Of The Early Life Of William Cowper, Esq.* Second Edition. (London, 1816), p. 20; hereafter listed as *Memoir*.

3. To Unwin, May 23, 1781. All letters are taken from the Wright edition. Since the letters are arranged chronologically in the Wright edition, they will be listed by date in the following notes.

4. *Memoir*, pp. 20–21.

5. "Tirocinium: Or, A Review Of The Schools," ll. 300–17. *Works*, p. 249.

6. *Memoir*, p. 43.

7. *Ibid.*, p. 22.

8. To Newton, July 19, 1784.

9. "Delia, Th'unkindest Girl On Earth," *Works*, p. 271.

10. "A Song," *Works*, p. 273.

11. "Of Himself," *Works*, pp. 269–70.

12. "Bid Adieu . . . ," *Works*, p. 278.

13. "R.S.S. Written In A Fit Of Illness," *Works*, pp. 280–81.

14. "R.S.S.," *Works*, pp. 279–80.

15. "Hope, Like The Short-Liv'd Ray," *Works*, pp. 282–83.

16. See Croft's preface to his edition of the early poems (1825), included in *Works*, pp. 643–45.

17. To Unwin, February 24, 1782.

18. To Lady Hesketh, April 17, 1786.

19. Some idea of the efforts of Cowper and his companions can be gained by examining the titles of the works. Thornton's best known poem was a "Mock Ode for St. Cecilia's Day. Adapted to the Ancient British Music Of The Salt Box, Jew's Harp, Marrow Bones, and Cleavers And Humdrum Or Hurdy-Gurdy." Cowper contributed the following essays to the *Connoisseur*: #111, "Letter Containing The Character Of The Delicate Billy Suckling"; #115, "Letter For Chris-

topher Ironsides An Old Bachelor, Complaining Of The Indignities Received By Him From The Ladies"; #119, "Of Keeping A Secret— Characters Of Faithless Confidants"; #134, "Letter From Mr. Village, Giving An Account Of The Present State Of Country Churches, Their Clergy And Their Congregation. The Chief Pests Of Society Pointed Out. Those Who Converse Irrationally Considered As Imitating The Language Of Different Animals."

20. *Memoir*, p. 26.

21. To Newton, September 24, 1785.

22. *Ibid.*

23. *Memoir*, p. 25.

24. *Ibid.*, pp. 27–29.

25. To Rowley, September 2, 1762.

26. *Memoir*, pp. 35–36.

27. The most celebrated of these has been the rumor that Cowper had a sexual deformity.

28. *Memoir*, p. 35.   The following account of Cowper's breakdown, except where otherwise indicated, is drawn from Cowper's *Memoir*, pp. 45–71.

29. "Retirement," 611–14, *Works*, p. 122.

30. To Lady Hesketh, August 9, 1763.

31. "Lines Written During A Period Of Insanity," *Works*, pp. 289–290.

32. "A Song Of Mercy And Judgment," *Works*, pp. 280–91.

33. *Memoir*, pp. 78–81.

34. *The Task*, I, 749.

35. *Ibid.*, I, 462–67.

36. To Hill, June 24, 1765.

37. *Ibid.*

38. To Lady Hesketh, July 5, 1765.

39. *Memoir*, p. 86.

40. To Lady Hesketh, September 14, 1765.

41. To Hill, October 25, 1765.

42. To Lady Hesketh, October 18, 1765

43. To Hill, November 5, 1765.

44. To Hill, July 3, 1765.

45. *Memoir*, pp. 88–91.

46. To Mrs. William Cowper, October 20, 1766.

47. *Memoir*, pp. 91–92.

48. To Mrs. William Cowper, October 20, 1766.

49. To Hill, July 16, 1767.

50. To Mrs. William Cowper, July 13, 1767.

51. To Hill, July 31, 1769.

Chapter Two

1. To Lady Hesketh, October 18, 1765.
2. To Newton, March 29, 1784.
3. To Unwin, November 18, 1782.
4. To Hill, May 8, 1770; to Mrs. Cowper, June 7, 1770; Cowper also wrote an account of his care for his brother and his brother's death.
5. To Lady Hesketh, January 16, 1786.
6. To Newton, August 21, 1781.
7. Newton's diary contains a record of Cowper's illness.
8. "Walking With God," *Olney Hymns,* I, iii.
9. To Lady Hesketh, January 16, 1786.
10. *Ibid.*
11. To Newton, July 12, 1780.
12. To Unwin, May 8, 1780.
13. To Newton, March 19, 1785.
14. To Newton, February, 1782; January 26, 1783.
15. To Hill, December 8, 1781; January 26, 1783; February 23, 1783.
16. To Unwin, July, 1779.
17. *Ibid.*
18. To Newton, July 12, 1780.
19. *Ibid.*
20. To Newton, February, 1782.
21. To Newton, August 21, 1781.
22. To Newton, March 19, 1784.
23. To Newton, September 8, 1783.
24. *The Task,* I, 357–66.
25. *The Task,* I, 367–71, 385–98.
26. *The Task,* I, 163–66.
27. *The Task,* I, 181–89.
28. *The Task,* I, 275–77.
29. *The Task,* I, 455–69.
30. *Aeneid,* VIII, 21–25.
31. Louis Antoine de Caraccioli, *La Jouissance de Soi-Meme* (Utrecht and Amsterdam, 1759), p. 88.
32. *Works,* p. 637.
33. *Ibid.,* p. 638.
34. *Ibid.,* p. 639.
35. *The London Magazine* LI (1782), 245.
36. *The Gentleman's Magazine* LII (1782), 130–31.
37. Cowper contributed an essay on his pets, Puss, Tiney, and

Bess, to a later issue of *The Gentleman's Magazine* LV (1785), 412–414.

38. *The Monthly Review* LXVII (1782), 262–65.
39. *The Critical Review* LIII (1782), 287–90.
40. To Unwin, May 27, 1782.
41. *Ibid.*
42. To Newton, August 21, 1781; to Unwin, September 26, 1781.
43. To Unwin, February 9, 1782.
44. To Unwin, February 24, 1782.
45. Kenneth Povey, "The Banishment of Lady Austen," *RES* XV (1939), 392–400.
46. *The Monthly Review* LXXIV (1785), 416–25.
47. *The Gentleman's Magazine* LIX (1786), 305–07.
48. *The Gentleman's Magazine* LVIII (1785), 985–88 and LIX (1786) contains a biographical account of the "facetious and well-known author of *John Gilpin*" intended to support this view of the poet's character and work.
49. To Unwin, 1784.
50. *Ibid.*
51. To Lady Hesketh, October 12, 1785.
52. To Lady Hesketh, 1785.
53. To Lady Hesketh, February 9, 1785.
54. To Unwin, July 3, 1786.
55. To Lady Hesketh, December 7 [1785].
56. To Lady Hesketh, February 27, 1786.
57. To Lady Hesketh, January 16, 1786.
58. To Lady Hesketh, May 8, 1786.
59. To Lady Hesketh, May 15, 1786.
60. *Ibid.*
61. To Newton, September 30, 1786.
62. To Newton, May, 1785; January 13, 1784.
63. To Lady Hesketh, May 8, 1786.
64. To Newton, July 27, 1783.
65. To Newton, November 17, 1786.
66. To Newton, December 16, 1786.
67. To Unwin, [May, 1784].
68. To Newton, December 16, 1786.
69. To Lady Hesketh, December 4, 1786.
70. To John Johnson, January 21, 1791.
71. To Mrs. Bodham, February 27, 1790.
72. To Rose, December 21, 1791.
73. To Lady Hesketh, June 11, 1792.
74. To Lady Hesketh, December 1, 1792.

75. To Lady Hesketh, May 24, 1792.
76. To William Hayley, July 22, 1792.
77. To Lady Hesketh, August 5, 1792.
78. To Hayley, September 21, 1792.
79. *Ibid.*
80. To Newton, April 11, 1799.
81. To Lady Hesketh, January 22, 1796; February 19, 1796; May 30, 1796; May 15, 1797; June 1, 1798; October 13, 1798.
82. *Works*, p. 428.
83. R. E. Spiller, "William Cowper, A New Biographical Source: J. Johnson's Holograph Memorandum Book," *PMLA* XLII (1927), 950.
84. *Ibid.*, pp. 954–55.
85. *Memoir*, p. iii.

Chapter Three

1. So that the reader may follow the discussion more easily, I include the arguments of each book.

Book I, The Sofa: Historical deduction of seats, from the stool to the Sofa—A Schoolboy's ramble—A walk in the country—The scene described—Rural sounds as well as sights delightful—Another walk —Mistake concerning the charms of solitude corrected—Colonnades commended—Above and the view from it—The wilderness—The grove—The thresher—The necessity and the benefits of exercise— The works of nature superior to, and in some instances inimitable by, art—The wearisomeness of what is commonly called a life of pleasure—Change of scene sometimes expedient—A common described, and the character of crazy Kate introduced—Gipsies—The blessing of civilized life—That state most favourable to virtue—The South Sea islanders compassionated, but chiefly Omai—His present state of mind supposed—Civilized life friendly to virtue, but not great cities—Great cities, and London in particular, allowed their due praise, but censured—Fete champetre—The book concludes with a reflection on the fatal effects of dissipation and effeminacy upon our public measures.

Book II, The Time-Piece: Reflections suggested by the conclusion of the former book—Peace among the nations recommended, on the ground of their common fellowship in sorrow—Prodigies enumerated—Sicilian earthquakes—Man rendered obnoxious to these calamities by sin—God the agent in them—The philosophy that stops at secondary causes reproved—Our own late miscarriage accounted for—Satirical notice taken of our trips to Fontainbleau—But the pulpit, not satire, the proper engine of reformation—The reverend Advertiser of engraved sermons—Petit-Maitre parson—The good preacher—Pictures of a theatrical clerical coxcomb—Story-tellers and jesters in the pulpit reproved—Apostrophe to popular applause —Retailers of ancient philosophy expostulated with—Sum of the whole matter—Effects of sacerdotal mismanagement on the laity— Their folly and extravagance—The mischiefs of profusion—Profusion itself, with all its consequent evils, ascribed, as to its principal cause, to the want of discipline in the universities.

Book III, The Garden: Self-recollection and reproof—Address to domestic happiness—Some account of myself—The vanity of many of their pursuits who are reputed wise—Justification of my censures —Divine illumination necessary to the most expert philosopher— The question, What is truth? answered by other questions—Domestic happiness addressed again—Few lovers of the country—My tame hare—Occupations of a retired gentleman in his garden— Pruning—Framing—Greenhouse—Sowing of flower-seeds—The country preferable to the town even in the winter—Reasons why it is deserted at that season—Ruinous effects of gaming and of expensive improvement—Book concludes with an apostrophe to the metropolis.

Book IV, The Winter Evening: The post comes in—The newspaper is read—The world contemplated at a distance—Address to winter—The rural amusements of a winter evening compared with the fashionable ones—Address to evening—A brown study—Fall of snow in the evening—The waggoner—A poor family-piece—The rural thief—Public houses—The multitude of them censured—The farmer's daughter: what she was—what she is—The simplicity of country manners almost lost—Causes of the change—Desertion of the country by the rich—Neglect of magistrates—The militia principally at fault—The new recruit and his transformation—Reflection on bodies corporate—The love of rural objects natural to all, and never to be totally extinguished.

Book V, The Winter Morning Walk: A frosty morning—The foddering of cattle—The woodman and his dog—The poultry—Whimsical effects of frost at a waterfall—The Empress of Russia's palace of ice—Amusements of monarchs—War, one of them—Wars, whence —And whence monarchy—The evils of it—English and French loyalty contrasted—The Bastile, and a prisoner there—Liberty the chief recommendation of this country—Modern patriotism questionable, and why—The perishable nature of the best human institutions—Spiritual liberty not perishable—The slavish state of man by nature—Deliver him, Deist, if you can—Grace must do it—The respective merits of patriots' and martyrs' states—Their different treatment—Happy freedom of the man whom grace makes free— His relish of the works of God—Address to the Creator.

Book VI, The Winter Walk At Noon: Bells at a distance—Their effect—A fine noon in winter—A sheltered walk—Meditation better than books—Our familiarity with the course of nature makes it appear less wonderful than it is—The transformation that spring effects in a shrubbery described—A mistake concerning the course of nature corrected—God maintains it by an unremitted act—The amusements fashionable at this hour of the day reproved—Animals happy, a delightful sight—Origin of cruelty to animals—That it is a great crime proved from scripture—That proof illustrated by a tale—A line drawn between the lawful and unlawful destruction of them—Their good and useful properties insisted on—Apology for the encomiums bestowed by the author upon animals—Instances of of man's extravagant praise of man—The groans of the creation shall have an end—A view taken of the restoration of all things—An invocation and an invitation of him who shall bring it to pass—The retired man vindicated from the charge of uselessness—Conclusion.

2. October 10, 1784.

3. December 13, 1784.

4. *Ibid.*

5. Morris Golden, *In Search of Stability, The Poetry of William Cowper* (New York, 1960), 119–55.

6. *The Task*, VI, 149–82.

7. To Teedon, November 17, 1792.

Chapter Five

1. Isaac Watts, Preface to *Hymns and Spiritual Songs, Works,* ed. Rev. George Burder (London, 1810–11), IV, 253.

2. Numbers in parentheses refer to book and number of hymn in the *Olney Hymns.*

3. *Olney Hymns,* II, lxii.

4. *Ibid.,* II, viii.

5. *Ibid.,* III, xv.

6. *Ibid.,* I, iii; III, viii; III, xx.

7. *Ibid.,* II, lxii.

8. *Ibid.,* I, lxvii.

9. *Ibid.,* II, liii.

10. *Ibid.,* II, lv.

11. "Discourse of the Love of God," *Works,* II, 633.
12. *Hymns and Spiritual Songs,* IV, 280.
13. *Hymns and Sacred Poems* (London, 1739–1740), p. 10.
14. *Ibid.,* p. 187
15. *Ibid.,* p. 150.

Selected Bibliography

PRIMARY SOURCES

1. Collected Works

Works, Ed. John Johnson. 10 vols. London: Baldwin, Cradock, and Joy, 1817.

Works, Comprising His Poems, Correspondence, And Translations. Ed. Robert Southey. 15 vols. London: Baldwin and Cradock, 1835–37; 8 vols. London: H. G. Bohn, 1853–55 (Bohn's Standard Library).

Works, His Life And Letters By William Hayley. Ed. T. S. Grimshawe. 8 vols. London: Saunders and Otley, 1835, 1836.

2. Collected Poetry

Poems. 2 vols. London: J. Johnson, 1782.

Poems, The Early Productions of William Cowper, Now First Published. With Anecdotes From Letters Of Lady Hesketh. Ed. J. Croft. London: Baldwin, Cradock, and Joy, 1825.

Poetical Works. Ed. J. Bruce. Aldine Edition. 3 vols. London: Bell and Daldy, 1865.

Poetical Works. Ed. W. Benham. Globe Edition. London and New York: Macmillan, 1870.

Unpublished and Uncollected Poems. Ed. Thomas Wright. London, 1900.

Complete Poetical Works. Ed. H. S. Milford. Oxford Standard Authors. London: Oxford University Press, 1907. Fourth Edition, 1934. Repr. 1959.

3. Translations and Editorial Work

The Iliad and Odyssey. London: Joseph Johnson, 1802.

The Poetical Works of John Milton. 4 vols. Chichester: J. Johnson, 1810.

4. Letters

Life and Letters. Ed. William Hayley. 4 vols. Chichester: W. Mason, 1809.

Letters. Ed. J. Johnson. 3 vols. London: Baldwin, Cradock, and Joy, 1817.

Private Correspondence With Several Of His Most Intimate Friends. Now First Published. Ed. J. Johnson. 2nd Edition. London: H. Colburn, 1904. 2 vols.

Correspondence. Arranged In Chronological Order. Ed. Thomas Wright. 4 vols. London: Hodder and Stoughton, 1904. The standard edition.

Selections From Cowper's Letters. Ed. E. V. Lucas. World's Classics Edition. London: H. Frowde, 1908.

Unpublished And Uncollected Letters. Ed. Thomas Wright. London: C. J. Farncombe, 1925.

Letters. Ed. Sir J. S. Frazer. 2 vols. London: Macmillan, 1912.

Letters. Ed. W. Hadley. Everyman's Edition. London: J. M. Dent; New York: E. P. Dutton, 1926.

Selected Letters. Ed. Mark Van Doren. Great Letters Series. New York: Farrar, Straus, and Young, 1951.

5. Autobiography and Related Biography

Adelphi. A Sketch Of The Character And An Account Of The Last Illness Of The Late John Cowper. Ed. John Newton. London: C. Whittingham, 1802.

Memoir Of The Early Life Of William Cowper, Esq. Written By Himself. 2nd edn. London: R. Edwards, 1816. A reprint edited by Maurice Quinlan is in *Proceedings Of The American Philosophical Society*, XCVII (1953), 359–82.

SECONDARY SOURCES

1. Biographies

HAYLEY, WILLIAM. *The Life And Posthumous Writings Of William Cowper.* 3 vols. Chichester: W. Mason, 1803–04. Based on Hayley's personal knowledge of Cowper and published with the approval of Lady Hesketh.

SOUTHEY, ROBERT. *The Works Of William Cowper, Comprising His Poems, Correspondence, And Translations.* 15 vols. London: H. G. Bohn, 1835–37 (Bohn's Standard Library). 8 vols. 185–55. Contains material not included by Hayley.

TAYLOR, T. *The Life Of William Cowper, Compiled From His Corre-*

spondence. London: R. B. Seeley and W. Burnside, 1835. Based on Haley and Johnson. Sympathizes with evangelicalism.

POLLOCK, J. M. *The Life, Genius, And Poetry Of Cowper.* London: 1860.

SMITH, GOLDWIN. *Cowper.* English Men Of Letters Series. London: Macmillan, 1880. Discusses relationship between Cowper's religion and his works. Minimizes the harmful effects of Cowper's evangelicalism.

WRIGHT, THOMAS. *The Life Of William Cowper.* London: T. Fisher Unwin, 1892. Details of Cowper's world in Olney and Weston, the product of Wright's antiquarian interest.

FAUSSET, HUGH I. *William Cowper.* London: Jonathan Cape, 1928. The harmful effects of Cowper's religious experience on his writing and personality.

CECIL, LORD DAVID. *The Stricken Deer: Or, The Life Of Cowper.* London: Constable, 1929; Indianapolis: Bobbs-Merrill, 1930. A brief critical life.

THOMAS, GILBERT. *William Cowper And The Eighteenth Century.* London: Allen and Unwin, 1935. 2nd edn., 1948. The most complete life, partially outdated by more recent historical and psychological research.

NICHOLSON, NORMAN. *William Cowper.* London: J. Lehmann, 1951. A brief appreciation, which emphasizes *The Task* and gives less credit to Cowper's performance as a satirist and comic poet.

QUINLAN, MAURICE. *William Cowper: A Critical Life.* Minneapolis: University of Minnesota Press, 1953. Presents a psychological analysis of Cowper's malady. Shows the effect of his mental state on his works.

RYSKAMP, CHARLES. *William Cowper Of The Inner Temple, Esq. A Study Of His Life And Works To The Year 1768.* Cambridge: Cambridge University Press, 1959. Contributes many new insights and much heretofore unpublished information, including several letters. A careful analysis of Cowper's environment tends to reduce the previous emphasis on his mental instability.

2. *Related Biographies And Letters*

BULL, JOSIAH. *John Newton. An Autobiography And Narrative.* London: Religious Tract Society, 1868. Memoir of Newton by his and Cowper's friend.

MARTIN, BERNARD. *John Newton. A Biography.* London: William Heinemann, 1950. The most recent and thorough study.

HESKETH, HARRIET. *Letters Of Lady Hesketh To The Rev. John Johnson, Concerning Their Kinsman William Cowper.* Ed. Catharine

B. Johnson. London: Jarrold and Sons, 1901. A basic source of information about Cowper's last years.

HURDIS, REV. JAMES. *Letters Of The Rev. J. Hurdis To Cowper,* 1791–1794, ed. J. F. Tattersall. Eastbourne: T. R. Beckett, 1927.

3. Bibliographies And Concordances

BATESON, F. W., ed. *Cambridge Bibliography Of English Literature.* New York: Cambridge University Press, 1941.

HARTLEY, LODWICK. *William Cowper: The Continuing Revaluation.* Chapel Hill: University of North Carolina Press, 1938, 1960. A complete annotated bibliography with introductory remarks on the present state of Cowper scholarship.

NEVE, JOHN. *A Concordance To The Poetical Works of Cowper.* London: Sampson Low and Co., 1887.

RUSSELL, NORMA. *A Bibliography Of William Cowper To 1837.* Oxford Bibliographical Society Publications. Oxford: Oxford University Press, 1963.

4. Criticism

BROOKE, STOPFORD A. *Theology In The English Poets.* London: J. M. Dent, 1874. "The revolutionary idea of the unity of Man was in Cowper's mind grounded on a theological one." Cowper's evangelicalism offered him no comfort.

BROWN, WALLACE C. *The Triumph Of Form: A Study Of The Later Masters Of The Heroic Couplet.* Chapel Hill: University Of North Carolina Press, 1948. Cowper's use of the heroic couplet.

CARMICHAEL, MONTGOMERY. "Cowper And The Throckmortons," *Dublin Review* CXC (1932), 195–210. The Throckmortons' Catholicism and their friendship with Cowper.

COLDICOTT, H. R. S. "How Cowper Got His Pension. From A Manuscript Of William Hayley," *Cornhill Magazine* XXXIV (1913), 493–507. Hayley's attempts on Cowper's behalf.

"Cowper's Last Years," *Times Literary Supplement,* October 5, 12, 1951. Entries from a manuscript volume containing extracts from the diary of John Johnson, July 28, 1795 to February 3, 1800.

CRAVEN, DOROTHY H. *Cowper's Use of "Slight Connection" In "The Task": A Study In Structure And Style.* Dissertation, University of Colorado, 1953. A summary appears in *University of Colorado Studies* XXIX, ii (1954), 4–6.

DAVIE, DONALD A. "The Critical Principles Of William Cowper," *Cambridge Journal* VII (1953), 182–88. De-emphasizes the Pre-Romantic element in Cowper; maintains that the poet held "defiantly" to Neo-Classical principles.

DOBSON, AUSTIN. *Eighteenth-Century Vignettes.* London, Edinburgh, New York: Oxford University Press, n.d. Does not treat Cowper as a serious poet.

DOWDEN, E. "Cowper and William Hayley," *Atlantic Monthly* C(1907), 74–87. Hayley's attempts in the 1790's to rescue Cowper from his chronic melancholy.

FAIRCHILD, H. N. "Additional Notes On John Johnson's Diary," *Publications of the Modern Language Association.* Discusses Johnson's manuscript diary at Cambridge, which contains accounts of Cowper's dreams.

———. *Religious Trends in English Poetry.* New York: Columbia University Press, 1942. Vol. II. Cowper's use of evangelical formulations makes his poetry less subjective than many critics have held.

FORSTER, E. M. "William Cowper, An Englishman," *Spectator* CXLVIII (1932), 75. Cowper's work has little relevance to modern England.

GILBERT, DOROTHY L., AND RUSSELL POPE. "The Cowper Translation Of Mme. Guyon's Poems," *Publications of the Modern Language Association* LIV (1939), 1077–98. The ingenuity and technical excellence of Cowper's translations. Cowper modifies erotic imagery of the originals.

GOLDEN, MORRIS. "Churchill's Literary Influence On Cowper," *Journal of English Germanic Philology* LVIII (1959), 655–65.

———. *In Search Of Stability.* New York: Bookman Associates, 1960. Cowper's writing manifests his struggle for mental stability.

GREGORY, HOOSAG K. "The Prisoner And His Crimes: Summary Comments On A Longer Study Of The Mind Of William Cowper," *Literature and Psychology* VI (1956), 53–59.

———. *The Prisoner And His Crimes: A Psychological Approach To William Cowper's Life And Writings.* Dissertation, Harvard University, 1951. A Freudian analysis which explores the possibility of genital deformity and latent homosexuality. Cowper's poetry did not resolve conflicts but instead allowed him to escape from them.

HARTLEY, LODWICK. " 'The Stricken Deer' And His Contemporary Reputation," *Studies in Philology* XXXVI (1939), 637–50. Cowper enjoyed a high reputation among his contemporaries.

———. *William Cowper, Humanitarian.* Chapel Hill: University of North Carolina Press, 1938. Cowper's values are those of his age.

———. "The Worm And The Thorn: A Study Of Cowper's *Olney Hymns,*" *Journal of Religion* XXIX (1949), 220–29. Disagrees with Fairchild and Keck, who find little that is personal in Cowper's hymns.

HOLMES, E. D. "The Question Of Cowper's Indebtedness To Churchill," *Modern Language Notes* XIII (1898), 165–70. Cowper's debt has been overemphasized.

HUANG, RODERICK. *William Cowper: Nature Poet.* Oxford: Oxford University Press, 1957. Influences of Methodism and the landscape poetry tradition.

KECK, WENDELL M. *Cowper's Olney Hymns: A Theological Study.* Dissertation, Stanford University, 1941. Examines doctrinal content of hymns; what seems to be personal revelation results from religious conventions.

KER, W. P. *On Modern Literature: Lectures And Addresses,* Ed. Terence Spencer and James Sutherland. Oxford: Oxford University Press, 1955. Cowper's diction and blank verse.

MacLEAN, KENNETH. "William Cowper," *The Age Of Johnson: Essays Presented To Chauncey Brewster Tinker.* New Haven: Yale University Press, 1949. Cowper's poetry appeals to the modern reader because of its autobiographical content, but the poet was not a Romantic.

MANNING, BERNARD L. "History, Politics, And Religion In Certain Poems Of William Cowper," *Congregational Quarterly* VII (1929), 326–43. Cowper's Whig values.

MARTIN, BERNARD. "Fresh Light On William Cowper," *Modern Language Quarterly* XIII (1952), 253–55. New Letters from Newton to Cowper.

MARTIN, L. C. "Vaughan And Cowper," *Modern Language Review* XXII (1927), 79–84. The poets have similar attitudes toward nature.

NORMAN, H. J. *Cowper and Blake.* London: Cowper Society, 1914. Both poets were friends of Hayley.

POVEY, KENNETH. "The Banishment of Lady Austen," *Review of English Studies* XV (1939), 392–400. The banishment did not leave hard feelings and was probably by mutual consent.

———. "Cowper and Lady Austen: New Documents And Notes," *Review of English Studies* X (1934), 417–27. Refers to Greatheed's memorandum on Lady Austen to Hayley which characterizes her as pious, witty, but physically unattractive.

———. "Cowper's Spiritual Diary," *London Mercury* XV (1927), 493–96. Text of a fragmentary diary written in 1795, taken from a copy made by J. Johnson.

———. "Further Notes For A Bibliography of Cowper's Letters," *Review of English Studies* VII (1932), 316–19.

———. "Notes On Cowper's Letters III," *Review of English Studies* X (1934), 67–68.

————. "Notes On Cowper's Letters IV," *Review of English Studies* XII (1936), 333–35

————. "The Text Of Cowper's Letters," *Modern Language Review* XXII (1927), 22–27. Texts of published letters are often inaccurate and incomplete.

————. "The Hurdis-Cowper Letters. Unpublished Letters Addressed By James Hurdis, The Sussex Poet To William Cowper," *Sussex County Magazine* (April, 1927), 223–25.

QUINLAN, MAURICE J. "Cowper's Imagery," *Journal of English and Germanic Philology* XLVII (1948), 276–85. Relates Cowper's imagery to his psychological state.

SAINTE-BEUVE, C. A. "William Cowper, ou de la poesie domestique," *Causeries du Lundi* XI (1856), 139–47. Cowper's poetry as a portrait of his domestic life.

SHAFER, R. "William Cowper," *Bookman* LXXIV (1931), 287–97. Cowper as "silver" poet.

SHERBO, ARTHUR. "Cowper's *Connoisseur* Essays," *Modern Language Notes* LXX (1955), 340–42. Relates the essays to "Conversation."

SPILLER, R. E. "William Cowper. A New Biographical Source: Rev. J. Johnson's Holograph Memorandum Book, 1795–1800," *Publications of the Modern Language Association* XLII (1927), 946–62. A transcript of the memorandum book, an important primary source of information about Cowper in these years.

STEPHEN, SIR LESLIE. "Cowper And Rousseau," *Hours In A Library*. Vol. II. London: Smith and Elder, 1879.

————. *English Literature And Society In The Eighteenth Century*. New York and London: G. P. Putnam, 1907.

THEIN, ADELAIDE E. "The Religion of John Newton," *Philological Quarterly* XXI (1942), 146–70. Emphasizes the harshness of Newton's Calvinism.

————. *The Religion Of William Cowper, An Attempt To Distinguish His Obsession And His Creed*. Dissertation, University of Michigan, 1940. *Dissertation Abstracts* V, i (1943), 24–25. Cowper not an extreme Calvinist; believes in freedom of spirit and the light of conscience and reason.

WAUGH, ARTHUR. "William Cowper," *Fortnightly Review* CXXXVI (1931), 590–603. Cowper's sincerity makes his poetry worthwhile.

WHITING, MARY B. "'A Burning Bush': A New Light On The Relations Between William Cowper And John Newton," *Hibbert Journal* XXIV (1926), 303–13. An account of Newton's funeral sermon on Cowper.

Index